Feathers From the Prairie

A Short History of Upland Game Birds

By Morris D. Johnson
Upland Game Biologist

Sketches by Ted Cornell, Medora, North Dakota

Pittman-Robertson Project W-67-R-5

Published by the
NORTH DAKOTA GAME AND FISH DEPARTMENT
Russell W. Stuart, *Commissioner*
Bismarck, North Dakota

1964

Price $1.50

Foreword

North Dakota is fortunate in having been endowed with an impressive variety of upland game birds. Some of these have been on the North Dakota scene since the coming of white man. Others have since been introduced in an effort to provide additional species for man to hunt and otherwise enjoy. Some species, both native and introduced, have flourished under changing economic conditions and some have drastically declined. They have all played a significant role in the history of the state and are a cherished part of our heritage.

It is important that historical records of our upland game be preserved. These records will contribute to a full understanding of what has happened to various species over the years and will have a practical value in documenting information which will be an aid in future management of game species.

The completion of this publication has been made possible through funds provided by the Federal Aid program for wildlife restoration. This program enables the North Dakota Game and Fish Department to undertake investigational and development work that will contribute to better game management.

We are proud to have the author of this publication, Mr. Johnson, on our Game Management staff. Mr. Johnson received a B.A. degree from Parsons College in 1948, a B.S. degree in Zoology from Iowa State University in 1954 and a M.A. degree in Wildlife Management from the University of Missouri in 1956. This excellent training prepared him well for the Upland Game Biologist's position that he has held with the North Dakota Game and Fish Department for the past eight years. During this time he developed a deep interest in documenting for posterity an accurate account of our upland game fauna as it was and is found in North Dakota.

A tremendous amount of effort has been expended in researching literature from many scattered sources and interviewing scores of people who were eye witnesses to important events in the past. The author skillfully presents a chronological record of these events which will prove valuable as reference material to the professional worker and will be interesting and informative to all.

It is fitting that such a comprehensive account of our upland game species should be published on the 75th anniversary of North Dakota statehood.

C. R. GRONDAHL, *Project Leader*
Surveys and Investigations
Game Management Division

Acknowledgments

"Feathers From the Prairie" would not have been possible without the excellent cooperation of many people. During the three years the project was conducted hundreds of persons were contacted for information on the wildlife of North Dakota and in no instance did they fail to lend assistance. In many cases these persons continued to supply information to the final stages of the project.

I am indebted to North Dakota Game and Fish Department Commissioners the late Dr. I. G. Bue and Mr. Russell W. Stuart, Deputy Commissioner Wilbur J. Boldt, who approved the project and permitted the writer to pursue the work at his own digression.

Special thanks are extended to Mr. C. R. Grondahl, Project Leader of the Game Division, for his constructive criticism and edit of the original manuscript, and to Mr. C. M. Linkletter, English Department, University of North Dakota, Grand Forks, for his painstaking work of editing the final manuscript.

Nearly all the personnel of the State Game and Fish Department contributed to the project at some time during the course of work. No words can express my gratitude to these people who worked extra hours contacting old-timers and running down historical material so necessary to the writing of the book.

I would like to express my gratitude to Staff Photographers Shin Koyama and Ed Bry for their work in recopying photographs and to Mr. Koyama for his many hours of layout work on the entire publication. Bill McClellan of the Game and Fish Department and Ted Cornell of Medora endeavored to meet every request for artwork on maps and sketches.

I appreciate the many overtime hours of typing humbly granted by Department stenographers Mrs. Terry Burlingame and Miss Darlene Dohrmann in preparing all copies of the manuscript. Special thanks too, to Betty Stephens Morgan for proofreading the printed manuscript.

I am indebted to Mr. Russell Reid, Miss Margaret Rose, and all members of the North Dakota State Historical Society and its affiliated library, for valuable assistance and criticism. I particularly thank them for opening their doors so that I might make use of the vast file of books, manuscripts, photos, and legal documents under their jurisdiction.

Finally, I would like to express my appreciation to the following individuals who loaned historical material that could not be obtained from the usual sources: Howard Berg, Devils Lake; Arvid Berggren, Hampden; Mrs. Harry Byrnes, Lakota; Len Carroll, Dickinson; Dr. C. H. D. Clark, Fish and Wildlife Branch, Toronto, Ontario, Canada; Harold Duebbert, U. S. Fish and Wildlife Service, Devils Lake; Duane Green, Bottineau; Carl and Nancy Hendrickson, Mandan; Eric Jacobsen, Bismarck; Harold Jensen, Esmond; Frank Johnson, Fullerton; M. A. Johnson, Larimore; Robert Johnson, Fullerton; Mr. and Mrs. Percy Judd, Cando; A. T. Klett, U. S. Fish and Wildlife Service, Devils Lake; Everett Knudson, Walhalla; Joseph Kooker, Bismarck; Mr. and Mrs. W. A. Leach, Pebble Beach, California; Anna and Charlotte Leutz, Hebron; William B. Mershon, Jr., Saginaw, Michigan; Mrs. Elizabeth Roberts, Dickinson; Paul E. Slabaugh, Bottineau; and Henry V. Williams, Grafton.

MORRIS D. JOHNSON
Upland Game Biologist

TABLE OF CONTENTS

1

Sharp-tailed Grouse

Scientific name: *Pediocetes phasianellus*

Size:

Length, 16-20 inches. Wingspan, 26-29 inches. Weight, 1¾-2¼ lbs. Cocks slightly larger than hens. Average weight for 287 birds in North Dakota (1955-56) was 31.3 oz.; largest cock, 37.0 oz.

Coloration:

Drab gray-brown bird mottled with white. Cocks indistinguishable from hens except at close range or in the hand. V-shaped markings on breast, feathered legs, and purple air sacs on the throat of cocks.

Flight:

Characterized by a rapid takeoff and sharp turns. Once airborne the bird takes several rapid wing beats, glides for some distance, and then repeats the pattern. Sharptails "chuckle" or "cluck" loudly during flight. The pointed tail distinguishes it from other North Dakota grouse.

Flock habits:

Adult cocks "pack" throughout the year. Adult hens and immature birds remain together from hatching time until the following spring when immature cocks join adult cocks on the courtship grounds. Flocks of 100 or more birds are common in fall and winter.

History

Although the pheasant is rated the favorite game bird of the average North Dakota hunter, the sharp-tailed grouse has more genuine interest for the hunter who appreciates history. The latter has more to talk about because the sharptail has lived in the state for centuries. This game bird is an example of an unsophisticated native living in its natural environment — the grasslands. No other upland bird has been in the state so long or in such numbers.

Probably the sharptail has lived in North Dakota for thousands of years. Scanty records exist, and some of the earliest white fur traders mention "chicken." But there are few detailed records concerning grouse, which in the fur trader's

opinion was a relatively unimportant species. Early white inhabitants did not record history, as has been mentioned by State Museum Director Russell Reid:

> Most of the employees of the large fur companies were illiterate and have left us no record of their adventures. With some exception, the bourgeoises in charge of the trading posts were either too busy or lacked the inclination to write about the animal life about them. Most of our material is from the pen of the scientist, the sportsman, and the adventurer, who were attracted to the upper Missouri by the stirring tales of fur traders. Some of these men have left elaborate journals giving good accounts of the fauna and flora of the region.[1]

Sharp-tailed grouse were commonplace on the prairie, and people do not usually write about things which are commonplace. The larger animals, elk and buffalo, were common, but they were also a chief source of food and clothing. Hence, they were more frequently mentioned in frontier accounts. Birds were of minor importance in all respects.

The French explorer Verendrye visited North Dakota in 1733, but left little information on sharptails. On the other hand, Lewis and Clark, seventy-one years later in 1804-05, left much. They referred to the "pointed tail prairie hens" and compared them with the "prairie fowl common to Illinois" [pinnated grouse] that were better known in the eastern parts of the United States. The Lewis and Clark expedition saw "Great Numbers of Grouse" below the mouth of the Grand River in South Dakota in the fall of 1804 and at Ft. Mandan in North Dakota the same winter. The species was abundant throughout this area.[2] Clark noted the differences between the pinnates and sharptails in the journals dated September 2, 1806, on the expedition's return trip while camped near Yankton: "I saw 4 prairie fowls common to Illinois, these are the highest up which have been seen."[3] It is apparent that the men on this early expedition readily recognized the difference between the pinnates and sharptails. Their references all were made to the sharptail, and Lewis wrote in considerable detail explaining the difference between the two species.

Grouse in South Dakota were also recorded by the Loisel expedition which established a fur post on the Great Bend of the Missouri River, 1796-1804. They reported "pheasants" in every season as abundant.[4] And in 1812 John Luttig, another fur trader at Ft. Manuel Lisa near the present South Dakota - North Dakota line, wrote, "killed 1 pheasant".[5] "Pheasants" in both these cases were, of course, sharptails.

By the mid-1800's several competent observers were recording excellent natural history notes. Among these men was the naturalist, Audubon. After his arrival in North Dakota in 1843, he wrote that his party "started the first and only Prairie Hen we have seen since our departure from St. Louis"[6] at the Great Bend of the Missouri River fifty miles from Pierre. This reference was to

---

[1]Crawford, L. F. *History of North Dakota*, Vol. I, p. 142.

[2]Burroughs, R. D., *The Natural History of the Lewis and Clark Expedition*, p. 211.

[3]Ibid, p. 211.

[4]Tabeau, P., *Tabeau's Narrative of Loisel's Expedition to the Upper Missouri*, p. 88.

[5]Luttig, J. C., *Luttig's Journal of a Fur Trading Expedition on the Upper Missouri*, 1812-1813, p. 71.

[6]Audubon, M., *Audubon and His Journals*, Vol. II, p. 514.

the pinnated grouse whereas all later references specifically named the "sharptailed grouse". The sharptail is mentioned many times in his journals.

A few years after the Audubon trip to the Missouri River country, an English sportsman, John Palliser, visited Ft. Union to hunt. On short excursions from the fort "Rabbits and prairie hens were our principal game," he wrote. "The bird is evidently a species of grouse, and stands as tall, but perhaps not quite so heavy."[7] Here he apparently referred to a comparison with another grouse (pinnate) with which he was familiar. Although Palliser did not differentiate between the members of the grouse family, he was no doubt describing sharptails at Ft. Union.

Homesteading at Rock Lake around 1900.

The artist, Rudolph Kurz, at Ft. Union in 1851, also mentions "prairie hens" as being present in the fort's museum cases. ". . . we rode across the prairie into the west. The first day we saw nothing but prairie chickens, black birds, and in the evening several shy antelope."[8]

While living at Ft. Berthold in 1858-66, Henry Boller noted that the birds were very abundant and enough for a savory stew could be shot at almost any time, within a few hundred yards of camp."[9]

By the late 1800's homesteaders and other travelers began to move into North Dakota in considerable numbers. They left many accounts which indicated the prevalence of the sharptail. Among the visitors was Dr. Elliot Coues,

[7]Palliser, J., The Solitary Hunter or Sporting Adventures in the Prairies, p. 82.
[8]Kurz, R. F., Journal of Rudolph Friederich Kurz, 1846-1852, p. 108.
[9]Boller, H., Among the Indians. Eight Years in the Far West, p. 212.

whose voluminous report on the wildlife of the region outlined the range of the pinnate and sharptail and further differentiated between the two subspecies of sharptails (Columbian and prairie).[10] One of North Dakota's most beloved provincial historians, Joseph H. Taylor of Washburn, stated that grouse were more plentiful in 1873 than at any later period.[11] And Teddy Roosevelt, living and hunting on his Elkhorn Ranch in the Badlands near Medora, agreed concerning the large number of birds:

> The sharp-tailed prairie fowl is the most plentiful of the feathered game to be found on the northern cattle plains, where it replaces the common prairie chicken so abundant on the prairies to the east and southeast of the range of our birds. In habits, it is much like the latter, being one of the grouse which keep to the open, treeless tracts, though it is far less averse to timber than is its nearest relative, and often is found among the cottonwood trees and thick brush which fringe the streams.[12]

It is noticeable, however, that by the 1890's pinnated grouse were as common as sharptails in some areas of the state. Here are some of the statements of old-timers presently living in North Dakota concerning the number of grouse before and after 1900: (See old-timer list, back of book).

Southwest (Badlands):

Chris Rasmussen, Medora — We had thousands of grouse in the early days in the Little Missouri Bottoms (1908-23). When you'd shoot a bird out of the bottoms, there would be so many grouse getting up, the air was filled with a roar of wings.

Charles Stewart, Carson — In 1913-14 we had old white Flint corn piles in open bins near the farm buildings. The bins were made of woven wire and during the winter the sharptails packed around the food supply so thick they couldn't all feed at one time. They were practically all sharptails.

Virgil Carroll, Rhame — We'd have 200-300 (sharptails) around the strawstack in in the fall and winter in 1914. They are fewer in 1960 than in the teens. Bacon Creek was loaded with them as recently as 1951-52 so we still have highs and lows on them.

Harv Robinson, Dickinson — In this country in the 1890's they were all sharptails and there were lots of them.

Northwest:

J. B. Lyon, Williston — In 1904 the sand hills had the square tails thicker than sharptails but in the breaks where the Badlands begin the sharptails were predominant — in fact, practically all were sharptails. Pinnates were found in more scattered bands.

Harvey McConnell, Kenmare — Both species in about equal numbers (early 1900's). Sharptails were numerous in the hills west of here in 1915. You could get your limit at anytime.

North-central:

Edwin Peterson, Rugby — In 1906 the sharptails were about as plentiful as the pinnates at Souris, No. Dak. Both were numerous at that time.

Joseph Quamme, Westhope — At Hope in the late 1890's and early 1900's the birds were mostly pinnates but the white-breasted (sharptails) grouse were the most plentiful in the foothills of the Turtle Mountains.

[10]Coues, E., *Birds of the Northwest*, p. 408.

[11]Taylor, J. H., *Beavers and Their Ways*, p. 204.

[12]Roosevelt, T. R., *Hunting Trips of a Ranchman*, p. 74.

Northeast:

> *Dr. W. F. Sihler, Devils Lake* — There were lots of sharptails and prairie chickens when I first started hunting in 1899. Almost any time in those days you could hunt an hour at Grand Harbor (north end of Devils Lake) and have all the grouse you could use.

> *C. J. Ness, Cando* — The pinnated grouse hunting was good here in 1912-14. In 1916-17, the population began coming down and by the 1920's sharptails began replacing the pinnates. The Turtle Mountains were good hunting for sharptails earlier, however.

South-central:

> *Fred Petrie, Linton* — The birds here in this area from 1900-15 were mostly sharptails but six miles east of Linton pinnates were quite common.

> *Glen Wood, Emmonsburg* (Missouri River) — We always had more sharptails than pinnates here. In 1912, I killed sixty-four sharptails in a three week period while putting up hay on the Beaver Creek Bottoms. In winter you'd see flocks of 150-200 in those days.

Southeast:

> *Ben Baenen, Jamestown* — When I came to our homestead nine miles south of Jamestown in 1892, there were prairie chickens everyplace. They were mostly "broadtails." They were thick until the 1930's.

> *Everett Hyatt, Ludden* — They were all pinnates here in 1900 and shortly afterwards.

In summarizing the grouse history one is safe in assuming that the sharptail has been in North Dakota for hundreds, maybe thousands, of years. It has been here longer, and with more persistence, than its close relative the pinnate whose history is found in a later chapter. Although the sharptail has experienced ups and downs in population, the statewide numbers probably are much below those of the years before 1930 as most of the old-timers have stated. Sharptail populations have been governed by the amount of mixed prairie grasses, and the future of the species is in as much jeopardy as any of our game birds at this time.

Role

Whether a modern game species plays an important role living with the human race can generally be determined by answering several questions: Is the game good to eat? Is it fun to hunt? Almost as important: Is it compatible with man and his economic interests? And of tertiary importance: Can its by-products be utilized, or is it graceful and pleasing to look at?

The Indian and early white man were dependent on wildlife for their subsistence. A good example, the buffalo, was utilized for food, weapons, clothing and shelter. Large game animals were much preferred over small animals and birds because they provided larger quantities of food and materials. According to W. R. Wood, archeologist for the North Dakota State Historical Society, sharptail bones have been found at only one site in North Dakota, Kipp's Trading Post at the mouth of the White Earth River.[13] Although birds like the sharp-tailed grouse were used for food and other purposes, their role was perhaps equally as important from other points of view.

The sharptail, for instance, was mimicked in Indian ceremonies. The Red Man's "chicken dance" is a takeoff on the dance of this bird. There is the same wheeling and spinning motion, stamping of the feet, semi-crouched position of the body, mock aggressiveness, uttered sounds, and "trance-like attitude" of

[13]Wood, W. R., Letter, April 2, 1963.

the participant. At least some tribes used the feathers of the sharptail for orna-
mentation. Maximilian described one Cree warrior at Ft. Union in 1833 who
decorated his headdress with the "whole tail of the prairie hen."[14]

The Hidatsa Indians called the bird Sihska, and since that time names
have varied considerably. Lewis and Clark called him "sharptail" from the
beginning. The name was based on the physical appearance of the bird. In
the early 1800's, Loisel[15] and Luttig[16] referred to him as "the pheasant," probably
associating the bird with other species with which they were already familiar.
Down through the years the names multiplied as more people from faraway
places saw the bird.

The grouse has been called "spike-tailed," "pointed-tailed," "pin-tailed,"
"white-bellied," "speckle-bellied," "white-breasted," "black-footed," "willow
grouse," "white grouse," and "prairie grouse." Also "prairie hen," "prairie
chicken," "fool hen," "wild chicken," and just plain "chicken." At the present
time residents of western North Dakota commonly refer to him as "prairie
chicken" while in the eastern part of the state he is more often called "grouse"
or, more acceptably, "sharp-tailed grouse."

The courtship grounds of this bird have also gone under many different
titles. They have been called "walk-arounds," "tooting," "booming," "drumming,"
"strutting," "wooing," "stamping," "dubbing," "hooting," "cooing," and the currently accepted "dancing" grounds. One of the most appropriate local names
was coined by rancher Louis Schmeling, of Golden Valley County who in the
spring of 1963 stated he had plenty of grouse in his area and they were "jigging
around" on every hilltop.

The sound of the sharptail in flight has been called "kuk-kuk-kuk," "clucking,"
"cackling," "chattering," "crowing," etc. Likewise the sounds of the cocks on
the dancing grounds have been called many different things. This is understandable because the birds emit a variety of noises during their courtship
activities. The stamping of the feet, the rustling and clicking of the tail feathers,
the beating of the wings, the gobbling, the hooting and cackling as the bird

[14]Maximilian, *Travels in the Interior of North America, Maximilian of Wied,* Vol. II, p. 13.
[15]Tabeau, op. cit., p. 88.
[16]Luttig, op. cit., p. 71.

jumps off the ground, and the expulsion of air from the purple neck sacs, all add up to a confusing mixture of eerie sounds.

Because of its size, the sharptail was not heavily hunted for food except during periods of big game scarcity. It was, however, taken when the opportunity arose and contributed variety to the pot. Its dark meat is exceedingly palatable. Not everyone would agree that it is better than the pheasant, ruffed grouse, or other game; nevertheless, it is often placed near the top of the list of good eating.

One of the first men to note this was Audubon, who also stated that the season in which the meat is taken is essential to its enjoyment:

June 10, 1843 — Bell shot a Sharp-tail Grouse, which we ate at our supper and found pretty good, though sadly out of season.[17]

July 26, 1843 — We saw two Grouse one of which Bell killed, and it we found very good this evening for our supper.[18]

August 2, 1843 — The Sharp-tailed Grouse are first-rate eating now, as they feed entirely on grasshoppers, and berries of different kinds.[19]

Another observer who appreciated this food was easterner Charles C. Coffin who visited North Dakota on a sight-seeing tour in 1869. While traveling from Abercrombie to Georgetown (north of Fargo) by carriage and horseback in the latter part of July, he wrote:

Those who had shotguns went to hunt; while some of us tried the river [Red] for fish, but returned luckless. The supper was good enough, however, without trout or pickerel. Who can ask for anything better than prairie chicken [sharptail], plover, duck, pork, and pigeons? . . .

The prairie chickens are whirring in every direction, and one of our bluff and burly teamsters, who is at home upon the prairies, who in the First Minnesota Regiment faced the Rebels in all the battles of the Peninsula, who was in the thickest of the fight at Gettysburg, who is as keen-sighted as a hawk, takes the grouse right and left as they rise. His slouched hat bobs up and down everywhere. He seems to know just where the game is; now he is at your right hand, now upon the run a half-mile away upon the prairies. He stops, raises his gun . . . there is a puff of smoke, another, and he has two more chickens in his bag. We are sure of having good suppers as long as he is about.[20]

[17]Audubon, op. cit., Vol. II, p. 23.
[18]Ibid., Vol. II, p. 114.
[19]Ibid., Vol. II, p. 126.
[20]Coffin, C. C., *The Seat of Empire*, p. 59, 78.

Theodore Roosevelt in the 1880's told of the enjoyment of hunting and the quality eating the bird afforded:

Large game is still that which is sought after, and most of the birds killed are either simply slaughtered for the pot, or else shot for the sake of variety, while really after deer or antelope, though every now and then I have taken a day with the shotgun after nothing else but prairie grouse . . .

Like the latter bird [pinnate], and unlike the ruffed grouse and blue grouse, which have white meat, its flesh is dark, and it is very good eating from about the middle of August to the middle of November, after which it is tough. . . .

Occasions frequently arise, in living a more or less wild life, when a man has to show his skill in shifting for himself; when, for instance he has to go out and make a foray upon the grouse, neither for sport nor yet for a change of diet, but actually for food. . . .

By the middle of August the young are well enough grown to shoot, and are then most delicious eating. . . .

On more than one occasion I would have gone supperless or dinnerless had it not been for some of these grouse. . . .

Salt, like tea, I had carried with me, and it was not long before two of the birds, plucked and cleaned, were split open and roasting before the fire. And to me they seemed the most delicious food, although even in November the sharptails, while keeping their game flavor, have begun to be dry and tough, most unlike the tender and juicy young of August and September. . . .[21]

Shortly before the turn of the century Dwight Huntington came to North Dakota to hunt and soon after his arrival pronounced the sharptail as "the best of the American grouse." He commented, too, on its preparation for the table:

. . . Its flesh is always in fine condition for the table and the young birds are tender and delicious. I prefer all grouse broiled quickly, before a fire, but they are very good cooked in any way domestic chickens are, and in the winter they may be stewed or parboiled to advantage like domestic fowls of mature age.[22]

On the other hand, Coues was not altogether flattering:

I myself do not esteem it very highly. A tender young Grouse, early in the season, is not to be despised, but all such specially-flavored meat is likely to soon become distasteful, especially if, on one or two occasions, a person has been forced upon to surfeit of it. Confined to Grouse for a few days, most persons, I should judge, would find relief in mess-pork.[23]

There are many old-timers still living in North Dakota who enjoy grouse on the table, to say nothing of the modern "station wagon hunters" who will probably enjoy it again next fall. Glen Wood of Emmonsburg relishes grouse or he certainly wouldn't have partaken of it "practically every day for dinner" in a three week period in 1912. Louis Nostdal of Rugby says, "Of all the game, grouse was my favorite, and we used to cook them over an open fire at Smoky Lake in 1902." "We'd hang them and use them as food in the winter," adds Dr. W. F. Sihler of Devils Lake. And George Schiefer of Kenmare says, "We generally ate one or two whenever we wanted them at any time of the year. It was common for nearly everyone to live off grouse in those days (1890's)."

[21]Roosevelt, op. cit., p. 74-91.
[22]Huntington, D. W., *Our Feathered Game, A Handbook of North American Game Birds*, p. 75.
[23]Coues, op. cit., p. 418.

No doubt grouse on the table in the 1960's is more of a gourmet's dish than the commonplace item it was, at least in North Dakota, around 1900. There were even men in the early days who hunted game for the extra income. Times were tough here and grouse plentiful, while "back east" there were more people with money but grouse were rapidly on the decline. Even in the east the lower income men often made trips west to "market hunt." Pinnated grouse, waterfowl, and big game were their primary targets. Game they acquired was sold and served on tables of the upper-class epicureans of the day. Reuben Humes of Dickinson was one North Dakotan who benefited by hunting for the market in 1900: "Some mornings I would kill as high as fifty chickens [sharptails]. I kept a few and sold the others for fifteen cents in Dickinson. They were packed and shipped east." Presumably by "packed and shipped" he refers to the method of "boxing or barreling" the game with salt or charcoal and transporting it on the railroad.[24]

Market hunting was also referred to by the Dickinson Press:

> George Frye and W. L. Richards, (Cherry Creek area), being neighbors, and both sportsmen, often hunted prairie chickens together (late 1880's). Those were the days when flocks numbered many hundreds. One time the two men shot 500 birds and sold them to Joe Green for 20 cents apiece. He shipped them east and received high prices for them.[25]

References to wild game on the rich man's table "back east" did not always mean that "back east" was beyond the boundaries of North Dakota. The 1880 Christmas menu at the Dakota House in Jamestown listed "Galtine of prairie chicken a la jelee."[26] The year before on November 22, 1879, the Grand Pacific Hotel in Chicago listed "Roast Pin-tail grouse" among a long list of game delicacies.[27] These special menus were common at many cities all over the United States in the early settlement period, and no doubt many North Dakota sharptails ended up appeasing the appetites of customers who had never seen the bird in its natural environment.

Altogether, the role of the sharptail has not been controversial, especially when one considers the varying reputations of such game birds as the pheasant. It is a rare occasion, for instance, that the sharptail is condemned as a depredator of agricultural crops. There have undoubtedly been instances where large winter packs of grouse have consumed large quantities of grain in open cribs, but this has never necessitated mass campaigns to control their numbers. The bird's widespread reputation of eating grasshoppers in summer and "budding" in winter has counteracted what little adverse criticism may have been cast in his direction. The farmer looks at the grouse as he does the Hungarian partridge — as a friend rather than a pest.

The argument that the grouse chases pheasants and other birds out of the country is practically nonexistent. Generally the argument is reversed and the pheasant has sometimes been condemned for misconduct and strife among game

[24]*WPA Historic Data Project, 1938, Reuben Humes Biography*, p. 3.

[25]*Dickinson Press*, July 2, 1957.

[26]*Jamestown's Diamond Jubilee, 1883-1958*, p. 25.

[27]*North Dakota Outdoors*, Feb. 1943, p. 5.

bird populations. When pheasant stocking gained momentum in the early 1930's many people went along with the idea of introducing this new game bird. No doubt they realized that the grouse were on the decline and felt the pheasant would be a suitable replacement. One of few, however, who wrote in defense of the native birds, was Norman Wood:

> It is a question, however, if the money and effort needed to successfully introduce this species (pheasant) could not be better employed to protect and propagate the many fine native game birds which are better adapted to the natural conditions of the state.[28]

Dyed-in-the-wool grouse hunters may be a minority compared with the pheasant hunters, but North Dakotans are indeed fortunate in having such a fine all-around game bird as the sharp-tailed grouse. Eastern states have trapped and transplanted sharptails in the effort to gain another huntable species. The results have been largely unsuccessful. If the sharptail were to fade completely out of the wildlife picture in North Dakota, and it has been slowly losing ground, the bird would undoubtedly be missed by many people. On the other hand, as in the case of the heath hen and passenger pigeon, now extinct, the bereavement could be relatively short-lived. Some people seem to feel that the sharptail doesn't have any significant role in man's progress.

---

[28]Wood, N. A., *A Preliminary Survey of the Bird Life of North Dakota*, p. 82.

Harvest

There is no way of estimating the number of sharptails harvested by hunting the past two or three hundred years in the state. Annual harvest estimates have been kept for only the past twenty-five years.

Grassland that is required for sharptail survival is gradually being converted to cultivated crops, pasture for livestock, and other human economic interests. Thus the statewide grouse population has gradually declined the past fifty years. With this decline there has been public concern to control the grouse harvests. More hunters using modern shotguns, and more automobiles moving over more roads into areas that were relatively inaccessible in the past, have permitted more complete harvests of game. The Game and Fish Department has advocated annual open seasons under the realization that hunting alone has been only a minor limiting factor on the overall sharptail population. Harvests have been reduced by opening seasons only in the fall, limiting the bag, and closing some areas in the state for the past twenty years.

If one is to appreciate and evaluate the harvest of the sharptail, he must consider the methods of harvest in the past and present. Bow and arrow hunting employed by the Indians was for the most part extremely inefficient; it certainly did not deplete the grouse populations. Since the Indian was far more interested in big game than small, there is a question whether he spent much time hunting the sharptail. It is true that gophers, rabbits, and game birds were taken with snares, but most small game was left to boys just learning to hunt.

The introduction of firearms was a significant step forward for the hunter. First guns used by the fur trappers and frontiersmen were single-shot flintlocks which enabled the hunters to kill game with greater consistency. Sharptail kills with these weapons were made while the birds were perched in a tree, shrub, or standing on the ground. Many old-timers became expert shots who occasionally killed the birds in the air with long rifles, but not with the ease of the modern shotgun. It was difficult to kill great numbers of birds at one time with flint-locks. A fine description of these guns was recorded in the journals of Alexander Henry at Pembina shortly after 1800:

> The guns used in the Northwest were made in England especially for purposes connected with the fur trading business. They were imported by way of York Factory and exchanged at the posts for peltries at certain values. They continued to have flint fire locks long after the percussion cap had come into general use on account of the great distances to the points at which the latter might be obtained. If an Indian or other hunter got out of his supply of percussion caps, on the supposition that he used them, it might be a hundred or more miles from the nearest post, a percussion fire gun would be of no use, while the flintlock gun was serviceable at any time.[29]

Hunters of today may be surprised to learn that the shotgun was held in contempt by many of the early hunters and Indians. In fact, the shotgun was called the "squaw gun,"[30] a disrespectful term for the period.

In North Dakota the rifle was used more than the shotgun until 1900, and the rifle was the more popular weapon for many more years in the Badlands. It was essential for killing big game. Powder used for shotguns was of inferior quality, difficult to obtain and, although shotguns appeared in the territory by the mid-1800's, they were generally in the hands of the wealthy people. The Audubon Expedition carried shotguns and the weapon was preferred over the rifle for bird shooting. Audubon mentioned that Provost, a member of his party, "saw a Grouse within a few feet of him but did not shoot as he had only a rifle."[31]

As late as the 1880's Roosevelt, showing his disdain for the shotgun, claimed that "the expert with a rifle should not be compared with the shotgunner, the former being much more worthy of acclaim."[32]

A pair of North Dakota old-timers comment on the guns used for grouse hunting. H. B. Spiller of Cavalier says:

> The first gun I owned when I was 12 years old was an old Baker double-barrel, 12 gauge breechloader. This was the only breech-loading shotgun in the township (Yorktown, Dickey County) in 1887. It was a job to get black powder for the brass cases. Breech-loading shotguns were rare in those days.

Harv Robinson of Dickinson:

> In this country [the Badlands] in the 1890's we'd often kill two or three grouse to eat. We generally killed them with rifles as there were very few shotguns around in those days. The larger caliber rifle was felt to be more of a necessity. And I'll admit sometimes we'd tear up those grouse pretty bad.

[29]Lee, C. H., *The Long Ago*, p. 16.
[30]Bogardus, A. H., *Field, Cover, and Trap Shooting*, p. 15.
[31]Audubon, op. cit., Vol. II, p. 66.
[32]Roosevelt, op. cit., p. 74.

Buckboard hunting for sharptails at Dickinson, 1910.

The early rifle hunter was not merely content to take grouse with the rifle but added a technique which assured him of more than one bird at a time. Palliser was one of the first to comment on this procedure:

> They [grouse] do not mind the report of the rifle, and when a number are on the same tree you may bag most of them commencing with the lowest so that his fall from the tree may not alarm his companions. . . .

> One beautiful clear, cold morning in January, I started to shoot some prairie fowl. These birds were too wild to shoot with shot, especially with the very inadequate powder imported by the trader into the Indian country; so I took my single-barrelled rifle, and shot them off the branches of the high trees where they used to set sunning themselves, taking the lower first, that his fall might not alarm his companions. This sort of shooting is pretty rifle practice, especially as the prairie hen does not always fly away if you miss, but allows a second shot. Indeed, I have sometimes been amused at seeing the unconscious bird, on feeling the wind of the bullet, peck with his bill in the direction of it, giving an angry chuckle as it whizzed past him.[33]

Boller and Roosevelt also mentioned this step-by-step system of picking off grouse one by one with a rifle. Among the living old-timers who employed this unique method of harvesting grouse with a .22 caliber rifle are George Harvey of Williston and Glen Wood of Emmonsburg.

Another method seldom exploited by the modern hunter is blind shooting. Some present day hunters will follow a large pack of grouse to learn where they are feeding in a stubble or corn field. In late afternoon the hunters may hide nearby for a blind or pass shoot, or they may walk in with a party and do some

---

[33]Palliser, op. cit., p. 100.

flush shooting.   Sometimes the results are good.   Reuben Humes mentioned his successful sharptail hunting of 1900 which combined blind shooting and the .22 caliber rifle:

> In the fall of the year I shot many grouse with a .22 rifle.   I would find a large cottonwood tree that was located near a patch of bullberries.   Then I built a blind about thirty or thirty-five yards from the cottonwood tree.   To make the blind I made a depression in the ground and covered it with branches and grass.   I crawled into the blind and waited for the grouse to come.   Sometimes hundreds of them would light in the cottonwood tree.   I shot grouse that were in the lower branches and worked up.   I shot them in the head and as long as they tumbled to the ground the other grouse would not fly away, but if I just wounded one and it flew away the others would usually follow.[34]

In addition to the bow and arrow and snares there is the probability that the early Indians caught grouse with some type of baited traps.   They left written and verbal accounts of taking eagles, other large birds, and fish with traps constructed of willows and similar materials.   Early white settlers trapped sharptails for food.   Among those who still talk about it is Arthur Anderson of Belfield:

> When grouse were plentiful in the period 1890-1900 we even made traps for them out of lathes.   These traps were four feet square and three or four feet high. We used wheat straw as bait and sometimes we'd catch a half dozen birds in one catch.

"Jake" Bjornseth of Dunseith, a veteran fur trapper, also speaks of trapping grouse:

> During the years of high grouse populations around 1900, and later, we made grouse traps and used them to catch sharptails in the winter.   These traps were two by four feet and two feet high.   They were made of willows the size of your finger and had swinging drop doors where the birds could enter to feed on the bait.   Generally we set the traps around strawstacks and baited them with wheat and barley.   Sometimes we'd have our traps full of birds — which was about a dozen at one time.   They were real easy to catch.   After we caught them we dressed and froze them to be used for food. We'd trap all winter and had a ready food supply.

Early Indians walked to the hunting grounds and thus covered limited areas. Although the Indians kept dogs the animals were of minor importance in grouse hunting since the hunter did not have reliable weapons with which to kill the birds after the dogs winded them.   The later addition of the horse obviously permitted the Indian to cover more ground in a shorter time, but again, until firearms were added, grouse hunting was for the most part unproductive.

After the arrival of the shotgun, horseback hunting became a most satisfactory method of harvesting sharptails.   Theodore Roosevelt mentioned that he had killed four with one shot from horseback at "horse jog on a regular cowpony-gait, a kind of single foot pace, between a walk and a trot."[35]   Chris Rasmussen of Medora "hunted a lot of sharptails by horseback around 1900."   And Glen Wood shot the birds "from an old roan saddle horse, and many's the time I unloaded the magazine of six loads and shot six grouse."   Dan Connell of Medora, hunting from horseback in the Badlands, is shown on page 17.

---

[34]*WPA Historic Data Project*, op. cit., p. 3.
[35]Roosevelt, op. cit., p. 76.

Rancher Dan Connell with sharptails taken at the TIX Ranch in the Badlands in 1905.

The most common "horse hunting" in 1900, and later, was from democrat wagons, spring buggies, buckboards, and other horse-drawn vehicles. Sportsmen could hunt in company and enjoyed a certain degree of comfort. Furthermore, since they often camped out for several days during a hunting trip, it was possible to tote along their equipment in the vehicle. H. B. Spiller of Cavalier recalls hunting

> . . . from a 'spindle-body' road wagon, a light one-horse, one-seated affair with spindling around the seat and platform. On Sunday afternoons my wife and I would take a two or three hour ride east and south of Pembina and kill fifteen to twenty grouse in less than five miles of driving. We did this from spring until fall.

In 1911, Arthur Anderson and his wife of Belfield took a forty mile trip in a spring wagon drawn by a team of mules to visit her father's ranch in the Badlands north of the Little Missouri River. On this trip he relates, "We were gone over a week. It took two days to get where we were going. We killed, cooked, and ate sharptails for all the meals enroute. We called the trip our second honeymoon."

Sharptails on the dog cart at Kenmare, 1904. Left to right: George Child, John Persons, Ed Gross and Roy Smith.

Nonresidents who came to hunt in North Dakota during the early 1900's often rented buggies. Ben Bird of Medora operated three livery barns between Almont and the South Dakota line between 1905 and 1911 and traveled east as far as Dawson to provide transportation and guide service for nonresident hunters. He guided the famous railroad men, Jim and Walt Hill, and hauled them around the Lake Isabel area in a two-seated spring wagon. Ben kept bird dogs for the hunters' use and, on one occasion, received $25.00 per day for guiding while a Minneapolis calendar company photographed the hunt.

By the 1920's the automobile was well on the way to replacing the horse-drawn vehicle. Thus the method of hunting was changing. Roads were being improved in all counties of the state and it became common practice in the Red River Valley to hunt sharptails in the Coteau or Badlands, traveling to the hunting grounds and returning home all in one or two days.

Some aspects of harvesting sharptails are not covered in this chapter. The use of dogs, a controversial issue for many years, and a definite asset to hunting any game species, is presented in detail in Chapter 11. Some of the methods of harvest are also discussed in the pinnated grouse chapter.

Also, it is important to repeat here one implication in many of the statements of the old-timers. That is, sharptails should be harvested in the fall. The September grouse are excellent in flavor and their population is at its highest point for the year. Since grouse mature earlier than pheasants, the young are generally adult-sized. Veteran sharptail hunters recognize and appreciate the pleasant sixty degree, windless days of September for successful hunting. The birds hold well to dogs and they have not developed the wild characteristic so noticeable by the time they have "packed up" in November.

The harvest figures for the sharptail in recent years are shown in the following table.

TABLE 1   **SHARPTAIL HARVESTS**

Year	Sharptails per Hunter During the Season	Estimated Sharptail Harvest	Year	Sharptails per Hunter During the Season	Estimated Sharptail Harvest
1935	2.0	45,000	1950	0.9	50,000
1936-37	Information unavailable		1951	1.1	70,000
1938	4.2	71,000	1952	1.4	96,000
1939	4.7	127,000	1953	1.4	70,000
1940	4.6	133,000	1954	1.2	75,000
1941	3.9	150,000	1955	1.3	91,000
1942	3.5	144,000	1956	2.4	167,000
1943	2.7	110,000	1957	1.2	83,000
1944	2.2	110,000	1958	1.6	119,000
1945	1.0	70,000	1959	0.8	45,000
1946	0.6	38,000	1960	1.7	99,000
1947	0.2	10,000	1961	1.3	72,000
1948	1.8	130,000	1962	1.6	79,000
1949	0.7	50,000			

Seasons and Regulations

Any qualms the Indians may have had about killing sharptail grouse during the countless years before the arrival of white men have not been widely publicized. Because of the life Indians lived, one which made no drastic changes in the grassland, there was little need for any hard and fast seasons and regulations. Their methods of hunting were relatively ineffectual when it came to killing great numbers of grouse. And the number of Indians was small compared to the number of white men to come later. Any regulations that benefited sharptails were coincidences generated by Indian customs or taboos. Examples of these were the taboo concerned with the killing of the white buffalo or the custom of the hunting chief announcing the exact time and place for a buffalo hunt. The hunter who violated these restrictions was in for far more trouble from his companions than the poacher in modern times.

Once the white man laid claim to the Dakota Territory he asserted his own rules and regulations. Some of the first ones applied to hunting and wild game. As early as 1862 the first Dakota Territorial Legislature passed an act forbidding

> . . . all Indians to trespass or enter upon any ceded land within the territory for the purpose of hunting or fishing, or traveling to and from the land or hunting grounds of different tribes of Indians without having first obtained a written pass or permit for such purposes from the local United States agent of the tribe.[36]

It has been inferred that killing game was an important issue, but the 1932 Annual Report of the Game and Fish Department stated, "The sponsors of this legislation were actuated by a desire to restrain the roving propensities of the red man rather than by any awakened interest in game protection."[37]

The first legislation to directly affect the sharptail grouse was passed in 1875. The law stated that it would be unlawful for any person, except on his own premises, to kill any grouse "between the first day of March and the first day of August in each and every year."[38] The purpose of the law was to allow the birds to reproduce during the closed season. A section of the act specified a fine of "not less than two, or more than fifteen dollars"[39] to be paid if the birds, their nests, or eggs, were destroyed during the closed season.

During the session of 1877 the legislators prohibited the sale and traffic of grouse outside Dakota Territory and reduced the open season to the period August 15 to December 31.[40]

One of the currently accepted methods of regulating game bird harvests, bag limits, was inaugurated in 1887 when the legislature specified that not more than twenty-five grouse could be taken in one day or held in possession.[41]

The first law that prohibited such unscrupulous harvest methods as trapping, snaring, netting, bird lime, and artificial lights came in 1897.[42] This was the same year the first official game hunting license was required, although a special license to hunt with a dog had been initiated the previous year. (See page 205).

It is safe to assume that the laws prior to this time were of little consequence; after all, who was around to enforce them? There were no full-time game wardens. A game commissioner had been appointed in 1884 but this was a part-time operation for the appointee, a man who was not backed up with any wardens until ten years later. In 1893 forty-eight men were appointed by the governor as "game and fish protectors"[43] but it was difficult to prosecute many cases under the few existing laws of the period. Evidence of this haphazard

---

[36]*North Dakota State Game and Fish Dept., Third Annual Report,* 1932, p. 54.

[37]Ibid., p. 54.

[38]*Dakota Legislative Assembly Laws, 11th Session, 1874-75,* p. 205.

[39]Ibid., p. 205.

[40]*Dakota Legislative Assembly Laws, 14th Session, 1881,* p. 90.

[41]*North Dakota Game and Fish Records, 1891-1935,* p. 27.

[42]*North Dakota Legislative Assembly Laws, Fifth Session, 1897,* p. 130.

[43]*North Dakota Legislative Assembly Laws, Third Session, 1893,* p. 174.

Tommy Bry, Misty, and sharptails, 1963.

interest in protection has been verified by the statements of old-timers. Many first hunted in the 1890's and early 1900's and were unaware that a license was required until 1910 or later.

The natural elements were as important as the written laws in governing seasons and harvests for many years. Methods of travel, weather, and even insects played a far more important role in protecting sharptails than regulations. In the period before there were man-made laws early explorers noted these hardships. The Lewis and Clark Journals mention the difficulties of travel on land and water, storms that dispirited the party, diseases, food poisoning and bothersome insects.[44] The Loisel party directly blamed mosquitoes in limiting hunting success:

> Often, our hunters, not being able to endure them [mosquitoes], returned at full speed to throw themselves into the boats. What is more they could not aim their weapons when concerned with these insects. In short, the mosquitoes, not leaving the crew to take its food in the evening or its rest at night, exhausted it as much as did all the work of the day.[45]

At a later date (1890's), after a few game regulations were in effect, Frederic Remington noted that insects curtailed one of his party's pinnated grouse hunts in the Valley City area. In this case the nuisance was a swarm of flying ants and the party made a "precipitous retreat, leaving the covey of chickens and their protectors, the ants, in the field."[46]

With the arrival of more people the land was put to greater use in North Dakota and more hunting regulations were put into effect. Some were drawn up for the benefit of game, some for landowners, and some for hunters. First laws on posting and entering cultivated fields appeared in the 1890's. Hunting with dogs was prohibited from 1919-32 (see Chapt. 11). Market hunting was outlawed before 1900, and limiting the number of shells to three in the shotgun magazine was enforced after August 20, 1935, (Fed. Law). Shorter seasons were in effect by the 1930's. Finally, for the first time in 1931 some areas in the state were completely closed to sharptail hunting. All of these benevolent laws, plus many more, were perpetuated to benefit the grouse. No doubt some laws, such as closed seasons during the reproduction period, have served their purpose. Others, such as the completely closed seasons in the eastern quarter of the state for over twenty years, have not resulted in greater numbers of grouse. A changing agricultural picture has had much to do with the declining grouse populations.

Many of the problems of setting seasons and regulations are discussed in more detail in the pheasant chapter and apply to all game. The following table of sharptail seasons and regulations through the years will give the reader some idea of the changes that have taken place.

[44]*North Dakota History, Jan., 1948,* p. 24.

[45]Tabeau, op. cit., p. 63.

[46]Remington, F., *Pony Tracks,* p. 105.

TABLE 2   SHARPTAIL REGULATIONS THROUGH THE YEARS

Year	Season Length	Daily Shooting Hours	Total Days of Hunting*	Day of Week Season Opened	Daily Limit	Possession Limit	Open Area
1875	Aug. 1 - March 1	No limit	212	Sunday	No limit	No limit	All of Dakota Territory
1876	Aug. 1 - March 1	No limit	213	Tuesday	No limit	No limit	All of Dakota Territory
1877	Aug. 1 - Dec. 31	No limit	139	Wednesday	No limit	No limit	All of Dakota Territory
1878	Aug. 15 - Dec. 31	No limit	139	Thursday	No limit	No limit	All of Dakota Territory
1879	Aug. 15 - Dec. 31	No limit	139	Friday	No limit	No limit	All of Dakota Territory
1880	Aug. 15 - Dec. 31	No limit	139	Sunday	No limit	No limit	All of Dakota Territory
1881	Aug. 15 - Dec. 31	No limit	139	Monday	No limit	No limit	All of Dakota Territory
1882	Aug. 15 - Dec. 31	No limit	139	Tuesday	No limit	No limit	All of Dakota Territory
1883	Aug. 15 - Dec. 31	No limit	139	Wednesday	No limit	No limit	All of Dakota Territory
1884	Aug. 15 - Dec. 31	No limit	139	Friday	No limit	No limit	All of Dakota Territory
1885	Aug. 15 - Dec. 31	No limit	139	Saturday	No limit	No limit	All of Dakota Territory
1886	Aug. 15 - Dec. 31	No limit	139	Sunday	No limit	No limit	All of Dakota Territory
1887	Sept. 1 - Dec. 31	No limit	122	Thursday	25	25	All of Dakota Territory
1888	Sept. 1 - Dec. 31	No limit	122	Saturday	25	25	All of Dakota Territory
1889	Sept. 1 - Dec. 31	No limit	122	Sunday	25	25	All of Dakota Territory
1890	Sept. 1 - Dec. 31	No limit	122	Monday	25	25	All of Dakota Territory
1891	Aug. 20 - Nov. 30	No limit	103	Thursday	25	25	Statewide
1892	Aug. 20 - Nov. 30	No limit	103	Saturday	25	25	Statewide
1893	Aug. 20 - Nov. 30	No limit	103	Sunday	25	25	Statewide

SHARPTAIL REGULATIONS (Continued)

Year	Season Length	Daily Shooting Hours	Total Days of Hunting*	Day of Week Season Opened	Daily Limit	Possession Limit	Open Area
1894	Aug. 20 - Nov. 30	No limit	103	Monday	25	25	Statewide
1895	Aug. 20 - Nov. 30	No limit	103	Tuesday	25	25	Statewide
1896	Aug. 20 - Nov. 30	No limit	103	Thursday	25	25	Statewide
1897	Aug. 20 - Oct. 31	No limit	73	Friday	25	25	Statewide — First laws prohibiting traps, snares, nets, bird lime, or artificial light.
1898	Aug. 20 - Oct. 31	No limit	73	Saturday	25	25	Statewide
1899	Aug. 20 - Oct. 1	No limit	43	Sunday	25	25	Statewide
1900	Aug. 20 - Oct. 1	No limit	43	Monday	25	25	Statewide
1901	Sept. 1 - Oct. 15	Daylight hours only	45	Sunday	25	25	Statewide
1902	Sept. 1 - Oct. 15	Daylight hours only	45	Monday	25	25	Statewide
1903	Sept. 1 - Oct. 15	Daylight hours only	45	Tuesday	25	25	Statewide
1904	Sept. 1 - Oct. 15	Daylight hours only	45	Thursday	25	25	Statewide
1905	Sept. 1 - Oct. 15	Daylight hours only	45	Friday	25	25	Statewide
1906	Sept. 1 - Oct. 15	Daylight hours only	45	Saturday	25	25	Statewide
1907	Sept. 1 - Oct. 15	Daylight hours only	45	Sunday	25	25	Statewide
1908	Sept. 1 - Oct. 15	Daylight hours only	45	Tuesday	25	25	Statewide
1909	Sept. 7 - Nov. 1	½ hour before sunrise to ½ hour after sunset	56	Tuesday	10	20	Statewide

SHARPTAIL REGULATIONS (Continued)

Year	Season Length	Daily Shooting Hours	Total Days of Hunting*	Day of Week Season Opened	Daily Limit	Possession Limit	Open Area
1910	Sept. 7 - Nov. 1	½ hour before sunrise to ½ hour after sunset		Wednesday	10	20	Statewide
1911	Sept. 7 - Nov. 1	½ hour before sunrise to ½ hour after sunset	56	Thursday	10	20	Statewide
1912	Sept. 7 - Nov. 1	½ hour before sunrise to ½ hour after sunset		Saturday	10	20	Statewide
1913	Sept. 7 - Nov. 1	½ hour before sunrise to ½ hour after sunset	56	Sunday	10	20	Statewide
1914	Sept. 7 - Nov. 1	½ hour before sunrise to ½ hour after sunset	56	Monday	10	20	Statewide
1915	Sept. 7 - Nov. 1	Sunrise to sunset	56	Tuesday	10	20	Statewide
1916	Sept. 7 - Nov. 1	Sunrise to sunset	56	Thursday	10	20	Statewide
1917	Sept. 16 - Oct. 17	Sunrise to sunset	32	Monday	5	10	Statewide
1918	Sept. 16 - Oct. 17	Sunrise to sunset	32	Monday	5	10	Statewide
1919	Sept. 16 - Oct. 17	Sunrise to sunset	32	Tuesday	5	10	Statewide
1920	Sept. 16 - Oct. 17	Sunrise to sunset	32	Thursday	5	10	Statewide
1921	Sept. 16 - Oct. 17	½ hour before sunrise to sunset	32	Friday	5	10	Statewide
1922	Sept. 16 - Oct. 17	½ hour before sunrise to sunset	32	Saturday	5	10	Statewide
1923	Sept. 16 - Oct. 17	½ hour before sunrise to sunset	32	Sunday	5	10	Statewide
1924	Sept. 16 - Oct. 17	½ hour before sunrise to sunset	32	Tuesday	5	10	Statewide
1925	Sept. 16 - Oct. 17	½ hour before sunrise to sunset	32	Wednesday	5	10	Statewide

SHARPTAIL REGULATIONS (Continued)

Year	Season Length	Daily Shooting Hours	Total Days of Hunting*	Day of Week Season Opened	Daily Limit	Possession Limit	Open Area
1926	Sept. 16 - Oct. 17	½ hour before sunrise to sunset	32	Thursday	5	10	Statewide
1927	Sept. 16 - Oct. 17	½ hour before sunrise to sunset	32	Friday	5	10	Statewide
1928	Sept. 30 - Oct. 17	½ hour before sunrise to sunset	18	Sunday	5	10	Statewide
1929	Sept. 30 - Oct. 17	½ hour before sunrise to sunset	18	Monday	5	10	Statewide
1930	Oct. 5 - Oct. 15	½ hour before sunrise to sunset	11	Sunday	5	10	Closed in all of Dickey, Richland, and Sargent Counties
1931	Oct. 1 - Oct. 15 (noon)	Sunrise to sunset	14½	Thursday	5	10	Statewide
1932	Oct. 1 - Oct. 15 (noon)	Sunrise to sunset	14½	Saturday	5	10	Statewide
1933	Sept. 20 - Oct. 12 (noon)	Sunrise to sunset	22½	Wednesday	5	10	Statewide
1934	Sept. 22 - Oct. 1 (noon)	Sunrise to sunset	9½	Saturday	5	10	Statewide
1935	Oct. 12 - Oct. 20 (noon)	Sunrise to sunset	8½	Saturday	Unit 1-3 Unit 2-1	Unit 1-3 Unit 2-1	Closed in all or parts of 11 southeast counties
1936	Oct. 10 - Oct. 20 (noon)	Noon to sunset	5½	Saturday	3	3	(See map, page 30)
1937	Oct. 9 - Oct. 18	7:00 a.m. - 4:00 p.m.	10	Saturday	3	3	Closed in five southeast and eight southwest counties
1938	Oct. 1 - Oct. 10	7:00 a.m. - 4:00 p.m.	10	Saturday	3	3	(See map, page 30)
1939	Oct. 1 - Oct. 15	7:00 a.m. - 4:00 p.m.	15	Sunday	3	3	(See map, page 30)
1940	Oct. 1 - Oct. 20	Sunrise to 5:00 p.m.	21	Tuesday	3	3	(See map, page 30)
1941	Sept. 28 - Oct. 19	Sunrise to 6:00 p.m.	22	Sunday	3	6	Closed in five southeast, all or parts of six southwest, and six northeast counties

SHARPTAIL REGULATIONS (Continued)

Year	Season Length	Daily Shooting Hours	Total Days of Hunting*	Day of Week Season Opened	Daily Limit	Possession Limit	Open Area
1942	Sept. 26 - Oct. 25	Sunrise to sunset	30	Saturday	3	6	Closed in 2 southwest and 12 east counties
1943	Sept. 20 - Oct. 15	½ hour before sunrise to sunset	21	Saturday	3	6	Closed in all or parts of 27 east counties
1944	Sept. 20 - Oct. 15	½ hour before sunrise to sunset	26	Wednesday	3	6	Closed in all or parts of 16 east counties
1945	Sept. 30 - Oct. 30	½ hour before sunrise to sunset	21	Sunday	3	6	Closed in all or parts of 32 east counties
1946	Oct. 5 - Oct. 20	½ hour before sunrise to sunset	16	Saturday	3	6	Open in all or parts of 24 west counties
1947	Oct. 15 - Oct. 24	½ hour before sunrise to sunset	10	Wednesday	3	3	(See map, page 31)
1948	Oct. 8 (noon) - Oct. 17	½ hour before sunrise to sunset	9½	Friday	3	3	Open in all or parts of 32 west counties
1949	Oct. 7 (noon) - Oct. 30	Noon to sunset	12	Friday	3	6	Closed in all or parts of 24 east counties
1950	Oct. 6 (noon) - Nov. 5	Noon to sunset	15½	Friday	3	6	Closed in all or parts of 27 east counties
1951	Sept. 28 - Nov. 4	Noon to sunset except ½ hr. before sunrise to sunset on Sat. & Sun.	25	Friday	3	6	Closed in all or parts of 24 east counties
1952	Sept. 26 - Nov. 2	Same as 1951	25	Friday	4	8	Closed in all or parts of 17 east counties
1953	Oct. 1 - Oct. 11	Same as 1951	7½	Thursday	3	6	(See map, page 31)
1954	Oct. 1 - Oct. 17	Same as 1951	11½	Friday	3	6	Closed in all or parts of 20 east counties
1955	Oct. 1 (noon) - Nov. 6	Same as 1951	24	Saturday	3	6	Closed in all or parts of 20 east counties

SHARPTAIL REGULATIONS (Continued)

Year	Season Length	Daily Shooting Hours	Total Days of Hunting*	Day of Week Season Opened	Daily Limit	Possession Limit	Open Area
1956	Sept. 28 (noon) - Nov. 4 Nov. 16 - Nov. 25 (SW of Mo. River)	9:00 a.m. to sunset	47½	Friday	Unit 2-4 Unit 1&3-3	Unit 2-8 Unit 1&3-6	Closed in all or parts of 19 east counties
1957	Unit 1, Sept. 28 - Nov. 7 Unit 2, Sept. 28 - Oct. 13	9:00 a.m. to sunset	50	Saturday	Unit 1-3 Unit 2-2	Unit 1-6 Unit 2-2	Closed in all or parts of 18 east counties
1958	Unit 1, Oct. 4 - Nov. 6 Nov. 12 - Dec. 7 Unit 2, Sept. 27 - Nov. 6 Nov. 12 - Dec. 7	9:00 a.m. to sunset	67	Saturday	Unit 1-4 Unit 2-3	Unit 1-8 Unit 2-6	Closed in all or parts of 19 east counties
1959	Sept. 26 - Nov. 8	9:00 a.m. to sunset	44	Saturday	3	6	Closed in all or parts of 19 east counties
1960	Oct. 1 - Nov. 10	9:00 a.m. to sunset	41	Saturday	3	6	(See map, page 32)
1961	Sept. 30 - Nov. 9	9:00 a.m. to sunset	41	Saturday	3	6	(See map, page 32)
1962	Sept. 15 - Nov. 18	9:00 a.m. to sunset	65	Saturday	4	8	Closed in all or parts of 15 east counties
1963	Sept. 21 - Nov. 7 Nov. 18 - Dec. 15	Sunrise to sunset	76	Saturday	4	8	Closed in all or parts of 15 east counties

*Based on eight hours per day of hunting (Exp., two half days = one day).

Examples of Sharptail Hunting Seasons Since 1936
1936

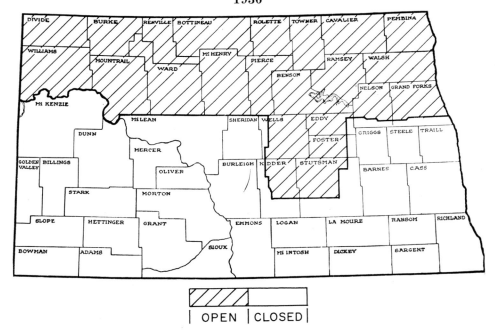

1938-40

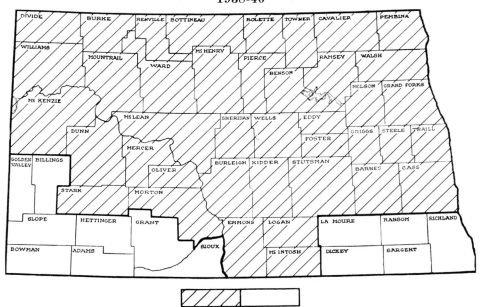

Examples of Sharptail Hunting Seasons Since 1936

1947

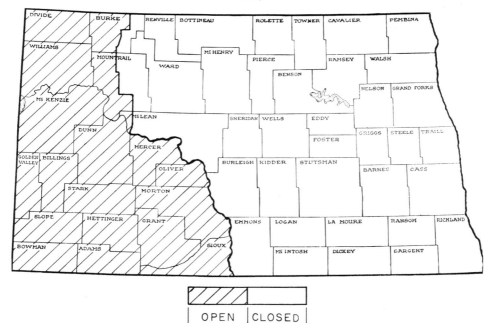

1953

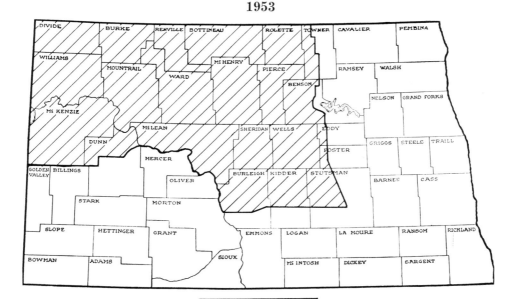

Examples of Sharptail Hunting Seasons Since 1936
1960-61

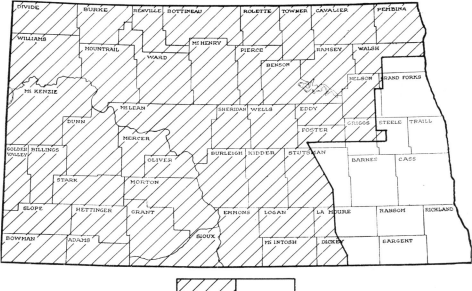

| OPEN | CLOSED |

Limiting Factors

Most people recognize the sharptail as a bird of the prairies. It is found in greatest numbers where there is an abundance of grassland interspersed with 5-30 percent brushland. Maintaining good quality grassland should insure the well-being of the sharptail, but it is not an easy task. A look around will prove this. Raising crops and livestock and building roads and cities have for obvious reasons taken precedence over the preservation of grouse and other wildlife species. But whatever benefits civilization has brought to the grouse, and there have been a few, the preponderant effect has been limiting.

History has shown us the sharptail survived for hundreds, probably thousands of years in North Dakota in the wild, natural state. The bird is acclimated to this region, much more so than the pheasant and other introduced species. In fact, this is the way through evolution, that any bird or animal becomes acclimated to a region — simply living with the conditions in that area for many generations. The sharptail with its heavy undercoating of feathers on the body and legs, special nares in the beak for cold weather breathing, and snowshoe feet, is adapted for the Dakota climate. Sometime in its evolution it rose to feed, or "bud", as we now call it, in trees above the level of snow cover. When blinding blizzards dropped temperatures below zero the

TED CORNELL

bird took to burrowing beneath the snow's surface and weathered out storms. In brief, it became an extremely hardy inhabitant of the prairies. And through the years the grouse survived severe blizzards, drought, prairie fires, and heavy populations of predators. All of these natural elements were of greater magnitude in the past than in modern times. The sharptail survived these possible limiting factors, experiencing highs and lows in the population, but maintaining itself in all areas of the state until the late 1920's. Only in the last thirty years has the species been virtually eliminated in eastern areas of the state. There may be minor reasons for this but, beyond a doubt, the most obvious one is destruction of its habitat — the grasslands.

It is true this destruction has been taking place for hundreds of years in the form of grazing and fire. Wild buffalo, numbering into the millions before their annihilation in the 1800's, were long in a kind of competition with the sharptail. Many early travelers commented on overgrazing in particular areas all over the western United States. However, it is doubtful that the buffalo had the same drastic effect on grasslands as did the arrival of civilization. In most cases the buffalo could move to fresh pastures when one area was overgrazed. Damage may not have been as permanent as domestic grazing that is going on today. And, if the buffalo did stay in one area and overgraze, the grouse could readily move. Early hunters state that they were often forced to travel long distances to find the vast herds, so buffalo could not have been crowded on the prairie. More important was the fact that the buffalo was the main force utilizing the grasslands. In the present day this utilization of the grasslands, accomplished now by many of the forces of civilization, is far more intensive than it ever was in the buffalo years.

Fires, too, may well be more destructive in modern times. Although the early red man and white man often started fearsome fires which swept over hundreds of miles of prairie, the sharptail — except during the nesting season when the results were disasterous — could move to an unfired area where grassland could still be found. Some observers have stated that these early, limited fires even benefited grouse in the long-range scheme of events. Fire held down trees and opened areas to new vegetative growth that added variety to food and cover. However, in the present days of intensive farming, when nearly all available soil is cultivated, and when many farmers practice burning and plowing, the effect on grassland birds can be fatal. Few unmolested areas are available for their escape.

Closely associated with cover requirements for any species is the subject of food. Lewis and Clark noted the sharptail

> Feeds in grass, insects, the leaves of various shrubs on the plains, and on seeds of several species of spelt and wild rye which grow in the richer parts of the plains. In winter their food is the buds of the willow and cottonwood. . . ."[47]

Audubon mentioned in 1843 that the sharptail fed on "rose-berries and the seeds of the wild sunflower and grasshoppers,"[48] and Palliser in 1848, not differenti-

---

[47]Burroughs, op. cit., p. 213.
[48]Audubon, op. cit., Vol. II, p. 166.

ating between the sharptail and pinnate, stated that its flavor was much affected by what it fed on — usually rosebuds in this part of the country.[49]

Some early settlers had a destructive effect on several grouse foods, according to Joseph H. Taylor of Washburn:

> From my observation dating from the first winter here [Painted Woods], grouse or prairie chickens were more plentiful at that time [1873] than at any later period. Besides their feed of rosebuds and dried buck berries, the larger timber's points were well festooned with grape vines, the fruit of which dried in clusters on the vines and furnished delicious chicken feed the long winter through. Besides this the bulberries were everywhere plentiful in the bottomlands from September until February, and the wild cherries of the woodlands cured on the bushes for a much longer period. But as the settlers came in and occupied the land, the more grasping and wanton of their number and those heedless of the rights of their fellows, in a few years had destroyed the greater part of the bulberry bushes and grape vines and in lieu thereof the grouse held to the straw stacks and stubble fields of the farms for a part of their winter sustenance, and thus in many ways fell easy victims to the pot hunter.[50]

Both the sharptail and pinnate attained high populations in the early 1900's. Their comparative numbers in years gone by will never be known but the farming that was taking place before 1930 was not so intensive that it eliminated cover or food required by the birds. Adrian Larson noted this in McKenzie County in the years 1912-26:

> The plains form a distinct life area characterized by the grasses, such as the buffalo, grama, and blue-joint grasses. The wild rose, buckbrush, and silverberry are to be found in the coulees and depressions. This area includes, of course, all of the farm lands. This country has been homesteaded and farmed more or less since 1903. Many artificial groves of trees are scattered over the prairies, and on the whole it is more than likely that there are more birds now than there was prior to 1903.[51]

Larson listed the sharptail as the "common prairie chicken" that "nested abundantly in the area."

The somewhat mixed "benefit" of strawstacks to grouse (Taylor) has already been mentioned; other more recent observers believe the stacks were even more beneficial. C. J. Ness of Cando feels that "the strawstacks were important as both food and cover . . ."

Both Ben Bird of Medora and "Shorty" Foreman of Marmarth stress the importance of food supply for game birds. Foreman recalls:

> The first noticeable decline in sharptails, as I remember it, was about 1918. I attribute this decline to food supply. When there are no bullberries and other berries there are few grouse. We still get years when grouse are plentiful when there's a good supply of berries.

Another locally limiting factor for waterfowl, songbirds and other wildlife is migration. There are also numerous accounts of antelope, buffalo, prairie chicken, and sharptail migrations in North Dakota. Such mass movement is influenced by search for food, desire to escape the cold, or is of hereditary

[49]Palliser, op. cit., p. 83.
[50]Taylor, op. cit., p. 204.
[51]Larson, A., *Birds of Eastern McKenzie County, North Dakota,* p. 40.

nature; it is not completely understood.   Sometimes, as in the case of the sharptail, it is difficult to separate migration from the short movements of the bird.
Traveling several miles to feed is common among grouse but some of the movements during the early settlement years were of broader magnitude involving
greater numbers of birds and longer flights.   Norman Wood wrote of the sharptail, "In winter the species migrate southward and enters all the timber tracts in
numbers."[52]

Elmer T. Judd studied the birds in the Cando area in 1890-96:

> The Prairie Sharptail Grouse.   The most abundant of the grouse family and seen
> the year round, but the winter birds are thought to be those raised farther north.
> There appears to be a marked migration of this sub-species.[53]

There have been more spectacular accounts of pinnated grouse migrations
(see page 103).   It is not uncommon to hear a person say, "We had lots of sharptails until a few years ago but they all moved out."   One man stated that he
remembered when the birds flew to Canada just a few years ago.   The question
remains, if they did migrate where did they end their journey?   Did they move
because of a need for food or cover, or something else?   They may have moved
to escape a fire or the weather in the past, but where would they go today?   The
food and habitat at the end of their flight are often no different from the spot
they vacated.

In addition to migrations, mankind for generations has blamed predators
for declines in game.   If this were the nineteenth instead of the twentieth
century, many observers would undoubtedly be saying, "Kill the coyote or in
five years there won't be any grouse left."   Both the coyote and wolf were,
along with the grouse, once abundant over the Dakota territory, the coyote and
grouse both lasting in numbers into the 1940's.   Lewis and Clark, Audubon,
Boller, and living old-timers have described the large populations of predators,
but forty years of food habit studies have shown the coyote is not a serious
predator on grouse populations.   Grouse formed only a fraction of the coyote's
diet.   The two species lived in harmony for hundreds of years and the grouse
was not "wiped out."

---

[52]Wood, N. A., op. cit., p. 36.

[53]Judd, E. T., *List of North Dakota Birds Found in the Big Coulee, Turtle Mountains and
Devils Lake Region*, 1890-96, p. 15.

Also common on the prairie in greater numbers in the past than the present were aerial predators such as eagles, owls, hawks, and falcons, and a long list of carnivorous animals. Even the controversial red fox was abundant until the 1890's, as evidenced by the fur records from Ft. Union and Pembina and statements of old-timers. Practically all of these predators will kill sharptails when the opportune moment arises but the sharptail is accustomed to living with them and has survived predation for countless generations.

Another common reason presented for the decline of a game bird population is overhunting. As recently as 1946 the North Dakota Museum Review referred to this:

> Our native grouse, the sharptail and the pinnated were formerly found in North Dakota in immense numbers. The change in their natural habitat resulting from the settlement of the state may be one of the principal reasons for their present reduced numbers but without question excessive hunting has been a contributing factor.[54]

Many old-timers who shot hundreds, or "buggy loads," of grouse express regret that they killed so many. Others say they shot them because there were plenty of birds to be shot — the general public condoned indiscriminate killing at one time because the birds were available and the human population was small. But there is no doubt there has been too much indiscriminate shooting. The innovation of the breech-loading shotgun and the influx of humans speeded up the process. Some of the first attempts at conservation were the restriction of market hunting and closing seasons except during the fall and winter months. At the present time, however, the 40 to 60 day sharptail seasons are held annually with no significant damage to the grouse populations. Game managers are certain that the decline in sharptail populations is not due to overhunting, but to habitat destruction. Game bird numbers change rapidly when habitat conditions are right or wrong; populations can recover or drop suddenly. It is obvious that if overhunting did occur forty years ago, or as recently as five, it would have no effect on present populations. In those instances where small isolated populations of grouse are shot out hunting cannot be entirely blamed as the final limiting factor; the condition that resulted in reduced habitat was the primary factor in reducing the population.

Although there are approximately 65,000 upland game hunters in the field each fall in North Dakota, most of these are after pheasants. It is possible that sportsmen do not hunt sharptails as much as forty years ago when the birds were more abundant. Present bag limits and closed seasons ten months of the year are good insurance against overhunting.

Other decimating factors are often discussed, but generally these are not important enough to limit the populations at any time. Some of these are accidents such as flying into high wires or towers, getting trapped under the snow in an ice storm, and being exposed to insecticide spraying. Some accident factors were noticed early in the history of the state; others have been brought about by the modern age. Normal population cycles, too, played a role.

---

[54]*Museum Review*, Oct., 1946, p. 8.

We will never know the exact numbers of the sharptail in the days before the game census, but several things seem clear.   The sharptail once existed in the state in enormous numbers, and with increases in both cultivation and urbanization, these numbers have severely declined.   The past one hundred years of the sharptail are summed up best by Mrs. H. E. Crofford, a pioneer school teacher who traveled from Fargo in 1871:

> The grass that year was more than two feet high.   Prairie chickens [sharptail] were thick.   When we went out for a drive, as we sometimes did, the wheels of the vehicle or the horse's feet often crushed their eggs.   I hated to see the wheel come up, dripping egg yolks.   That wonderful grass waved like a sea in the sunlight, a fore-runner of the wheat fields that would wave there in after years.[55]

---

[55]*North Dakota History, Jan., 1928,* p. 130.

Research and Management

First attempts at sharptail management arrived in the late 1880's when hunting restrictions were imposed.

Since grassland was recognized as essential to sharptails, it was not long before someone conceived the idea of setting aside game refuges where birds could reproduce unmolested by man and domestic livestock. The first refuges were privately owned easement types and some were in operation shortly after 1900. Most of these private lands were under ten year easement to the state but some municipal and state lands were under perpetual easement. Perhaps the original idea of these refuges was well-intended, but the benefit to wildlife was often sadly deficient. On most private easement refuges the owners could continue to graze livestock and cultivate the land and, because of this fact, wildlife did not benefit to any marked degree. Some areas were so small that they were of little value. Finally, the landowner often desired the refuge solely for the purpose of keeping hunters off his land; he had state enforcement at all times which alleviated him of bothersome trespassers.

The second type of refuge, the state-owned, was set up with about the same purpose in mind as the first. Some of the early state refuges, where sharptails were common residents, were Morton County Refuge (640 acres) in 1917 and Dawson Refuge (2,958 acres) in Kidder County in 1921. Most of these were acquired by the state because they had poor quality soil or were misused by man. Although hunting was not permitted on these areas for many years, the current practice has been to permit hunting of most wildlife species. This is in accord with modern concepts of harvest management.

The third type refuge set aside for wildlife was the federal under control of the U. S. Fish and Wildlife Service. Most of these were set aside primarily for waterfowl but many other wildlife species have benefited from these large areas. Some of the first lands set aside as federal refuges included twenty-seven acres of islands at Stump Lake (Nelson County) in 1905, and 1,500 acres of the now 4,400 Chase Lake Refuge (Stutsman County) in 1908. Examples of large federal refuges which have benefited sharptails are Lostwood (15,900 acres) in Burke-Mountrail Counties and Arrowwood (26,700 acres) in Stutsman County, both obtained in 1935. Several other federal refuges were obtained in the 1930's. Although there has been little public hunting, except for deer, permitted on these, there has been some indication that limited hunting may be permitted in the future. Parts of Lake Tewaukon Refuge (6,300 acres) in Sargent County have been opened to pheasant hunting in recent years.

Other public lands where sharptails have benefited because the grassland has not been destroyed are the Theodore Roosevelt National Park Units, some of the lands controlled by the U. S. Forest Service, and Indian Reservations such as Standing Rock and Ft. Berthold. Hunting is permitted on most of the Forest Service and Indian Reservations, but no hunting is permitted in the National Parks.

Most of the Federal Aid projects* (see page 148 for Pittman-Robertson Act, 1937) conducted by the North Dakota Game Department can be termed management projects and include a considerable number of census jobs. A lack of funds and personnel have limited the amount of research undertaken.

The census method most widely used in North Dakota for sharp-tailed grouse is counting birds on spring dancing grounds. Known grounds in all areas of the state are mapped and counts made on male birds occupying these grounds each year. Data obtained is important over a long-term period and population trends are noted. The census is made on approximately four hundred dancing grounds each spring and was first introduced as a Federal Aid project in 1952. (Table 3.)

Roadside (automobile) counts were originated in 1940 for upland game in North Dakota and have proven an excellent method of censusing pheasant and Hungarian partridge populations. These counts are not considered as reliable for sharp-tailed grouse, however, simply because grouse do not frequent the roadsides as consistently as pheasants and Huns. Nevertheless, data obtained on sharptails from late summer roadside counts is used in determining reproduction for the current year.

---

*Federal aid to wildlife restoration projects enable the State Game and Fish Department to carry out research, development, and management of game birds and animals. These projects are called P-R projects in this book.

Spring dancing ground counts indicate sharptail population trends.

Other P-R management type projects conducted on the sharp-tailed grouse are winter aerial census work on specific areas and sex and age work derived from wing samples during the hunting seasons. The aerial census is self-explanatory, but the wing sample work is more comprehensive and can be termed research in some respects. The information obtained from the annual wing sample collections is helpful in predicting population trends before they occur. This project was started in 1949 in North Dakota and 1,500 to 2,000 wings are received from cooperating hunters each fall. (See Table 4.)

Some of the first research work performed on sharptails in North Dakota was undoubtedly food habit studies carried on by Coues and S. D. Judd, already mentioned here. And by 1937, Aldous conducted a modern research project on sharptails in north-central North Dakota in the vicinity of Lower Souris National Wildlife Refuge. He published information on trapping and banding, food habits, parasites, and other life history facts.[56] Klett added excellent research on sharptails in the 1950's after an extensive trapping and banding program on a township study area.[57] The work included new findings on longevity, nesting, habitat requirements, movement, hunting pressure, predation, and other pertinent subjects.

There have been many other short-term management and research projects conducted on the sharptail grouse in North Dakota the past twenty-five years. Several nesting and predation projects have been carried on. Some "timely" projects have been conducted as illustrated by a study of parasitized grouse collected during the 1943 hunting season. No doubt both long-term and short-term studies will be made. Some will add considerably to the knowledge of the species, others may add little. But both types must be accepted as an attempt to benefit the species. Added to the practical application of habitat, research is our best guarantee for maintaining grouse in the future.

---

[56]Aldous, S. E., *Sharp-tailed Grouse in the Sand Dune Country of North-Central North Dakota*, p. 23-31.

[57]Klett, A. T., *Banding and Marking Methods in Studying Seasonal Movements of the Sharp-tailed Grouse in Morton County, North Dakota*, p. 1-53.

TABLE 3
STATEWIDE SHARP-TAILED GROUSE DANCING GROUND COUNTS, 1952-63

Year	No. of Grounds	No. of Cocks	Avg. No. of Cocks/Ground
1952	25	209	8.4
1953	25	177	7.1
1954	80	1186	14.8
1955	157	2256	14.4
1956	191	2580	13.5
1957	156	2364	15.2
1958	192	3168	16.5
1959	192	2306	12.0
1960	205	1550	7.6
1961	207	2373	11.5
1962	117	1664	14.2
1963	117	1585	13.5

TABLE 4   AGE RATIOS OF SHARP-TAILED GROUSE
(taken from wing samples), 1949-63

Year	Juvenile	Adult	Total Birds	Juvenile: Adult Ratio
1949	107	77	184	1.39:1
1950	188	103	290	1.82:1
1951	200	109	309	1.83:1
1952	216	206	422	1.05:1
1953	199	138	337	1.44:1
1954	367	228	595	1.61:1
1955	946	647	1593	1.48:1
1956	725	464	1189	1.56:1
1957	1136	628	1764	1.81:1
1958	926	865	1791	1.07:1
1959	345	413	758	0.84:1
1960	854	365	1219	2.34:1
1931	1079	477	1556	2.26:1
1932	1234	495	1729	2.49:1
1933	1821	725	2546	2.51:1
10-year average (1954-63)				1.69:1

2

Sage Grouse

Scientific name: *Centrocercus urophasianus*

Size:

Length, 22-30 inches. Wingspan, 36-38 inches. Weight, 3-8 lbs. The cocks are about twice as large as the hens and weigh 6-8 lbs.; hens weigh 3-4 lbs.

Coloration:

Predominately gray-brown mottled with white and black. Cocks show considerable dark brown or black at throat and underside of body, and white at breast and tail.

Flight:

Recognized by straight-line, lumbersome takeoff and gradual ascent. "Chuckles" in flight but not so noticeably as the sharptail.

Flock habits:

Like other grouse the sage grouse remain in family groups until spring when immature cocks separate from hens to join adult cocks. Large flocks common in winter on good grouse range.

History

The sage grouse is the largest member of the North American grouse family and second only to the wild turkey in size of all the gallinaceous birds in America. In pioneer times this grouse was the leading upland game bird in nine western states. The species was never widespread over North Dakota and is presently confined to the southwestern portion of the state.

Credit for first records of the sage grouse has been extended to the Lewis and Clark Expedition. Although these men apparently did not see the bird in North Dakota they did report it in the vicinity of the Marias River in Montana on June 5, 1805. They later reported it to be common west to the plains of the Columbia River.[58]

[58]Burroughs, op. cit., p. 214.

Although Audubon himself did not see sage grouse, members of the 1843 expedition on the Missouri River sighted the bird. Excerpts from Audubon's Journals are as follow:

August 1, 1843 (Ft. Union): Owen told me that he had seen, on his late journey up the Yellowstone, Grouse, both old and young, with a black breast and with a broad tail; they were usually near the margin of a wood. What they are I cannot tell, but he and Bell are going after them tomorrow morning.

Aug. 2, 1843: Bell and Owen started on their tour up the Yellowstone after Cocks of the Plain.

Aug. 5, 1843: Owen and Bell returned this afternoon; they had seen no Cocks of the Plains.[59]

By the 1870's several observers were more explicit. Coues noted that the bird was dispersed over the western interior of the nation where it was ". . . coextensive with the treeless, arid, and almost desert regions where grow the various species of Artemesia or wild sage, upon which it chiefly feeds. . . ." He wrote that it was common on the plains of western Kansas and Nebraska and in southwestern portions of Dakota west to California and Oregon. He did not find it at Ft. Stephenson on the Missouri River in North Dakota nor did he believe it to be "Northward and east of longitude 103°."[60]

Cooke wrote: "In the Mississippi Valley district the Sage Cock is found only along the extreme western edge of Kansas, Nebraska and Dakota."[61]

S. D. Judd reported the sage grouse was breeding

. . . on the sagebrush plains of the Upper Sonoran and Transition zones, from the east slope of the Sierra Nevada and Cascade Mountains in Nevada, California and British Columbia east to Assiniboia (Sask.), Dakota, Nebraska and Colorado.[62]

Norman Wood, during his work in North Dakota in 1920-21, reported a letter from former State Historical Director Lewis Crawford who had seen "thousands

[59]Audubon, op. cit., Vol. II, p. 125-131.

[60]Coues, op. cit., p. 402.

[61]Cooke, W. W., *Report on Bird Migration in the Mississippi Valley in the years 1884 and 1885*, p. 309.

[62]Judd, S. D., op. cit., p. 23.

of cocks" at one place on the Cannonball River. Wood wrote that the bird could be found only on the sage brush plains west of the Badlands.[63]

Some of the old-timers interviewed for this book report as follows:

> *Charles Cornell,* who has lived south of Medora on the old Collis Ranch since 1919: "I have never seen over 20 to 30 sage hens around since I've lived in this country. There are more of them south of here."

> *Harv Robinson,* who has lived in the Badlands since 1891: "There were lots of them in the Marmarth area in those early days."

> *G. L. Wingstrand,* a resident of Rhame since 1907, reports: "Common in this area and I hunted them after September 1st."

Some idea of present range can be ascertained by talking with residents of the southwestern part of the state. Wes Hardin of the U. S. Forest Service in Dickinson saw one bird nine miles southwest of Grassy Butte in southern McKenzie County during the summer of 1962. And State Game Warden Ed Bry of Belfield reported a small active strutting ground ten miles north of Sentinel Butte in Golden Valley County in both 1960 and 1961. Bry and ranchers Willard Porter and "Jiggs" O'Connell also saw a "good-sized" flock at Pyramid Park in Billings County on several occasions in 1961. Counts are made on twenty-five strutting grounds each spring by Game and Fish Department personnel in Bowman and Slope Counties and the largest ground near Marmarth was frequented by forty-five cocks in 1959 and thirty-eight cocks in the spring of 1961. A rough estimate of the total population of sage grouse in North Dakota at the present time is about 3,000 to 4,000 birds.

---

[63]Wood, N. A., op. cit., p. 36.

Role

Due to its limited numbers the sage grouse has never been an important game species for North Dakota hunters. Though the bird is large the quality of its flesh is considered by some persons to be inferior. It is a straightaway flier and not particularly "sporting" to the gunner. The habitat it requires is sparsely settled by man so it does not conflict with the economic interests of mankind. In brief, the sage grouse is not a controversial game species.

The first popular name applied to sage grouse was the "cock of the plains" coined by Lewis and Clark.[64] It has also been referred to as "sage hen," "sage fowl," "sage cock," "sage chicken," and "fool hen."

Its place of courtship is called a strutting ground. On these grounds the large cocks make their "jugging" sound in the spring of the year.

---

[64]Burroughs, op. cit., p. 214.

TED CORNELL

Most early observers considered the bird to be unimportant on the dinner table. Lewis felt the meat was only "tolerable in flavor," and did not think it as good as either the pheasant (ruffed grouse in this case) or pinnated grouse.[65] Eastern sportsman Parker Gillmore claimed that it was almost inedible from living on the buds of the wild sage.[66]

Coues claimed the sage cock was

> . . . one offering attraction to the sportsman, it is, nevertheless, of the least consequence of all from an economic point of view, since the nature of its harsh and bitter food renders its flesh little acceptable — indeed unpalatable under ordinary circumstances.[67]

Later in his book Coues tempered his criticism somewhat by quoting a friend, Dr. Newberry, who said, "The young bird, if parboiled and stewed is very good; but, as a whole, this is inferior for the table to other species of American Grouse."[68]

J. H. Schoenberger, who hunted the North Dakota Badlands in late August, 1875, wrote:

> I picked the bird which was about the size of a half grown turkey and Felix then took charge of it. He prided himself on being a much better cook than teamster and our breakfast of sage hen broth was ample proof that he was right.[69]

Roosevelt apparently subjected the flesh of sage grouse to a thorough test:

> It is commonly believed that the flesh of the sage fowl is uneatable, but this is very far from being the truth; on the contrary, it is excellent eating in August and September, when grasshoppers constitute their chief food, and if the birds are drawn as soon as shot, is generally perfectly palatable at other seasons of the year . . .

> An old bird, which had fed on nothing but sage, and was not drawn when shot, would, beyond question, be very poor eating. Like the spruce grouse and the two kinds of prairie fowl [sharptail and pinnate], but unlike the ruffed grouse and bluegrouse, the sage fowl has dark meat . . .

> We carried eleven birds back, most of them young and tender, and all of them good eating.[70]

Long-term residents of the Badlands interviewed the past three years sav this about sage grouse as food:

> *Chris Rasmussen, Medora:* In the summer of 1902 while in the Boyce Creek area we ate quite a few sage hens, always the young birds. Tht old birds aren't worth eating.

> *G. L. Wingstrand, Rhame:* I've always preferred getting the sage grouse about September 1st because nobody wants to eat the old birds. The taste of sage is too strong. But the young birds are good eating. In fact they are excellent. I like the young ones better than sharptails but not as well as pheasants.

[65]Ibid., p. 215.

[66]Gillmore, P., *Prairie and Forest, A Description of the Game of North America*, p. 215

[67]Coues, op. cit., p. 402.

[68]Ibid., p. 405.

[69]Schoenberger, J. H., *From the Great Lakes to the Pacific*, p. 34

[70]Roosevelt, op. cit., p. 100-104.

In summary we can readily see the quality of sage grouse as a food item is once again a matter of individual taste, but it is probably last on the preferred list of upland game birds in the opinions of old-timers. Since the season has been closed for many years there are few, outside of the Badlands, who have tasted the bird.

The sage grouse has never been recognized as a particularly "sporting" bird for the "man-with-the-gun." Descriptive adjectives "elusive," "streaking," "darting," and "wheeling," denoting speed and evasive action, do not apply. On the contrary, the big bird is a lumbersome, straight-line flier that raises gradually like a "pre-jet age bomber" when flushed. Many old-timers claim to have shot them on the wing with the rifle, no easy feat for other members of the grouse family. Roosevelt stated that early in the season they were

> . . . tame and unsuspicious to the very verge of stupidity . . . are rarely as wild as the sharptails . . . they move along in a strong, steady flight, sailing most of the time. . . . They are very easy marks but require hard hitting to bring them down. . . . Most of the sage fowl I have killed have been shot with a rifle.[71]

G. L. Wingstrand of Rhame who hunted in the period 1910-20 says:

> We always hunted them with a .22 cal. repeating rifle. It was easy to pick up half a dozen of these birds at early morning or at dusk. I've hit big ones on the wing with a .22 cal. rifle because of the way they fly. It's just like shooting jackrabbits.

The "cock of the plains" is not destined to become an important game bird in North Dakota. Neither will he ever come under severe criticism by ranchers of the Badlands. Because the wastelands are his element he is not in serious competition with man.

---

[71]Ibid., p. 100-102.

Harvest

The last sage grouse season was held several years before the Game and Fish Department began estimating harvests of upland game birds. Because of their limited range in the state the numbers of sage grouse killed in the past would be minor compared with pinnates and sharptails. At the present time, largest harvests in the United States are in Wyoming where 41,000 birds were taken by hunters in 1961, and Montana where 27,000 birds were legally bagged. Several other western states harvest 10,000 to 20,000 sage grouse annually.

Many of the harvest methods employed for pinnates and sharptails were used in taking sage grouse. As mentioned in the last section, the rifle was used by residents of the Badlands during the early settlement years. At the present time the shotgun is the accepted weapon.

If the sage grouse were placed on the game list in North Dakota in the near future the harvest could probably be controlled with permit hunting similar to current antelope seasons. A conservative estimate of the number of birds that could be harvested without endangering the population would be in the neighborhood of five hundred.

Seasons and Regulations

The last open season on sage grouse in North Dakota was in 1922. Prior to that year, seasons and regulations on all the prairie grouse were the same. Therefore, the sharp-tailed grouse regulations listed on page 24 are applicable to the sage grouse through 1922.

North Dakota Legislative Laws for 1923 stated: "It shall be unlawful to shoot, kill, or trap in any manner the Sandhill, Little Brown or Whooping Crane, Swans, the Sage Hen or Sage Grouse."[72] During this period it was the common vogue to close seasons with the belief that a game species would be saved from extinction, and even increase in numbers, but this has not proved practical for sage grouse. R. L. Patterson in his exhaustive book, *The Sage Grouse in Wyoming*, expressed the modern concept of management:

> Practically every state has recognized the imperative need for shooting all other upland game birds and waterfowl during the fall harvest period, yet few states have awakened sufficiently to the need for extending the same sporting chance to either the sage grouse or the sage grouse hunter. In the fall, the sage grouse is a distinctly different type of bird than it is in the summer. It becomes more wary, flies more readily, and for longer distances, and in general exhibits more intelligence than is commonly displayed during the warm summer months.[73]

As in the case of the antelope, on which seasons were closed for fifty years in North Dakota, a season could be annually held for sage grouse. The harvest should certainly be controlled, but limited hunting could be allowed each fall without damaging the grouse population. Perhaps forty thousand of these birds could have been harvested the past forty years in North Dakota with no effect whatsoever on present numbers.

Sage grouse seasons in the western states customarily opened in July and August during the years around 1900, but in recent years the seasons are opened in mid to late September. Although juvenile birds are at best quality for eating in August they are often small and selective shooting of hens "burns out" populations in certain areas. Also, early seasons allow the hunters to kill birds still in the molt, and consequently, in poor condition. The best time for a season in North Dakota would undoubtedly be September at about the same time as the permit season on antelope.

---

[72]*North Dakota Legislative Assembly Laws, 18th Session, 1923*, p. 315.

[73]Patterson, R. L., *The Sage Grouse in Wyoming*, p. 175.

Limiting Factors

A clear-cut example of the importance of habitat to a wildlife species is illustrated by the life history of the sage grouse. In North Dakota, and other areas of western United States, this grouse is found only where black sage (*Artemesia tridentata*) and closely related plants are growing. Many early travelers noted the grouse-black sage relationship. Roosevelt wrote that the bird was found "only where the tough, scraggly wild sage abounds, and it feeds for most of the year on sage leaves."[74] Another early observer, Captain Bendire, believed the sage plant to be important to the bird but quoted other persons who thought the plant important only when other more desirable foods were lacking.[75]

[74]Roosevelt, op. cit., p. 99.
[75]Bendire, C., *Life Histories of North American Birds*, p. 107-109.

The bird utilizes the sage plant for both food and cover. Most nests are found in this cover and over 75 percent of its annual food supply comes from the plant. In winter the grouse feeds almost entirely on sage. Young birds in the first three or four months of life feed on insects, but by their first autumn have turned to the plant for their sustenance. As already noted, late in the season the flesh of the bird takes on a "sagey tang" which is particularly noticeable in mature grouse.

Many early observers believed this bird unique because it did not have a gizzard. In recent years, however, it has been proved that it does, although the organ is relatively undeveloped when compared with the gizzard of other game birds. According to Patterson:

> The sage grouse possesses the typical fowl-like digestive system, although there are many persons who will proclaim vociferously that the bird does not have a gizzard. This belief arises from the fact that the sage grouse stomach is a thin-walled muscular organ and membranous in structure as compared with the heavy walled organ found in most other upland game birds and domestic fowl.[76]

Since the sage grouse feeds primarily on the herbaceous leaves of the sage plant, and does not require grit in its diet, there is no need for a highly developed gizzard.

The bird is restricted to extreme southwestern sections of North Dakota because the black sage is found only in that area. A letter from the state's Dean of Botanists, Dr. O. A. Stevens of North Dakota State University, says:

> The distribution of Artemesia tridentata in North Dakota has not changed materially since 1880. . . . I still cannot map it accurately. . . . It seems to occupy mainly the severely eroded places or sometimes wash from such places; essentially limited to the Badlands, especially the southern part.[77]

Because black sage grows in arid wastelands the problems of habitat destruction for this grouse are not as pronounced as for other species. An example is the sharp-tailed grouse which lives on grasslands that are more susceptible to cultivation and changing land use patterns. Overgrazing of rangelands in western United States was an important limiting factor on sage grouse and other game species in the early 1900's. Populations of many of these species declined until the 1930's. Since that time, largely through efforts of the U. S. Bureau of Land Management, U. S. Forest Service, and individual ranchers, there has been a more intelligent utilization of land. Overgrazing and range deterioration are not the problems they once were. Domestic livestock and wildlife have both profited by this more proper land management.

Weather is not an important limiting factor on sage grouse in North Dakota. Average annual precipitation in this grouse's range is about fifteen inches. There are no abrupt changes in elevation of the land that are common in mountainous areas of the west and which result in heavy depths of snow at certain seasons of the year. In western states flocks migrate 40 to 50 miles in search

[76]Patterson, op. cit., p. 172.

[77]Stevens, O. A., Letter, March 29, 1963.

of food or to escape snow, but no noticeable migrations have been reported in North Dakota. This fact may be partially due to the small population of birds in the state. The sage grouse, like the sharptail, is physically adapted to rough weather snowstorms, and flock movement is influenced by the need for food. Winterkill, as we know it for pheasants, is of no concern.

Both Coues and Roosevelt noted that the sage grouse spent most of its life in one area. Coues quoted Ridgeway when he wrote, "I have heard it said that the Sage Grouse migrates, but this is not so, as I have seen them at all seasons of the year on the same ground."[78]

Roosevelt wrote:

> Unlike the sharptail the habits and haunts of the sage fowl are throughout the year the same, except that it grows shyer as the season advances, and occasionally wanders a little further than formerly from its birthplace.[79]

Modern studies on sage grouse point up the fact that predation is not a limiting factor on populations. In Wyoming, ground squirrels, badgers, and magpies, in the order listed, were the biggest depredators on sage grouse nests. The magpie was important only in the regions where there was considerable settlement by humans. Other aerial predators involved are the golden eagle and two or three species of hawks. The chief mammalian predators, coyote and bobcat, have been reduced in numbers in recent years, and have not been considered a serious threat.

Since 1900 many persons have condemned overhunting as a major limiting factor. In 1907, Huntington included sage grouse on a list of birds he believed were being overhunted primarily because of the breech-loading shotgun, speeded up travel, and greater numbers of hunters.[80] Patterson reported that sage grouse populations in the west dropped steadily from 1900-30 largely in the face of habitat destruction but, in part, due to spring and summer shooting: "Summer shooting of sage chickens offers equally poor chances for the sustained production of harvestable quantities of birds." Patterson advocated seasons which opened no earlier than September 20.[81]

In summary, the sage grouse in North Dakota must be considered as living on the marginal range for the species. Since it is controlled by distribution of the sage plant it probably will continue to be confined to southwestern portions of the state.

---

[78]Coues, op. cit., p. 404.

[79]Roosevelt, op. cit., p. 99.

[80]Huntington, op. cit., intro.

[81]Patterson, op. cit., p. 33.

Research and Management

North Dakota has conducted little research on the sage grouse. And, management-wise, the only project applicable to the bird is an annual census.

This work was inaugurated in 1946. Department personnel walked over standardized areas of range, counting the birds as they were flushed. The project was conducted annually in February from 1946 through 1951.

In 1951 a new method of censusing the birds was initiated. Birds were located and counted while they were on their strutting grounds in March and April. Grounds were located through use of the automobile as listening stops were made in the sage grouse range.

By 1953 the airplane was used, and both airplane and automobile are used at the present time. Approximately twenty-five strutting grounds are censused each spring and the numbers of sage grouse recorded varies from 300 to 600. These counts serve as indicators to the overall population and must be compared on a year-to-year basis.

In the western states, where the sage grouse is ranked as an important game species by hunters, there has been some excellent research. Much has been learned about food habits, reproduction, daily and seasonal movements, parasites and disease, effects of hunting, effects of weather, and many other factors. Since the bird is a minor species in North Dakota there will probably be little research here. The Department expends more time and effort on major species. Several upland game species, waterfowl, big game, and furbearers rate research priority at the present time.

3

Ruffed Grouse

Scientific name: *Bonasa umbellus*

Size:

Length, 15-18 inches. Wingspan, 22-25 inches. Weight, 1-1½ lbs.

Coloration:

Generally darker colored than the prairie grouse. Both gray and red-brown color phases, and mixtures between, are found in North Dakota. Difficult to distinguish cocks from hens except when held in hand. Central tail feathers longer on cocks than hens. Broader and longer tail on this grouse than the sharptail.

Flight:

Noisy, explosive takeoff followed by an erratic, dodging flight as the bird darts through the trees. One of the most difficult birds to hunt.

Flock habits:

May be located in singles or family groups during the hunting season. Cocks are solitary during the breeding season, different from the prairie grouse. Seldom found in large flocks like other grouse.

History

Another member of the grouse family that has lived in North Dakota for thousands of years is the ruffed grouse, or woodland partridge. This excellent game bird inhabits the woodlands of the Pembina Hills and Turtle Mountains at the present time. There is reason to believe that in the past it may have been found along river bottoms and other wooded areas of the state. A small population exists today in the Killdeer Mountains where a small release of wild-trapped birds was transplanted from the Turtle Mountains in the early 1950's.

Although the ruffed grouse is present in only limited areas of North Dakota, it is one of the most widespread game birds in North America. Its range extends east and west from Atlantic to Pacific and north and south from Alaska to Georgia. It is present in forty-six states and provinces of North America. Several subspecies have been recognized, generally based on coloration, and the gray ruffed

Drumming cock in Walsh County, Pembina Hills, 1952.

grouse (*Bonasa umbellus umbelloides*) is the accepted subspecies for this state. Examination of birds by Department members the past fifteen years indicates that the gray phase outranks the red phase by a two to one ratio. Judd, reporting on state bird life from 1890-96, noticed the gray phase was predominate.[82] Wood, in 1920, wrote, "Most of these birds were light gray with black ruffs and tail bands, but a few were a dark reddish chestnut with red ruffs and copper tail bands.[83] Williams stated that North Dakota grouse in 1926 were mostly of the gray phase and emphasized that only an occasional red phase bird was found.

Few references were made to ruffed grouse in the early history of the state. The bird was discovered in only a small area of the territory, and most well-known early explorers traveled the thoroughfares of the Big Missouri River which was outside the bird's range. Lewis and Clark, Audubon, and others, did not see ruffed grouse along the Missouri.

One of the earliest notes on the bird was that of Alexander Henry who operated a fur trading post at Pembina:

> Sept. 26, 1800, a few pheasants killed.
> Oct. 24, 1800, pheasants killed near mouth of Park River.
> Oct. 30, 1805, one of my people had been out shooting pheasants [ruffed grouse] the day before. . . .[84]

Wood mentioned that G. J. Keeney, writing in *Forest and Stream*, "Found ruffed grouse along the Red River in scrub timber near Fargo, October, 1875."[85] the farthest south the bird was ever reported.

Finally, Coues recognized the probability of the ruffed grouse's presence in the Pembina area, but did not see the bird. He was reluctant to verify its existence in the state because, like other birds, it had been called many names. (The population was apparently at a low level when Coues visited the Turtle Mountains and Pembina Hills in 1874.)

> It is somewhat singular that a misapprehension should subsist, even among well-informed persons in regard to this species. The confusion in the minds of some is, doubtless, partly due to the fact that the bird goes under different names in different parts of the country; and we are often asked, is it a Partridge, or is it a Pheasant? to which reply may be made that it is neither, but a Grouse.[86]

One early writer claimed that the ruffed grouse was called "partridge" in the eastern states, "pheasant" in the middle, and "grouse" in the west.[87] Another stated that the bird was known as "partridge" in New England and "pheasant" in the southern states.[88]

---

[82]Judd, E. T., op. cit., p. 15.

[83]Wood, N. A., op. cit., p. 35.

[84]Henry, A., *The Manuscript Journals of Alexander Henry, Fur Trader of the Northwest Company and David Thompson, 1799-1814*, Vol. I, p. 103, 124, and 271.

[85]Wood, N. A., op. cit., p. 35.

[86]Coues, op. cit., p. 421.

[87]Lewis, E. J., *The American Sportsman*, p. 135.

[88]Judd, S. D., op. cit., p. 26.

Perhaps one of the most interesting notes is that of J. V. Brower in reference to the naming of the Mandan Indians, one of the oldest tribes living in North Dakota:

> The name — Mandan, is a corruption from the word Mantane, written by the Chevelier de la Verendrye, in 1742. The true meaning of the name is in doubt.
>
> The Mantane nation of people had a true name — the Pheasants; so called because they originally resided at the land of the pheasants [ruffed grouse]. The greatest pheasant region in America extends from Lake Superior and St. Croix River westwardly and northwestwardly to the head branches of the Red River of the North. Millions of those native birds are hatched each year in the fastness of that timbered expanse of country, where they flourish on buds, wild fruits and the seeds of native shrubs, vines and grasses. Less abundant the pheasants are known to extend to innumerable parts of North America to such an extent that their habitat is almost universal. It is therefore practically impossible to identify what land of pheasants was intended to be described when the early Indian tribes named the Mantanes — the Pheasants.[89]

Occasionally, the Department receives reports of this grouse at some distance away from the Pembina Hills and Turtle Mountains. Birds are often reported from the Forest and Park Rivers in the northeastern part of the state. Occasional reports come from the aspen, sandhill areas near Upham and Towner. Rare reports come from the Goose and Turtle Rivers and the city of Minot as evidenced by the following letter written by Frank Martin, Federal Refuge Manager at Upper Souris National Wildlife Refuge, to Commissioner H. R. Morgan on October 29, 1956:

> Dear Mr. Morgan:
>
> The upland game biologist in your department might be interested to know that we found a dead ruffed grouse on Highway 52 within the city limits of Minot near the Nash-Finch Warehouse.
>
> The bird was apparently car-killed. The body showed no signs of having been shot and it had not been field dressed.

Ruffed grouse fly to areas away from their normal range during the "crazy flight" so well-known to sportsmen and game men (See page 75). As mentioned earlier, the two major ruffed grouse areas in the state are the deciduous forest stands of the Pembina Hills and Turtle Mountains along the Canadian border. Presumably, these will continue to be the major areas in the future.

---

[89]Brower, J. V., *Mandan Contributions by E. R. Steinbreuck. Mem. of Explor. in the Basin of the Miss.,* p. 153.

Role

Although the bird's range is limited in North Dakota, sportsmen who hunt it rate it most popular. There are hunters from all areas of the state who consider the season a success if they have made at least one trip to the ruffed grouse woods in the fall. There are many living in, and near, the Turtle Mountains and Pembina Hills who devote more hunting hours to this than any other game species.

On a continental scale this grouse is one of the most important game birds. In fact, there are only three upland birds on which more ammunition is expended: bobwhite quail, pheasant, and mourning dove. More than two million hunters spend better than twenty million man-hours on ruffed grouse each year. Though the language used to describe such hunting may appear somewhat flowery or over-dramatic, those who go after the bird generally agree with the publicity. The species needs little fanfare either as food or sport; it sells itself. It is often called "the king of game birds" and is recognized as the official state bird of Pennsylvania. Unlike many of the stocked species, who have been pre-sold by enthusiastic supporters on one or two outstanding features, the ruffed grouse is a proven game

bird backed up by three centuries of hunting in North America. It is not great because of one quality but because it is a fine all-around game bird.

> Everything about the grouse merits our admiration. It lives gloriously and embodies all the qualities we cherish: skill, cunning, strength, speed, grace, courage, all love, all intense in quality and developed to a high degree. As a game bird it is unexcelled.[90]

Dr. W. A. Allen, who hunted western United States around 1900, spoke even more dramatically:

> The American ruffed grouse has probably been more discussed than any other bird of the west. The grouse is always a favorite bird with the sportsman, and its habits are governed largely by existing circumstances. With the eye of an eagle, the cunning of the fox, the carriage of a queen, the plumage of the peacock, it has the boldness of a lion. It is a wild adventurer who unconcernedly penetrates the deepest forest, and depends upon the unbroken wilderness for its daily bread.[91]

To digress a moment, the ruffed grouse, like other game birds, has been known by many different names. As was mentioned in the preceding section the bird was known as "partridge" in the east, "pheasant" in the south, and "grouse" in the west. The local names are even more varied: "fan-tail," "timber pheasant," "mountain pheasant," "wood partridge," "wood hen," "fool hen," and "ruffed grouse." In North Dakota there is some confusion when the term 'partridge' is used because both ruffed grouse and Hungarian partridge are known as "partridge," depending on the locality of the state that the hunter is visiting.

Hunting ruffed grouse is not often an easy undertaking. It is a definite challenge to sportsmen because the woods present an obstacle.

> In flight it is one of the swiftest of upland game birds and considerable skill, a quick eye, and a steady hand are needed to shoot it on the wing. Most shots must be made in cover, and the bird's habit of putting a tree between itself and the sportsman as it flies away adds to the difficulty.[92]

The challenge, however, is a major reason why many sportsmen enjoy this hunting. The hunter who uses a dog, or shoots the birds before they fly, increases his success with grouse. But the boastful hunter who brags about "doubles" and "triples" on other game birds should be just as full of admiration for the hunter who "singles" with this one. The grouse is that tough a target. The concensus of opinion is that the shooter who consistently hits the flying ruffed grouse should have little trouble hitting other game birds.

It is as highly prized on the dinner table as on the hunt. It was a preferred food of the northern Indian tribes and later served as an important food for pioneers. Rivaled only by wild turkey for its excellent eating qualities, this fine flavored white meat is appreciated by everyone. The bird was one of the first in demand in the days of market hunting. In the early 1800's a pair of ruffed grouse could be purchased for .25¢ in the east and in 1871 they sold for $4.00 a dozen at the Chicago markets. Demand was governed by the supply

[90]Trippensee, R. E., *Wildlife Management, Upland Game and General Principles,* p. 262.

[91]Allen, W. A., *Adventures with Indians and Game, or Twenty Years in the Rocky Mountains,* p. 296.

[92]Judd, S. D., op. cit., p. 28.

and at certain periods in the late 1800's the birds sold for as much as $2.00 apiece. Excellence of the grouse as a table delicacy caused the market supply generally to fall far short of the demand, and the price was always high.

There are no recorded accounts of market hunting for ruffed grouse in North Dakota, but Ed Peterson of Rugby speaks for many sportsmen, "One thing is for certain, ruffed grouse are the best eating of all game birds in North Dakota and that includes the pheasant."

The ruffed grouse is rarely criticized as competing with man and his economic interests. Since it lives in the woodlands, the bird feeds largely on insects, berries, nuts, greens, and a variety of foods not coveted by man. There have been rare and isolated instances where the grouse was criticized for budding too heavily on apple trees, but in North Dakota where orchards are few, there is little reason for concern. Judd cited one case where 180 apple buds were taken from the crop of one ruffed grouse and added that a bounty of .25¢ per head was paid for this bird in Massachusetts in the 1800's.[93] As recently as 1930, some states paid apple growers for damages where they occurred. Fortunately, the interest of bird admirers and hunters far exceeds the damage that the birds might be blamed for in most areas today. Like most game birds this one has been applauded for the good it does in eating many kinds of insects, such as chinch bugs, that are detrimental to crops. Even in the pursuit of hunting the ruffed grouse is not often criticized because the trespass nuisance is usually negligible to the landowner.

From the aesthetic standpoint this bird also deserves admiration. Spring courtship activities are spectacular and unique. Unlike other North Dakota grouse, the ruffed male performs on his own individual drumming ground in the woods. Usually this spot is on a log, brush pile, or in some secluded place where the bird sets up a commotion by beating its wings to attract the hens. Activity is most pronounced in the spring, but it occasionally "drums" at other times throughout the year. As the wings are moved forward there is a rush of air and a long drawn-out, low, and reverberating "thump-thump-thump" is the result. Beloved poet, William Cullen Bryant, described it as follows, "He beat 'gainst his barred sides with speckled wings and made a sound like distant thunder; slow the strokes at first then fast and faster, till at length they passed into a murmur and were still."[94] Another observer, less poetic, likened it to the starting of a one cylinder gas engine. Others are reminded of a basketball bouncing on a hollow gymnasium floor and slowly losing the bounce. Many of the expressions describing the courtship of the prairie grouse have been used for the ruffed grouse courtship, but most observers have accepted the "drumming" to distinguish the latter.

The ruffed grouse in North Dakota is not nearly as important as the three major upland game birds: pheasant, sharptail, and Hun. However, for those who do hunt the species each fall, it is important. Huntable populations will be maintained, it is hoped, in the future.

---

[93]Ibid., p. 33.

[94]Bryant, W. C., *Poems*, p. 317.

Harvest

Harvest figures have never been recorded for ruffed grouse in North Dakota. It is not known what percent, or how many North Dakotans go afield for the species each fall. But during years of high grouse populations, those who are confirmed ruffed grouse hunters experience excellent success with their sport. Mrs. Louise Olson of Rolla reports that during the 1959 season their party of two to six hunters took 60 to 70 ruffed grouse. The season's bag in 1961 for two to eight hunters was 125 birds. And during fifty-one days in 1962 their party, which varied from two to nine hunters, shot 170 grouse.[95]

Old-timer Ed Peterson of Rugby, who has hunted in the Turtle Mountains since 1906, states that he has shot 10 to 12 birds per day on many occasions in the years gone by. It should be kept in mind, however, that although individual harvests of ruffed grouse sometimes exceed the individual hunter's harvest of other game, the overall harvest of pheasants, Huns, and sharptails far surpasses that of ruffed grouse in any given year.

[95]Olson, L., *Letter,* May 26, 1963.

Ready for the hunt in the Turtle Mountains, 1900.

The annual take in North America during the abundant years is about four million birds with the largest harvests taking place in the lake states and eastern provinces of Canada. Minnesota, Wisconsin, and Michigan each harvest about 400,000 annually. In our neighboring state, Montana, from 30,000 to 70,000 were taken annually in the period 1958-61. And in 1961, when 72,000 birds were killed, the ruffed grouse was the second most important bird in Montana; the pheasant was the only species experiencing a greater harvest. At the present time the ruffed grouse is legally harvested in thirty-nine states and provinces.

The ruffed grouse was once an important food to northern Indian tribes. Many birds were harvested by traps and snares. The shotgun is the most common weapon today. While not used as widely as for pheasants, dogs are still quite commonly used on this grouse. In fact, the ruffed grouse dog is, like the ruffed grouse hunter, a rather specialized individual. Often the small dog, even the terrier, is best. Edminister commented in 1954, "Most bird dogs in the northern states are used on pheasants, and once they have pursued the running ringneck they are somewhat spoiled for use with grouse."[96]

The ruffed grouse dog is likely to be a close ranging hunter who merely flushes the bird to a tree. Then while the bird is focusing its attention on the dog the hunter makes the kill. Some hunters are critical of this "perch shooting" but one modern researcher reported that, although nearly three out of four Michigan hunters used a dog, their success was not much better than those who hunted without a dog.[97] The strongest selling point for dogs is that fewer crippled birds are left to die in the woods.

Another technique is road hunting in the early morning or late afternoon when the birds are out walking. Quite a number of North Dakota grouse are taken in this manner. Vehicle hunting is condemned by many sportsmen, but in ruffed grouse country modern automobile hunting is not as easily managed as it is for prairie grouse. Obviously, cars cannot drive through the woods as easily as across the prairie. Those who prefer to get out and walk while hunting are not bothered by automobile hunters.

Sometimes the hunting can be extremely easy. During the early years of settlement the birds were often called "dumb" because they were so easy to kill. In areas seldom hunted today they are sometimes so unwary of man that they can be knocked off the limbs of trees with a stick. After they've been hunted, however, they become very difficult targets, flushing far ahead of the hunter and dodging quickly away through the trees.

The Game Department is currently planning a questionnaire which should furnish information on future harvests.

---

[96]Edminster, F. C., *American Game Birds of Field and Forest*, p. 201.

[97]*Ruffed Grouse Society of America, (News Letter)*, p. 7.

Seasons and Regulations

Hunting ruffed grouse in North Dakota was covered under prairie grouse regulations until 1913. Since that time it has become a custom to specify open areas in four counties of the Turtle Mountains and Pembina Hills, and to hold shorter open seasons for this grouse than for other game birds. From 1918 to 1959 these seasons did not exceed thirty days.

Because of its prevalence across North America, and because it was one of the first game species to be hunted by pioneers, this bird was the object of some of the earliest game regulations. As early as 1708, the ruffed grouse, heath hen, quail, and wild turkey were protected in New York State. The Federal Lacey Act of 1900, which restricted sale and traffic of game between states, was important to the welfare of the bird in the eastern states, but probably had little bearing on the species in North Dakota. Nevertheless, North Dakota laws of 1901 stipulated that "pinnated grouse, sharp-tailed grouse, ruffed grouse, woodcock, or deer," could not be sold within or outside the state.[98] The fine was to be $10.00 for each bird or animal picked up in violation of the law.

In 1901 the State Game and Fish Board recommended "that turtle doves, plovers, and ruffed grouse should be given the protection of a closed season for a term of years."[99] Thus, in 1913 the season was closed for the first time for a four year period. Since that time ruffed grouse seasons have been closed for two periods (1929-30 and 1945-49).

The best time for the fall opening in North Dakota, as far as hunters are concerned, is after the first frost. This allows some of the leaves to fall and results in better hunting. The current rule is to open seasons by late September or early October. Late seasons permit better visibility, but snowfall is more apt to hinder walking.

During the period around 1930 ruffed grouse populations were low and bag limits and seasons were shortened in many parts of the country. As mentioned earlier, it has been realized in recent years that controlled hunting has little effect on grouse populations and the tendency has been for most states to lengthen seasons. In 1940 the average for twenty eastern states was thirty-nine days. By 1961 these same states averaged sixty-two days. During the four seasons, 1959-62, ruffed grouse populations were high in North Dakota and the seasons averaged forty-two days.

Ruffed grouse regulations in North Dakota, past and present, are shown in Table 5.

---

[98]*North Dakota Legislative Laws, Seventh Session, 1901*, p. 132.

[99]Ibid., p. 133.

TABLE 5   RUFFED GROUSE REGULATIONS THROUGH THE YEARS

Year	Season Length	Daily Shooting Hours	Total days of Hunting*	Day of Week Season Opened	Daily Limit	Possession Limit	Open Area
1875-1912	Same as for Sharp-tailed Grouse						
1913-1916	Closed						
1917	Sept. 16 - Oct. 17	Sunrise to sunset	32	Monday	5	15	Bottineau, Rolette, Cavalier and Pembina Counties
1918	Oct. 1 - Oct. 10	Sunrise to sunset	10	Tuesday	5	15	Bottineau, Rolette, Cavalier and Pembina Counties
1919	Oct. 1 - Oct. 10	Sunrise to sunset	10	Wednesday	5	15	Bottineau, Rolette, Cavalier and Pembina Counties
1920	Oct. 1 - Oct. 10	Sunrise to sunset	10	Friday	5	15	Bottineau, Rolette, Cavalier and Pembina Counties
1921	Oct. 1 - Oct. 10	½ hour before sunrise to sunset	10	Saturday	5	15	Bottineau, Rolette, Cavalier and Pembina Counties
1922	Oct. 1 - Oct. 10	½ hour before sunrise to sunset	10	Sunday	5	15	Bottineau, Rolette, Cavalier and Pembina Counties
1923	Oct. 7 - Oct. 16	½ hour before sunrise to sunset	10	Sunday	5	10	Bottineau, Rolette, Cavalier and Pembina Counties
1924	Oct. 7 - Oct. 16	½ hour before sunrise to sunset	10	Tuesday	5	10	Bottineau, Rolette, Cavalier and Pembina Counties
1925	Oct. 7 - Oct. 16	½ hour before sunrise to sunset	10	Wednesday	5	10	Bottineau, Rolette, Cavalier and Pembina Counties
1926	Oct. 7 - Oct. 16	½ hour before sunrise to sunset	10	Thursday	5	10	Bottineau, Rolette, Cavalier and Pembina Counties

RUFFED GROUSE REGULATIONS (Continued)

Year	Season Length	Daily Shooting Hours	Total days of Hunting*	Day of Week Season Opened	Daily Limit	Possession Limit	Open Area
1927	Oct. 7 - Oct. 16	½ hour before sunrise to sunset	10	Friday	5	10	Bottineau, Rolette, Cavalier and Pembina Counties
1928-1929	Closed						
1930	Oct. 11 - Oct. 15	½ hour before sunrise to sunset	5	Saturday	5	10	Bottineau, Rolette, Cavalier and Pembina Counties
1931	Oct. 11 - Oct. 15	Sunrise to sunset	5	Sunday	5	10	Bottineau, Rolette, Cavalier and Pembina Counties
1932	Oct. 8 (noon) - Oct. 12	Sunrise to sunset after first day	4½	Saturday	5	10	Bottineau, Rolette, Cavalier and Pembina Counties
1933	Oct. 7 (noon) - Oct. 12	Sunrise to sunset after first day	5½	Saturday	5	10	Bottineau, Rolette, Cavalier and Pembina Counties
1934	Sept. 28 (noon) - Oct. 1	Sunrise to sunset after first day	3½	Friday	5	10	Bottineau, Rolette, Cavalier and Pembina Counties
1935	Oct. 18 - Oct. 20	Sunrise to sunset	3	Friday	3	3	Bottineau, Rolette, Cavalier and Pembina Counties
1936	Oct. 16 (noon) - Oct. 20	Noon to sunset	2½	Friday	3	3	Bottineau, Rolette, Cavalier and Pembina Counties
1937	Oct. 9 - Oct. 18	7:00 a.m. - 4:00 p.m.	10	Saturday	3	3	Bottineau, Rolette, Cavalier and Pembina Counties
1938	Oct. 1 - Oct. 10	7:00 a.m. - 4:00 p.m.	10	Saturday	3	3	Bottineau, Rolette, Cavalier and Pembina Counties
1939	Oct. 1 - Oct. 15	7:00 a.m. - 4:00 p.m.	15	Sunday	3	3	Bottineau, Rolette, Cavalier and Pembina Counties

RUFFED GROUSE REGULATIONS (Continued)

Year	Season Length	Daily Shooting Hours	Total days of Hunting*	Day of Week Season Opened	Daily Limit	Possession Limit	Open Area
1940	Oct. 1 - Oct. 21	Sunrise to 5:00 p.m.	21	Tuesday	3	3	Bottineau, Rolette, Cavalier and Pembina Counties
1941	Sept. 28 - Oct. 19	Sunrise to 6:00 p.m.	22	Sunday	3	6	Bottineau and Rolette Counties
1942	Sept. 26 - Oct. 25	Sunrise to sunset	30	Saturday	3	6	Bottineau and Rolette Counties
1943	Sept. 25 - Oct. 15	Sunrise to sunset	21	Saturday	3	6	All of Bottineau; Rolette County north of Highway No. 5
1944	Sept. 20 - Oct. 15	½ hour before sunrise to sunset	26	Wednesday	3	6	All of Bottineau and Rolette Counties; Cavalier County west of Highway No. 1
1945-1949	Closed						
1950	Oct. 6 - Nov. 5	Noon to sunset each day	15½	Friday	3	6	Bottineau, Rolette, Cavalier and Pembina Counties
1951	Sept. 28 (noon) - Nov. 4	Noon to sunset except ½ hour before sunrise to sunset on Saturday and Sunday	25	Friday	3	6	Bottineau, Rolette, Cavalier and Pembina Counties
1952	Sept. 26 (noon) - Nov. 2	Noon to sunset except ½ hour before sunrise to sunset on Saturday and Sunday	24	Friday	4	8	Bottineau, Rolette, Cavalier and Pembina Counties
1953	Oct. 1 (noon) - Oct. 11	Noon to sunset except ½ hour before sunrise to sunset on Saturday and Sunday	7½	Thursday	3	6	Bottineau, Rolette, Cavalier and Pembina Counties
1954	Oct. 16 (noon) - Oct. 31	Noon to sunset except ½ hour before sunrise to sunset on Sunday	9½	Saturday	3	6	Bottineau, Rolette, Cavalier and Pembina Counties

RUFFED GROUSE REGULATIONS (Continued)

Year	Season Length	Daily Shooting Hours	Total days of Hunting*	Day of Week Season Opened	Daily Limit	Possession Limit	Open Area
1955	Oct. 21 (noon) - Nov. 6	Noon to sunset except ½ hour before sunrise to sunset on Saturday and Sunday	11½	Friday	3	6	Bottineau and Rolette Counties
1956	Oct. 12 (noon) - Nov. 4	9:00 a.m. to sunset after first day	23½	Friday	3	6	Bottineau and Rolette Counties
1957	Oct. 12 - Oct. 31	9:00 a.m. to sunset	20	Saturday	3	6	Bottineau and Rolette Counties
1958	Oct. 11 - Nov. 6	9:00 a.m. to sunset	27	Saturday	3	6	Bottineau, Rolette, Cavalier and Pembina Counties
1959	Oct. 3 - Nov. 8	9:00 a.m. to sunset	37	Saturday	3	6	Bottineau, Rolette, Cavalier and Pembina Counties
1960	Oct. 1 - Nov. 10	9:00 a.m. to sunset	41	Saturday	4	8	Bottineau, Rolette, Cavalier and Pembina Counties
1961	Sept. 30 - Nov. 9	9:00 a.m. to sunset	41	Saturday	4	8	Bottineau, Rolette, Cavalier and Pembina Counties
1962	Sept. 29 - Nov. 18	9:00 a.m. to sunset	51	Saturday	4	8	Bottineau, Rolette, Cavalier and Pembina Counties
1963	Sept. 21 - Nov. 7	Sunrise to sunset	48	Saturday	3	6	Bottineau, Rolette, Cavalier and Pembina Counties

*Based on a full day's hunting. (8 hrs. = one day.)

Limiting Factors

This bird requires woodland habitat for its survival. Consequently, it is found in only two major areas of North Dakota. Fortunately, the ruffed grouse has proven a more adaptable species than the spruce and pinnated grouse which require specialized habitat. The ruffed has adjusted to many of the changes resulting from man's activities and is found in both deciduous and coniferous forest stands in North America. Although the bird requires timber land, the cover type it utilizes may vary from one area to another and from season to season. Heavier cover is utilized in spring and winter than in the summer and fall. And, like many other wildlife species, this grouse is benefited by periodically opening patches in mature woods where annuals and brushy vegetation develop.

Many North Dakota game species make use of farmland for food and cover, but the ruffed grouse is dependent on the natural succession of vegetation occurring in the woodlands. Population may vary from year to year on a given area because the plant

Fire used for clearing, Turtle Mountains, 1962.

species and amount of cover is constantly changing. The bird is versatile, however, and may utilize 400 to 500 species. Some of the most common of these
in the Pembina Hills and Turtle Mountains are Alder (*Alnus rugosa*), Bur
Oak (*Quercus macrocarpa*), Chokecherry (*Prunus virginiana*), Highbush Cran-
berry (*Viburnum trilobum*), Dogwood (*Cornus stolonifera*), Bearberry (*Arcto-
staphylos uva-ursi*), Juneberry (*Amelanchier alnifolia*), Nannyberry (*Viburnum
lentago*), Pin Cherry (*Prunus pennsylvanica*), Rose (*Rosa sp.*), Willow (*Salix
sp.*), Aspen (*Populus tremuloides*), and Birch (*Betula papyrifera*). Very few
conifers are found in the ruffed grouse range in North Dakota, but where sites
are suitable, the most common species are Creeping Cedar (*Juniperus hori-
zontalis*) and Dwarf Juniper (*Juniperus communis*). Among the many other
common plants are the buckwheats, clovers and grasses.

Some clearing of timber by burning or bulldozing benefits ruffed grouse,
but extensive clearing occurring in North Dakota the past fifteen years has
eliminated the species in many areas. Extensive clearing was an accepted
practice during the early settlement of the United States, but in the lake states
forests are currently being reestablished and the ruffed grouse has benefited. In
the mid-Mississippi Valley, once a good range, the land is intensively farmed for
crops and livestock and the birds are extinct or scarce. This same thing could
happen in North Dakota if the present trend of "chopping off the woodlands"
continues.

Extensive cutting and bulldozing, Turtle Mountains, 1963.

At the present time there are 127,000 acres of woodlands remaining in the original 342,000 acres of the Turtle Mountains. There are 80,000 acres of timberlands left from the original 286,000 acres in the Pembina Hills. Clearing operations by man are taking 1.2 percent, or 1,500 acres, of timber in the Turtle Mountains each year. Removal of timber in the Pembina Hills is even more extensive. About 3.9 percent, or 3,200 acres, are cleared each year.[100] There is no question that this clearing, primarily through the use of the modern bulldozer, can be viewed as a major limiting factor on North Dakota's ruffed grouse populations.

Like the sharptail, the ruffed grouse is little affected by winter. It feeds above the snow and burrows beneath it for protection. It is an extremely winter-hardy species. Only during a cold, wet spring are the young birds susceptible to disease and exposure resulting from the weather. Although predators may take a heavier toll during winters of heavy snow, the overall winterkill of ruffed grouse, as we know it for pheasants, is not common.

Predators most important in one state may not be the most important in another. In North Dakota the raccoon, badger, red fox, skunk, weasel, crow, several species of squirrels, feral dogs and cats, and many species of hawks and owls are found in the ruffed grouse woods. Some of these animals are primarily nest predators; others are destructive to adult birds in winter. In Wisconsin the fox snake was found the most important nest predator. And in the southern part of the ruffed grouse range the gray fox is considered important at all times. Skunks, feral dogs and cats are troublesome in some areas of the eastern United States. Finally, in the northern parts of the range horned and snowy owls, lynx and bobcat are leading enemies of ruffed grouse.

As in the case with most game species, predation is most important as a decimating factor when the birds are scarce. Generally, the danger period for grouse is in late winter or early spring. Predators are short of food at this time and hunt more persistently than in periods when food is plentiful.

The accusation that the ruffed grouse was overhunted was common prior to 1930. Hornaday mentioned that the decline of ruffed grouse was due to "90% over-hunting and 10% vermin."[101] Modern wildlife observers believe hunting can be a decimating factor, but do not believe that it is a primary limiting factor on grouse populations. Pollack pointed out in a *Ruffed Grouse Society of America* newsletter that when ruffed grouse populations declined in the lake states in the 1940's, Minnesota quickly closed the season for four years and Wisconsin closed for three.[102] Michigan, on the other hand, continued to hold open seasons and harvested about 300,000 birds per year. When the Minnesota and Wisconsin seasons were reopened harvests in those two states were no larger than Michigan's. "The significant fact is that Michigan's harvest was as large as the other two states in spite of the fact that the season remained open during four years of relative grouse scarcity."[103]

[100]Green, D. L., *Letter*, May 28, 1963.
[101]Hornaday, W. T., *Thirty Years War for Wild Life*, p. 111.
[102]*Ruffed Grouse Society of America (news letter)*, p. 1.
[103]Ibid., p. 1.

Ammann, writing in the same publication as Pollack, stated that the average annual harvest (1955-60) of 350,000 ruffed grouse taken by 665,000 hunters in Michigan could be "at least twice as many birds" without damaging the grouse population.[104]

Mass migrations reported for pinnated grouse, squirrel, and other game species have rarely been observed for ruffed grouse. The young of practically all game species are prone to disperse from their rearing areas in the fall of the year. Dispersal is most evident during the years of good reproduction and some birds or animals show up in places well outside of their normal habitat. When ruffed grouse disperse in such a manner the phenomenon is called the "crazy flight" and individuals may fly into buildings or end up in downtown areas of a big city. Just why they undertake these "crazy flights" is not completely understood.

The ruffed grouse population builds up to a high every ten years. Buildup is gradual and there is, of course, a low population at one point during the cycle. Like the "crazy flight", it is not completely understood.

Although several decimating factors of ruffed grouse populations have been discussed in this section, the major concern of North Dakota hunters should be the extensive and progressive clearing of the forested areas. This complete destruction of habitat is the main limiting factor.

_____

[104]Ibid., p. 7.

Aspen and hazel are among the many excellent plants found in ideal ruffed grouse habitat as shown by this 1950 photo in the Pembina Sand Hills.

Research and Management

Because it is a minor game species hunted by a comparatively small group in North Dakota there have been only a few research and management jobs conducted on the ruffed grouse in the state. In many sections of North America where the bird constitutes a sizeable portion of the hunter's bag it is one of the most thoroughly studied game birds.

One of the first projects initiated in North Dakota was a census. A grid census was first employed in 1944. This technique was developed by Ralph T. King in Minnesota in the 1930's. North Dakota Game Department personnel systematically walked over areas of known size, flushed, and counted ruffed grouse. Work was performed in the fall and winter months and the results furnished a grouse-per-acre figure to be used in estimating trends in the population. Data was important when used on a year-to-year basis. The work was modified in 1952 and the grouse-per-acre information is no longer used. Information is now tabulated on a grouse-per-mile figure. Some of the data obtained in the walking counts is presented in Table 6.

Another method of censusing ruffed grouse is the roadside drumming count first used in 1950. Department members driving along specific routes in the ruffed grouse area record the numbers of drumming cocks during the months of May and June. Information from these counts is believed to be more reliable than the flushing counts and furnishes much needed information on spring populations. Here again the information is most important when used over a period of years. This census method is currently in use and the data collected for the past thirteen years is presented in Table 7.

During the fall of 1950 the Game Department began collecting ruffed grouse wings and tail feathers from hunters. These feather samples provide sex and age information on the ruffed grouse population. The work furnishes valuable reproduction information for the current year and helps in the prediction of population trends for the next year. Unfortunately, the number of wings and tail feathers sent in each year is small and the results are sometimes based on an inadequate sample. Information from wing samples and tail feather collections the past fourteen years is shown in Table 8.

Among the jobs which are not regularly conducted has been a trapping and transplanting project. In the winter of 1950-51 the Department tried several methods of capturing grouse in the Turtle Mountains. Few were taken that first winter, but the second winter (1951-52) between twenty and thirty grouse were captured through the use of traps and spotlighting at night. These birds were held for a few weeks at the Spiritwood Lake Field Station and then released in the Killdeer Mountains. From this small release there is still (1964) a wild population of ruffed grouse in the Killdeers. Because of this successful transplanting there may be future stockings attempted in the Sully's Hill area near Devils Lake or the aspen stand areas of Lower Souris National Wildlife Refuge. These, plus other possible areas, have limited habitat for ruffed grouse and might support small populations. Stocking would be done with wild-trapped birds since the pen-raising of all grouse species is more difficult than for pheasants and some other game birds.

At the present time there are no plans for any intensive studies on ruffed grouse in North Dakota. Current projects are aimed at obtaining population information which is an aid to setting the hunting seasons, providing sportsmen with information on the abundance of the species, and providing long-term trend information to show that hunting has little long-range effect on ruffed grouse populations. Similar projects will be continued in the immediate future.

TABLE 6   RUFFED GROUSE FALL FLUSHING COUNTS, 1944-59

Year	Turtle Mountains		Pembina Hills	
	Miles/Bird	Total Miles	Miles/Bird	Total Miles
1944*	2.7	57	2.1	36
1945	10.5	74	11.0	88
1946*	20.0	120	No counts made	
1947	6.0	72	28.0	84
1948	2.5	60	1.8	60
1949	2.5	48	2.8	48
1950	3.2	48	2.0	48
1951	3.3	33	1.5	36
1952	1.3	21	1.5	32
1953	1.6	64	2.0	62
1954	2.3	21	4.1	62
1955	3.8	60	6.1	55
1956	1.9	62	2.5	33
1957	1.8	42	3.2	35
1958	1.4	64	4.0	89
1959	1.5	64	3.9	39
14 year avg.**	3.1	52	5.3	54

*Winter counts.

**Average does not include years when winter counts were made.

TABLE 7   RUFFED GROUSE SPRING DRUMMING COUNTS
(Ten routes, 240 stops per season)
1951-63

Year	Average Drums Per Stop	
	Turtle Mountains	Pembina Hills
1951	5.0	2.6
1952	4.2	2.1
1953	5.4	4.0
1954	3.1	1.4
1955	1.9	1.3
1956	1.5	2.1
1957	1.3	2.0
1958	1.4	2.7
1959	1.5	No counts made
1960	3.3	3.6
1961	2.4	No counts made
1962	3.3	1.6
1963	1.1	1.2

TABLE 8   AGE RATIOS OF NORTH DAKOTA RUFFED GROUSE
Taken from Wing and Tail Feather Samples, 1950-63

Year	No. of birds in Sample	Juv.:Ad. Ratio
1950	32	3.3:1.0
1951	150	2.6:1.0
1952	312	2.0:1.0
1953	269	1.4:1.0
1954	48	1.3:1.0
1955	29	3.1:1.0
1956	56	2.3:1.0
1957	19	1.1:1.0
1958	92	2.1:1.0
1959	38	1.5:1.0
1960	144	2.6:1.0
1961	215	2.5:1.0
1962	414	1.5:1.0
1963	24	3.0:1.0

TED '63'
CORNELL

4

Pinnated Grouse

Scientific name: *Tympanuchus cupido pinnatus*

Size:
Length, 16-19 inches. Wingspan, 27-29 inches. Weight, 2-2½ lbs. Cocks slightly heavier than hens. Plump appearing bird.

Coloration:
Rather drab, predominately brown. Key markings are the barred feathers on the breast. Less feathering on the legs than the sharptail. Cocks have yellow colored air sacs at throat and pinnae feathers which are voluntarily erected overhead during spring courtship. Little difference noted between sexes until held in the hand.

Flight:
Similar to sharptail. "Chuckles" in flight. Broad, squared-off tail is different from sharptail and is distinguishing feature in the air.

Flock habits:
Adult cocks pack together throughout the year. Adult hens and immature birds remain together until the spring breeding period. Large flocks of 100 or more birds commonly sighted in the years prior to 1940 in North Dakota.

History

Long-term residents of North Dakota have witnessed the nearly complete history of the pinnated
grouse in the state. The rise and fall of this elegant,
immigrant species have taken place in less than eighty
years. All accounts of "prairie chickens" prior to 1870
were in reference to the sharp-tailed grouse because
the pinnated grouse was not yet living in the state.

The range of the pinnate has been unstable during the past two hundred years. A native of the tall
grass prairies, and more truly a grassland species than
the sharptail, it was found in great numbers in eastern
sections of the United States in the early 1800's. As
human settlements sprang up in midwestern sections of the continent the pinnate populations also
showed remarkable increases. When there were large
populations of pinnates in eastern United States the
birds were scarce or absent further west. But by the
time the pinnate populations built up in the midwest,
the birds were already decreasing along the east coast.

The range, at one time or another, reached from
Massachusetts and Vermont to Georgia along the eastern extremities and from British Columbia and Alberta
to New Mexico and Texas on the western edge of the

TED CORNELL '67

range. Living within this large area of land were two main species: (1) the greater pinnate (*Tympanuchus cupido*) and (2) the lesser pinnate (*Tympanuchus pallidicinctus*). There were three subspecies of the greater pinnate: (1) the heath hen (*Tympanuchus cupido cupido*) of the east coast, now extinct, (2) the Attwater prairie chicken (*Tympanuchus cupido attwateri*) of the Gulf of Texas-Louisiana, and (3) the greater prairie chicken (*Tympanuchus cupido pinnatus*) of the midwestern United States.[105] According to Dr. Fred Hamerstrom of of Wisconsin, the leading authority on prairie chickens in the United States, only about 15 percent of the original range was still occupied by the birds in 1959.[106]

The exact date of the pinnate's arrival in North Dakota is not known. Fortunately, however, since the bird did follow man's agricultural activities, there were human observers nearby when pinnates moved into this state. Accounts of "first" pinnates in several areas are well worth repeating. Dr. Elliott Coues, already noted in other chapters as providing excellent information about Dakota wildlife in the 1870's, reported that he did not find the pinnated grouse at Pembina in 1873. On his travels on the Missouri River, however, he found them to be the most common grouse species up to Yankton, Dakota territory.[107] Lewis and Clark recorded Yankton as the most northerly limit of this grouse about seventy years earlier. Coues went on to relate that between Yankton and Ft. Randall both pinnates and sharptails were present, but above Ft. Randall all grouse were sharptails. One of Coues' informants noted that the first pinnated grouse killed by hunting at Ft. Ripley in Minnesota was in the year 1873. In summary, Coues wrote:

> I have no reason to believe that it [the pinnate] occurs at all in Northwestern Minnesota or Northern Dakota, where the other species [sharptail] is so abundant. Its progress upon the Missouri River has been traced by Dr. Hayden further than by myself to the Niobrara; and the writer adds that it may proceed to the White River.[108]

A few years later Cooke mentioned that the pinnate was forty miles from the southeastern corner of North Dakota at Herman, Minnesota, in 1879. He went on to say that the bird was also present on the Minnesota side across from Grand Forks at the same time and, by the early 1880's, the species was occupying a strip 30 to 60 miles wide along the Red River over the whole eastern edge of North Dakota.[109] Spring booming of the pinnate was reported as early as 1884 at Barton, North Dakota, a considerable distance west of the "strip," so some of the birds were already extending beyond the recognized range.[110] The famous naturalist, Seton, reported the pinnate common at Pembina in 1883.[111]

Ole Syverson told the Game Department in 1943 that the pinnate was abundant at Fargo when he arrived there in 1895. He had talked with old-

---

[105]Baker, M. F., *Prairie Chickens of Kansas*, p. 4.

[106]Hamerstrom, F. N., *Trans. of Midwest Prairie Chicken Conf., unpub. paper, March 16-18, 1959*, Emporia, Kansas.

[107]Coues, op. cit., p. 410.

[108]Ibid., p. 420.

[109]Cooke, op. cit., p. 105.

[110]Ibid., p. 106.

[111]Wood, N. A., op. cit., p. 35.

timers, and believed himself that the first pinnates showed up in the Fargo area about 1885, which would coincide with the observations made by Cooke.[112]   Syverson moved to Tolley, North Dakota, near the Mouse River in 1895 and noted all grouse in that area were sharptails at that date.   The pinnate did not show up in any significant numbers until the early 1900's.

William B. Mershon, who made his first trip to North Dakota to hunt in 1883, left a reliable account concerning the Dawson area:

> The sand hills were full of grouse .... sharptails.   There were no true prairie chickens or pinnated grouse around Dawson until sometime in the early 90's.   Then we began finding a pinnated grouse mixed with the sharptails.   Pinnated grouse worked northward I believe in this same slow way as cultivation advanced.   I know in 1903 when I first began going into the Moose Jaw district of Saskatchewan it was a repetition of what I had found in Dawson twenty years earlier with sharptails. Gradually, however, as years went on the pinnated grouse made their appearance.[113]

Minnesota Chief separator at work in the Kenmare vicinity, 1888.

Judd corroborated this testimony: "As the prairies are settled and broken up for grain fields the sharptail gives way to the prairie hen which was practically unknown here in the early 90's."   Judd called the pinnate a "Common summer resident, and if it continues to increase as it has the past five years it can soon be classed as an abundant bird of this section."[114]

Just how much of North Dakota was occupied by the prairie chicken during the "good pinnate years" between 1900-30 is not exactly known.   Apparently the birds could be found over the whole of the state with the exception of the Badlands.   In that rugged terrain there were islands of pinnates occupying level tracts of land during the peak years.   Wood claimed these birds could be found as far west as Medora in 1921[115] and Munn Stone mentioned to the Game

[112]*North Dakota Outdoors, Sept., 1943,* p. 8.

[113]*North Dakota Game and Fish Dept., Eighth Biennial Report, 1923-24,* p. 21.

[114]Judd, E. T., op. cit., p. 15.

[115]Wood, N. A., op. cit., p. 35.

Department that there were pinnates present for a 12 to 14 year period four miles south of Beach, North Dakota — three miles east of the Montana line.[116]

Some of the best information on the pinnate population since the late 1800's has been provided by the old-timers of the state during the past three years:

Southeast:

Ben Baenen, Jamestown — When I came to our homestead nine miles south of Jamestown in 1892 there were prairie chickens everyplace. These "broadtails" were thick from the 1890's to the 1930's.

Everett Hyatt, Ludden — We had lots of prairie chickens here in 1900 and shortly afterwards. There were but a few sharptails here during those early years.

South-central:

Pat Malone, Linton — When I first came to Linton in 1901 we had both sharp-tails and "yellowlegs" by the thousands.

Northeast:

Henry Haugland (letter, Oct. 31, 1957) — When I first came to Erie (Cass Co.), North Dakota in 1896 we called all grouse "chickens" but I know for sure that I never shot any sharp-tailed grouse until I lived in the Bisbee area later. We lived at Loma in 1910 and they [grouse] were practically all pinnates and there were plenty of them.

John Bert Johnstone, Hansboro — In the late fall of 1892 my oldest brother, Harry N., went hunting on our farm eight miles south of Emerado and shot two game birds. He brought them into the house and said, 'These are the first pinnated grouse I've seen here.'

Northwest:

George Harvey, Williston — We had both sharptails and prairie chickens here in the late 1890's and early 1900's. We hunted mostly on the flats for prairie chickens.

Cecil N. Westlake, Kenmare — The grouse in the New Town area from 1905-08 were practically all "yellowlegs." In the Kenmare area after 1908 the ratio of sharp-tails and yellowlegs" was about equal. Not so in the area that later became New Town. I never remember seeing a sharptail there.

Southwest:

A. T. Foreman, Marmarth — There were no "yellowlegs" along the Little Missouri River Bottoms in the Badlands around 1900. It was common to see flocks of from 50 to 100 birds and they were always sharptails.

Arthur Anderson, Belfield — We have had both "yellowlegs" and sharptails since I moved here (5 mi. S. of Belfield) in 1883, but I killed "yellowlegs" on only two occasions. Both times it was in the period, 1920-25. One time I killed a few "yellow-legs" at our homestead and that is as far west as I ever saw them. I've never seen them in the Badlands. The Badlands birds are all sharptails.

In summary, it would appear the pinnated grouse first showed up in notable numbers in North Dakota along the Red River Valley in the early 1880's. In 15 to 20 years this species spread across the state. The Badlands was the only area where pinnates were not sighted at one time or another during the past eighty years. Present estimated populations (1964) of pinnates in North Dakota are in the neighborhood of 4,000 to 5,000 and most of these birds are living along the eastern edge of the Coteau, or the western edge of the Red River Valley.

---

[116]*North Dakota Outdoors, Mar., 1947,* p. **5.**

Role

Beyond a doubt the upland game bird that stirs the memories of North Dakotans who lived in the years before 1930 more than any other game bird is the "real old-time" prairie chicken — the pinnated grouse. "Old Yellowlegs" flourished in an era reminiscent of black smoke and belching steam engines with such prestige names as Aultman-Taylor, Advance, and Buffalo-Pitts. It was a period of great mechanical advancement but a time when the human population still utilized burlapped stone water jugs, buffalo robes, bobsleds, windmills, kerosene lamps, and hand-operated, wooden butter churns. The prairie chicken was the romance game bird of the time. Our grandfathers knew him for his reverberating courtship booming, exorbitant numbers and fine-flavored meat at the dinner table.

Common names for the pinnated grouse were many. Some called him "yellowlegs," "broadtail," "square tail," "brown prairie chicken," "smooth-legged grouse," "foolhen," "bar-breasted grouse," and "The kettledrummer." Others named him "the boomer," "heath hen," "prairie hen," "wild chicken," or "prairie chicken."

The sounds made by the pinnate male as he promenaded across the courting grounds, now called booming grounds, were in a class by themselves and inspired a galaxy of names. Among these were "cooing," "looing," "crowing," "tooting," "strutting," "drumming," "stamping," and "scratching," plus many of the ones used to describe the sharptail courting grounds. The distinctive sound could be heard at a distance of from two to three miles. Van Tramp, traveling across the heart of the pinnate range in the Mississippi Valley in the 1850's, compared it to an almost forgotten instrument:

> The males, strutting and erecting their plumage like a peacock, and uttering a long, loud mournful note, something like the cooing of the dove, but resembling still more the sound produced by passing a rough finger boldly over the surface of a tambourine. . . .[117]

Another observer defined the sound as "bum-booing," while the influence of the Irish immigrants who helped settle the nation is shown by the description that the pinnate was calling "Old Mul-doon!" Still another writer, possibly from some seashore setting, stated that the sound bore a resemblance to "blowing a conch shell from a remote quarter." Bendire compared the tone to the notes of a pipe organ. Probably the classic interpretation of all arrived in the modern age when one pinnate observer, jealous of losing the prairie chicken to man's progress, combined pathos with reality, and wrote that the bird was reminding mankind of his plight by calling "Yoo-poo-or-damned-foo-ools!" However the strange and nostalgic sound was interpreted by the interested listener, it is now lost in the echoes of the past, perhaps never to be heard again. In North Dakota nowadays, rarely is an early spring morning disturbed by the prairie chickens as was described by Mrs. M. B. Cowdrey near Fargo on April 21, 1888: "The prairie hens made the air whirr this morning. . . ."[118]

Aside from the novelty of making its presence known by courtship booming in the spring, pinnated grouse was a preferred item on the dinner table. There have been many verbal and written accounts relating to the quality of the meat. Most people agreed that the dark meat of the bird was excellent. There were some, however, who developed little taste for pinnates just as there are many who have never developed a taste for venison. It should be remembered that when a species is plentiful and can be used for food, such as the pheasant in the mid-1940's, those partaking of the product often tire of its continual use and no longer appreciate the flavor. One writer left the following unusual statement about the pinnated grouse when the bird was so abundant in the early 1800's in Kentucky, "As for eating them, such a thing was hardly dreamed of, the negroes themselves preferring the coarsest food to this now much admired bird."[119]

This same writer mentioned that the dark-meated pinnate was preferred over the white meat of the ruffed grouse in the Atlantic states where the pinnate was no longer plentiful. The birds, more of a novelty and luxury than the ruffed grouse, "are considered a great delicacy at the East and command extravagant prices."[120]

---

[117]Van Tramp, J. C., *Prairie and Rocky Mountain Adventures, or Life in the West,* p. 114.

[118]Cowdrey, M. B., *The Checkered Years,* p. 222.

[119]Lewis, op. cit., p. 148.

[120]Ibid., p. 152.

Proof that the pinnate was considered a choice food item in foreign countries is evidenced by the shipment of 14,200 prairie hens sold at the markets in Paris, France, in 1875. And in London, prairie chickens were on the menu at an important diplomatic banquet served to high ranking American and foreign dignitaries in 1871.

In the midwestern United States during the late 1800's and early 1900's the pinnated grouse was common food because it could be easily obtained. It was important to early homesteaders as these North Dakota old-timers indicate:

> *Charles Wenz, New Rockford:* I remember during the drouth and depression years the Red Cross passed out a rough type flour called "Red Dog." It made fairly good bread and we ate lots of jackrabbits and prairie chickens with it. If it hadn't been for the wildlife during the Depression (1929-30) we would have starved, and so would lots of other people.

> *H. B. Spiller, Cavalier:* While living in Dickey County during the years 1885-94 we actually tired of eating prairie chickens but nearly everyone ate them rather than kill their own domestic chickens.

It should be remembered that the best season for eating prairie chickens and sharptails is in late August and September. As Webb stated, "In August the birds were in their most delicate condition for the table."[121] At this season the young-of-the-year grouse are tender and, having a ready supply of insect and green plant food, are in a plump condition for the table. One early hunter wrote:

> As food the bird can compare favorably with any of the grouse family but is dissimilar in one respect from all the others — that the sooner it is cooked after being killed, the more delicate and savory it will be found.[122]

The homesteader often gathered the eggs of wildfowl for food. Herb Swett of Dickinson states that when he was a youngster in Kidder County in the 1890's he often collected duck, goose, and prairie chicken eggs for his family to eat. And Joseph Quamme of Westhope, who lived in Steele County near Hope, North Dakota, from 1884-91 says, "We gathered the eggs of the prairie chicken and prairie plover and used them for food."

In the early 1870's in northwestern Illinois, farmers in many places burned the prairies in the spring "and often gathered for household use large numbers of the eggs [prairie hens] thus exposed."[123]

Next to waterfowl and big game the pinnated grouse was the most sought after game of market hunters in North Dakota in the late 1800's and early 1900's. Unfortunately, there were many accounts of waste by hunters. This was particularly true for the pinnated grouse. There were as many birds shot and left to spoil as were used. Many hunters, either the sport or market class, shot the birds fully intending to use them as food. But weather would prevent this. "About half of the young birds are spoiled or wasted because of warm weather."[124] The hunters' greed, slow methods of travel, and inadequate methods of preservation all entered into the waste.

---

[121]Webb., W. E., *Buffalo Land*, p. 72.
[122]Gillmore, op. cit., p. 197.
[123]Judd, S. D., op. cit., p. 13.
[124]Bogardus, op. cit., p. 22.

Col. Clive (center) and party at Devils Lake, 1882.

Experienced hunters, who knew how to get the job done, found good prices waiting for them at meat markets all over the country. As for other mass-hunted species, prices were highest where there was the greatest demand, usually in the eastern United States where prairie chickens were scarce. In the 1820's pinnated grouse were selling for $1.00 a pair at New York markets. Twenty years later they were $3.00-$5.00 per pair at the same markets. A few years later in the midwest where grouse were more plentiful on the adjacent prairies, prairie chickens were selling from .20-.25¢ apiece. At the Chicago markets in 1871 the birds brought $3.50 per dozen or about .30¢ each. The price at New York in the 1870's was about .20¢ per pound. The North Dakota grouse, based on the Dickinson area prices in the 1880's, were about .25¢ each. Minneapolis prices in 1896 were about .60¢ each, or $7.00 per dozen for pinnates and $6.00 per dozen for sharptails. Although a law was passed for Dakota Territory in 1877 which restricted the shipment of game outside the Territory, many prairie chickens were sent to Minneapolis and Chicago by market hunters well into the 1900's. Few people were working on enforcement of game laws in those days and hunters had a free hand to operate as they chose.

Several old-timers mentioned the waste of grouse in North Dakota. Harv McConnell of Kenmare states that in the years around 1915 hunters often left large quantities in the fields to spoil. On one occasion he picked up several wheat sacks filled with grouse that had been shot, stuffed into the sacks, and then left to the elements. H. B. Spiller, in Dickey County around 1890, found a pile of approximately three hundred that had been killed and abandoned by railroad workers building the Soo Line between Fullerton and Oakes. And Otto Kretschmar of Venturia remembers his father condemning the market hunters from Minneapolis who hunted by buggy nearly every day during the fall in the years around 1890, and brought in buggy loads of birds.

Now that the pinnate populations have declined to a fraction of their original numbers in most parts of the range, there are rare reports of crop depredations by these birds. Because North Dakota farms are large there have never been many damage complaints against pinnates. The populations were on the decline before modern, clean farming operations became the vogue, so most of the crop damage complaints have been directed towards the pheasant. In eastern United States there were numerous complaints of crop damage in the 1800's. Audubon mentioned that the eastern prairie chicken (heath hen) was a problem to fruit growers and grainfields and he once saw fifty prairie chickens budding on one fruit tree in Massachusetts.[125] In some areas landowners considered the birds as detrimental as crows. Lewis wrote:

> So numerous were they [pinnates] a short time ago [1840's] since in the barrens of Kentucky and so contemptible were they as game birds, that few huntsmen would deign to waste powder and shot on them. In fact they were held in pretty much the same estimation, or rather abhorrence, that the crows are now in Pennsylvania or other of the Middle and Southern States, as they perpetuated quite as much mischief upon the tender buds and fruit of the orchards, as well as the grain in the fields, and were often so destructive to the crops that it was absolutely necessary for the farmers to employ their young negroes to drive them away by shooting off guns and springing loud rattles all around the plantation from morning till night.[126]

And Webb observed, "Usually, during the first few years of settlement, it [pinnate] increases rapidly, and is often a nuisance to pioneer farmers."[127]

The following indicates the irony of the situation in Minnesota in the 1880's and 1890's.

> The grain fields afforded both food and protection for them until the farmers complained of them bitterly, but not half so bitterly as they did afterwards of the bird-destroyers who ran over their broad acres of wheat, oats, and corn in the order of their ripening. The farmers are proverbially hard — for sportsmen — to please.[128]

By the early 1900's the pinnate populations were declining in many parts of the range and those persons interested in the bird's welfare began proclaiming its merits. Various observers produced evidence that it was valuable to the

---

[125]Judd, S. D., op. cit., p. 18.

[126]Lewis, op. cit., p. 148.

[127]Webb, op. cit., p. 71.

[128]Hatch, P. L., *First Report of the State Zoologist accompanied with notes on the Birds of Minnesota*, p. 163.

farmer because it ate thousands of injurious grasshoppers, crickets, other insects, and wild seeds. All of this publicity, however, had little effect in bringing the populations back to their original numbers.

For sportsmen, the pinnate has always ranked high in popularity. It was the number one upland game bird on the prairies of the midwest up until 1930. One of the finest tributes came from the pen of the English sportsman, Parker Gillmore:

> The first pheasant I killed in China I thought the noblest game bird that ever I had pulled a trigger upon, and truly he was a beauty. . . . For years the pheasant reigned paramount in my opinion; but a change has come in my ideas, and now superlative before all others I place two descriptions of American game birds and this species is one of them. What days of pleasure have I had in the pursuit of pinnated grouse! . . . He is truly a noble bird, and affords the best of sport. . . .[129]

There are varying opinions on the quality of pinnated grouse hunting. Some say this bird was easier to hunt than the sharptail. Some stated that pinnates flew farther than sharptails when flushed; others claimed it flew slower, in a straight line, and could be easily shot. Some said it was dumb and could be "pot-shot" easily and whole coveys could be shot at one time. Many hunters claimed the pinnate was a "sucker" for hunters with dogs because the bird held so well.

Now that the prairie chicken is gone from many places practically everyone, in retrospect, proclaims him to be one of the finest game birds. There were numerous attempts to restock the species in the east before 1900 and many pinnates were transported and released in foreign countries in hopes the bird would make a comeback. All attempts at stocking and restocking were unsuccessful. At the present time the pinnated grouse plays practically no role to the sportsman, farmer or nature lover of North Dakota. He arrived, thrived, and faded into obscurity all in a period of about sixty years.

---

[129]Gillmore, op. cit., p. 194.

Harvest

Large, spectacular harvests of this bird in North Dakota were a thing of the past before anyone attempted to estimate annual harvest figures for the species. The Game Department files show only five years of figures for the pinnate covering the period 1938-42.

Many of the factors which influenced sharptail populations also affected the pinnate. In fact, changes in specific land use practices affected pinnates more directly than sharptails. It should be kept in mind that the pinnate was an immigrant species and declined more rapidly and markedly when land use changes took place.

Like the buffalo, it has often been repeated, the pinnated grouse was a species exterminated by hunting. There is no question that year-round hunting helped to reduce pinnate populations. And how many times have you heard the statement, "We had lots of chickens before the hunters and railroad crews came out from Chicago, Minneapolis, Fargo, Timbuktu, or some nearby town, and shot them out!"? Of more importance in "harvesting" the birds were the great land use changes accomplished by burning,

plowing and grazing the grassland. This latter type of "harvest" is pathetic because it is a final and fatal harvest!

Undoubtedly, the biggest hunting harvest of pinnates occurred in the period 1890 to 1930. Probably more birds were killed per hunter during the early part of the period. As time went by, greater numbers of hunters with better methods of transportation and more efficient weapons increased the overall harvest.

Before there were laws and wardens to aid in controlling hunting, the birds were trapped or shot in large numbers at any season of the year. The rifle that played an important part in early sharptail harvests was not universally used in hunting pinnates. As mentioned earlier, by the 1880's, when the pinnate first arrived in North Dakota in significant numbers, the shotgun had become popular and practical for game birds. Its effectiveness increased as the gun was developed into the repeater and automatic. Many observers condemned these weapons.

Traveling to the hunting grounds of the pinnate before 1900 was generally by the horse-drawn vehicles mentioned in the sharptail chapter. Wealthy hunters often paraded to their favorite shooting grounds in surreys "with the fringe on top" and shot the birds with Greener, Parker, L. C. Smith, Davenport, and other well-known makes of guns. They were often accompanied by a group of four or five top quality pointer and setter dogs that came under as much criticism as the repeating shotguns of later years. Prominent nonresident hunters came in rented or private railroad cars and were sidetracked near their favorite areas to hunt for several days or weeks. James Hill, the railroad magnate, and Michigan sportsman, William Mershon, headed up several railroad car hunts. The following excerpt from the files of the *Bismarck Tribune* describes one prominent party:

> Oct. 13, 1897 — The Massachusetts hunting party occupying a private car are located at Dawson, where they will put in some time. . . . The party's manager says the 30 day outing costs only about $200 per person and they have the privilege of a private car and the best of everything.[130]

By the early 1900's the automobile was in popular use and sportsmen covered more areas in a shorter period of time. Some of these cars were specially designed and modified for hunting and camping.

Market hunters before 1900 used super shotguns in a 2 to 10 gauge size, nets, and traps to take large amounts of birds. Baited funnel traps and bird lime, a viscuous substance made from the holly and mistletoe, caught large numbers of waterfowl, grouse, and other birds. Old-timer Cecil Westlake of Kenmare reports:

> While living in the area that later became New Town my dad made traps for catching the "yellowlegs." These traps were about 18″ wide by 36″ long and 18″ deep. They were similar to egg crates and the top was hinged and operated as a trap door. We used corn as bait when we could get it. But more often popcorn from the kitchen was used because it was available. The bait was placed on top and when the bird hopped up to take the bait he dropped into the trap. They were used at any time during the year but took just one bird at a time.

---

[130]*Bismarck Tribune*, Oct. 13, 1962, p. 4.

H. V. Williams of Grafton says he used a sixteen foot, long-handled, fish landing net with a bag three by four feet in size when he trapped pinnates for the U. S. Biological Survey in 1915-17.

Persons, and there are many, who are critical of the indolent sportsmen of today shooting their deer and game birds from an automobile or the back of a pickup truck, need only review the past to realize that this philosophy of hunting has long been present. New tools and laws have been more instrumental in changing hunting methods than has human nature. One of the favorite illegal methods of hunting pinnates in 1900 was to pull a long rope or wire between two wagons moving parallel with each other. As the birds were flushed they were shot by hunters riding in wagons or walking along behind the rope.

The number of prairie chickens killed in the United States the past one hundred years is beyond comprehension. There are innumerable newspaper accounts of the numbers of grouse "barreled and boxed" and shipped to meat markets across the United States. Railroad depots often had barrels and boxes of grouse stacked on their platforms awaiting shipment. Seventy meat markets in Chicago in the year 1871 handled, and sold, more than 513,000 prairie grouse. The same markets in 1873 moved over 600,000 grouse across their retail counters. One large establishment (see picture below), in New York City, sold 2,400 grouse daily during the Christmas holiday season in 1878.

The sale was not so spectacular in North Dakota as it was in large eastern cities. One instance of promiscuously taking pinnates was recorded in 1896 when W. L. Wilder of Grand Forks wrote Governor Roger Allin that over two thousand North Dakota grouse had been seized by the Minnesota Game and

The Christmas Season, Fulton Market, New York City, 1878.

Fish Commission in St. Paul in early February. Mr. Wilder's informants in the Minnesota Department stated that none of the birds were carrying shot. They believed all had been trapped, removed from the traps, and their necks broken. Shipping tags showed that these grouse had been transported by train from the Williston area by persons using fictitious names. Although there was considerable correspondence between Minnesota and North Dakota game officials following this episode, there was no prosecution of the individuals committing the deeds. The major reason was that market hunting was not covered legally by the State Legislature.

Generally, those who wanted the birds could go afield and get them; they did not have to purchase them. Those who participated in the grouse business killed and shipped the birds out of state until 1900 when the Federal Lacey Act went into effect. Most North Dakotans used the birds they killed for their own families or distributed them to friends. Grouse were a source of food near at hand for those who wanted them. J. B. Lyon of Williston, states that his best hunt took place in 1904:

> . . . when four of us drove a buckboard into the sandhills about 25 miles north of Culbertson, Montana, and hunted four days along the Little Muddy. We brought back over 200 chickens. This did not include all the birds we used for camp meat. All were "squaretails". . . . We gave away a lot of grouse when we got back home.

Lifelong resident of Venturia, Otto Kretschmar, enjoyed one of his best hunts on September 7, 1922:

> My brother Bill and I drove around one section of land one mile west, one mile north, one mile east, and the mile back to Venturia, and in about five hours shot over 75 prairie chickens (pinnates). We had the back seat of our old 1918 Dodge automobile filled up. We felt pretty good about it until our dad took one look at the birds and gave us the devil! He could see no sense in killing so many at one time.

The best time of the year to harvest the pinnated grouse was almost universally agreed upon. Most old-timers felt that the season should open by the middle of August or the first of September. By this time the birds were prime for the table, and they could be easily approached by hunters and dogs. Tuttle, who authored the book *Wam-dus-ky* at Stump Lake (Nelson County), discussed the importance of early fall grouse seasons:

> The exhibition of hunting chickens, which we saw this morning was, however, though highly pleasing to most of the party [using five dogs], very imperfect for the reason that the season [Oct. 12-29] was so far advanced that the birds were not only scarce but too wild also to lie for the dogs, flying up and off permanently before the men could approach near enough to kill more than a half-dozen of them. This was a serious disappointment to some of the company. . . .
>
> On our first trip [Sept. 20-28], chickens were plenty and dogs were wanting; now dogs were plenty and chickens wanting. . . .
>
> The time for chicken shooting here is September.[131]

Another veteran hunter wrote that the pinnated grouse was easier to kill in August and September but added, "In the early part of the season the best

---

[131]Tuttle, J. H., *Wam-dus-ky*, p. 94.

Railroad boys with pinnates taken in Richland County, early 1900's.

shooting hours were early and late in the day.   Now [Oct.] it is the reverse; the middle of the day is the proper time."[132]

Gillmore, while in the choice pinnated grouse areas in Illinois, mentioned best times to hunt the birds:

> In the commencement of the season, and in fact as long as the weather is bright and mild, they lie remarkably well to dogs; but severe and cold weather causes them to pack and become wild.   However, late in October, or even in November, if you should hit upon a warm, summer-like day, the birds will become so disinclined for exertion between the hours of 10 A. M. and 3 P. M. that marvelous bags can be made.[133]

At the present time largest harvests of pinnated grouse in the United States are taking place in Oklahoma, Nebraska, South Dakota and Kansas.   Hunters in Kansas harvested 88,000 pinnates during the 1959 season.   This is a noticeable contrast to the North Dakota grouse harvest where practically all the birds killed by hunters are sharptails.   A pinnate that shows up in the season's bag is a rare occasion in North Dakota at the present time.   Harvest figures were kept for only five years on the pinnated grouse.   Roy Bach, co-ordinator for the Federal Aid Division of the Game Department, estimated harvests and pinnate populations for the period 1938-42 as follows:

TABLE 9   PINNATE HARVESTS, 1938-42

Year	Birds/ Hunter	Pinnates Harvested Numbers	Population Total Estimated
1938	1.2	29,000	300,000
1939	1.2	45,000	350,000
1940	1.2	47,000	450,000
1941	0.8	40,000	420,000
1942	0.7	36,000	400,000

[132]Bogardus, op. cit., p. 72.
[133]Gillmore, op. cit., p. 196.

Seasons and Regulations

The last open season for this bird in North Dakota was in 1945. Before that time seasons and regulations were the same as for the sharp-tailed grouse. Because the pinnate did not immigrate into North Dakota until the 1880's the seasons and regulations pertinent to the species covered a period of about sixty years, or from 1885 to 1945. Since the pinnate did not become common in the western half of the state until about 1900 the regulations there were important for less than fifty years. The eastern quarter of the state has been completely closed to both pinnates and sharptails since 1942.

Shortly after 1900 all states concerned began making drastic cuts in the seasons and regulations and by 1945 North Dakota was the only state open to hunting. After a short term of years several states were reopened to pinnate hunting in areas where there was suitable habitat. Game managers recognized the fact that annual harvests of 40 to 50 percent of the birds could be made without endangering the populations. In some of these states (Kansas, Oklahoma) there are more pinnates now than there were twenty years ago.

Several of the first hunting regulations directed towards game species were originated for pinnated grouse. The idea of closed seasons in the United States was applied as early as 1708 in New

York for ruffed grouse, wild turkey, quail, and the heath hen, eastern counterpart of the pinnate. An entirely new regulation, bag limits, was introduced for the first time on prairie chickens in Iowa in 1878.

When the great populations of pinnated grouse began to decline on the east coast during early settlement days it was understandable that seasons and regulations were employed in an effort to stop the decline. Many people believed that once hunting was stopped the birds would reproduce and return to their former large numbers. But there were other important considerations. Seasons and regulations are always intangible items left up to individual judgment. All too often the promiscuous killing continued. Secondly, and more important, human populations were rapidly increasing and, with the increase, pinnate habitat changed greatly. Man was constantly altering the habitat to fit his needs; as a result the grouse population declined.

Many changes in seasons and regulations were introduced in an attempt to stop this decline. Market hunting, the use of nets and traps, and large gauge guns were outlawed. Bird dogs were prohibited. Shooting hours were reduced to daylight and sometimes to only a few hours each day. Nonresident hunters were restricted or closely governed. Many local, specialized regulations, so common for pheasants today, were enforced. And finally, many states were completely closed to hunting prairie chickens.

One of the biggest problems, conservationists feel, has been persuading the public to really care about natural resources. Perhaps too many individuals or groups who destroy plants or animals, by one means or another, exhibit no regret. They realize, but care little, that they are a cause of the extinction of a wild species. Other persons are unaware of their own responsibility in the loss of natural resources. The first group is a serious problem; the second can sometimes be educated. Certainly the problem of public apathy has had much to do with the fate of the prairie chicken. As early as 1893-94 the annual report issued by the North Dakota Game Commissioner stated that people did not pay any attention to game laws or seasons. Few arrests were made on hunting violations because local sentiment would not allow it. W. W. Barrett, then Commissioner, wrote, "The game laws of North Dakota cannot be executed, public sentiment will not justify it." He believed, however, that progress was being made.[134]

By 1915-16 the Game and Fish Board stated that public sentiment was changing. Bag limits of five grouse per day and the setting back of the opening dates from September 7 to September 20 were well-accepted. This was a mark of progress as far as enforcement was concerned but it did not curtail the decline of the prairie chickens. During the 1920's and 1930's an accepted practice was to hold short seasons, later opening dates, and small bag limits. Finally, the season was closed for the last time in the eastern quarter of the state to all grouse hunting in 1942. The remainder of the state was closed to pinnated grouse shooting in 1945 and has been closed ever since. There has been a gradual decline in numbers of this bird since the early 1930's despite many closed seasons. Seasons and regulations for the pinnated grouse were the same as sharptails through 1945 and are shown on pages 24 to 28.

[134]*North Dakota State Game and Fish Dept., First Biennial Report, 1893-94,* p. 352.

Limiting Factors

When a wild species takes a drastic dip in numbers and does not recover, as occurred with the pinnated grouse in North Dakota, we hear a score of reasons offered for the decline. Each critic is convinced his pet belief is the primary reason the species was reduced in numbers. Consequently, there are many beliefs concerning what have been termed *limiting factors* on pinnated grouse populations.

Gradually, as pointed out later in the pheasant chapter (pages 138-40), a wildlife species declines because several decimating factors are in effect at the same time. In the case of the buffalo which gave way to man's livestock, cultivation and fences, numerous reasons have been presented as limiting factors. Each advocate firmly believes, however, that his reason was the single major factor. For example, overhunting. (Few settlers objected to the hunting because it was the quickest way to starve out renegade Indians and open the land to agriculture.) Many people today agree that overhunting exterminated the great herds. Certainly the buffalo was easier to overhunt than game birds because the animal produced slowly (after the age of three years, only one calf per year). Still, several old-timers interviewed for this book swear that the weather (blizzards) finished off the herds. Others blame prairie fires for

Breaking the prairie at Rock Lake, early 1900's.

the "coup-de-grace." No doubt these were factors, but quite probably the basic cause was simply that the great herds had to go; if each buffalo cow had calved a dozen times a year, the killing would only have been accelerated to remove this nuisance to man's advancement.

No one felt so strongly about removing the pinnated grouse. The bird was seldom looked upon as an obstacle to man. The huge flocks dwindled away because man simply went about his business of making a living and intensifying his use of the land. As the country was settled, areas of the nation, east to west, went through a period of high pinnate populations. There was a certain point in the utilization of the land when cover and food supply was in balance for prairie chickens. The pinnate has been called more of a grassland bird than the sharptail and flourished with some farming as long as it was not clean, intensive farming. When the intensive farming stage was reached, and few waste areas remained, the pinnate died out rapidly. Promiscuous hunting speeded up the process. Like the buffalo, the pinnate was doomed by man's advancements.

Trained game managers agree that the most important prerequisite for pinnated grouse, as for all wild species, is suitable habitat. There was a difference of opinion as to what was proper habitat in the 1800's. Roosevelt, Cooke, and Hatch, among others, stated that the pinnate kept pace with the settlement of the country and tolerated more grain farming than the sharptail. Bogardus was more explicit in his interpretation of habitat as he wrote about pinnate populations in the Illinois-Indiana region in the 1860's:

> . . . . The prairies were but sparsely settled and not an acre in a thousand had been broken up. The grouse were in immense numbers . . . the loss of breeding grounds far overbalances the thousands lost by nets and trapping and legal shooting. Too much plowing . . . before the great prairies of Illinois and other western states were broken up by the plough of the settler, the grouse were more numerous than they are now [1874] and they could not have fed on grain, because there were no fields of grain within hundreds of miles of them.[135]

North Dakota old-timers interviewed for this book stress the importance of uncultivated prairie lands to pinnates:

> *Everett Hyatt of Ludden* — The main reason I would say that we don't have prairie chickens is (1) Big farming. When people started breaking up everything the chickens disappeared. (2) Drainage or drying up of small potholes. We have had big drainage through this area. When we came here in the early 1900's the chickens boomed in every direction. Everything east of here [now Hyatt Slough] was prairie at that time.

> *Pat McMahon of Kenmare* — The reason we don't have grouse is because of plowing and grazing of the prairie. There has been a gradual population loss through the years. The grouse also used strawstacks . . . by the 1930's mechanical combines were already coming into use and the grouse began to lose the benefit of strawstacks.

When a person says that the pinnated grouse requires grassland he is speaking in broad generalities because the type and composition of the grassland is also important. Present populations of pinnates are found, for the most part, along the eastern edge of the Coteau and northern Red River Valley in roughly the

---

[135]Bogardus, op. cit., p. 20.

east-central portions of the state. It is currently believed that pothole vegetation is important to the few remaining. Several observers in the past mentioned the importance of moist habitat for prairie chickens, but there was some disagreement. In areas where there is a higher annual rainfall than North Dakota's 15 to 20 inches per year, the birds may not have as much need for potholes and their surrounding plants as in this state. Gillmore claimed that the pinnates of the Illinois-Indiana region showed a preference "to those places where the prairie is covered with bunch-grass, particularly if the sub-surface is moist, and the area not overstocked with cattle."[136] Larson wrote that North Dakota pinnates bred commonly "in the neighborhood of the prairie marshes."[137] On the other hand, Lewis noted that "dry habitat" was necessary for the heath hen, eastern counterpart of the pinnate, on the east coast, and stated that the birds avoided marshy or wet places.[138] Tuttle quoted the famous ornithologist, Alexander Wilson, as saying that pinnates "avoid wet and swampy places, and are remarkably attached to dry grounds."[139]

Fire has long been condemned as a decimating factor on prairie chickens. The prairie fire was described as the pinnate's "most deadly enemy" particularly in the spring when it "destroys every nest within its sweep." However, early spring burning, before the birds nested, was permissible.[140] Fire during the nesting season was a major problem in the conservation of the birds and fall burning destroyed the food supply and winter cover. North Dakotan Tom Hansen of Valley City, witnessed a spring fire on the Hansen homestead in 1903 that raged over eighty acres of prairie chicken habitat. Hansen noticed after the fire that most of the nests were located around a pothole, some of them situated 15 to 20 feet apart. Another resident, Everett Hyatt of Dickey County, states; "I think the heavy prairie chicken nesting (1900) was around the sloughs. The prairie chicken is not a persistent nester like the pheasant. . . ."

In Wisconsin, prairie chickens needed open country and too much human settlement limited the populations. Fires that opened up the peatlands resulted

[136]Gillmore, op. cit., p. 201.

[317]Larson, op. cit., p. 46.

[138]Lewis, op. cit., p. 151.

[139]Tuttle, op. cit., p. 94.

[140]Judd, S. D., op. cit., p. 13.

Surveying, Towner County, early 1900's.

David Herndon and Henry Hutchinson with mixed bag taken at Stump Lake, 1890's.

in too many woody stands of aspen. Some aspen and some cultivation was beneficial but there was too much of both.[141] Modern research has shown that early spring burning is not necessarily destructive to the pinnate. In fact, fire has proven an important management tool in that burning permits the reestablishment of many plants utilized by prairie chickens as food or cover. Some observers believe that completely undisturbed areas of grassland which grow tall and dense over a period of years do not furnish all the necessary food and cover plants.

Observers who have rated the weather an important factor in reducing pinnate populations are quick to condemn a cold, damp spring. In the Second Biennial Report of North Dakota Fish and Game Commissioner, Mr. W. W.

---

[141]Hamerstrom, F. N., A *Study of Wisconsin Prairie Chicken and Sharp-tailed Grouse*, p. 118.

Barrett wrote, "The cause of the decrease in the numbers of this class of birds was owing mainly to the large rains at hatching time, causing small broods."[142]

Through the years it has been stressed by many observers that pinnated grouse do not renest as commonly as pheasants, Huns, and other species. This was one reason the first nesting attempts were believed so important to reproduction for a given year and those who observed the chickens hoped for favorable weather in the spring.

There are few references to winter losses of pinnated grouse in North Dakota. The *History of Dickey County* mentions homesteaders who endured the unusually cold winters of the 1880's. One old-timer spoke of a bitter cold April 26th (in 1884 or 1885) when little birds were found frozen and the old-timers "found a number of prairie chickens frozen." He did not state whether the mortality was caused simply by the cold itself or a layer of ice that sometimes entraps ground roosting birds.[143]

Since this bird feeds largely on the ground, and is not known as a "budder" like the sharp-tailed grouse, it is possible that pinnates may have suffered for a lack of food in North Dakota in the past. However, it is important to realize that prairie chickens migrated south from the northern states in the fall. These migrations were more obvious in the days when there were large populations of the birds. Reasons offered for migrations were that the birds were traveling to reach areas of greater food supply and to escape the cold. Several observers, through trapping records, found the longest flights were made by females and young of the year. The food supply during the pre-1900 period was adequate in the states of Illinois, Iowa, and Missouri during the winter because those areas raised larger quantities of grain than the northern states and clean farming was not yet practiced. Corn, which was being raised in the lower midwest, was a staple food item for the pinnate.

Although there is little evidence of fall migrations in North Dakota during the past 30 or 40 years it is believed that some of the North Dakota birds now winter in the vicinity of Sand Lake in northeastern South Dakota. Migrations may easily go unnoticed because the birds are scarce and, secondly, there is little difference in the meager food supply in the northern or southern parts of the range. The literature shows that migrations were witnessed by at least some observant North Dakotans in the past. Bent mentioned that Glen Berner, a competent wildlife observer from Jamestown, saw a large extensive migration of pinnates in 1924. Berner saw approximately thirty flocks ranging in size from 10 to 100 birds at one location on a northward spring migration. Dr. O. A. Stevens of Fargo (North Dakota State University) witnessed a large fall pinnate migration on October 8, 1930.[144]

In addition to the widely publicized deficiencies of food and cover, many other decimating factors have been blamed for the decline. Overhunting has often been blamed, as have predators, basically the same ones associated with

[142]*North Dakota Game and Fish Records, 1891-1935*, p. 12.

[143]Black, R. M., *History of Dickey County, North Dakota*, p. 228.

[144]Bent, A. C., *Life Histories of North American Gallinaceous Birds*, p. 260.

the pheasant, sharptail and Hungarian partridge. The overall population of predators may not have changed much the past fifty years but the proportion of certain ones (coyotes, hawks, etc.) has changed. Condemned as limiting the pinnate populations have been the coyote, bobcat, fox, weasel, mink, hawk, owl, and feral dogs and cats. The nest robbers were the same familiar raccoons, skunks, crows, and other species. Because the coyote was so common at the time the pinnate populations were rapidly declining, much criticism in the past was directed and written about him.

Young observers today may not have thought much about the pheasant being classed as a strong competitor with pinnated grouse. But many old-timers firmly believed the pheasant had much to do with limiting pinnate populations. Everett Hyatt, a reliable old-timer from Dickey County, states:

> When the pheasant was coming in and the prairie chicken going out in the 1930's the pheasant cocks would pick the eggs of the prairie chicken and ruin the nests. I saw many prairie chicken nests destroyed by pheasants and saw the pheasants do it.

Sharp, who studied the pinnate, sharptail, and pheasant of the Nebraska Sandhills in the period 1937-43, witnessed a dozen instances of fighting between pheasant and pinnate cocks on booming grounds. The pheasants were hostile to the pinnates, won all encounters, and several times chased the pinnates to a distance of a mile or more. This observer wrote that competition, "could eventually eliminate existing isolated pockets of prairie chickens."[145]

This competition has been considered a minor factor, as noted by Shrader and Erickson in Minnesota, "Studies so far completed indicate the bird [pinnate] was not driven out by the pheasant; in fact they were gone in certain areas before the pheasant became common."[146]

Several North Dakota old-timers mentioned that the installation of telephone lines, electric lines, fences, and other structures took a heavy toll on pinnates, sharptails, and other birds. The pinnate seemed more prone to hit overhead wires than any other game bird.[147] As early as the 1870's, observers had begun to notice the high wires as a mortality factor. A Kansas man was quoted in *Harpers Weekly* as having picked up thirty-two birds (several species) along a one-half mile stretch of new telegraph lines. Prairie chickens were among the birds most commonly picked up and the observer estimated thousands were lost annually to this innovation.[148]

Many of the outside factors such as cycles, inbreeding, and others, were condemned from time to time as reducing the populations. But the chief cause recognized by most persons is the same one recognized today — the pinnate populations declined because of destruction or alteration of their environment.

[145]Sharp, W. M., *Social and Range Dominance in Gallinaceous Birds, Pheasants and Prairie Grouse*, p. 244.

[146]Shrader, T. A., and A. B. Erickson, *Upland Game Birds of Minnesota*, p. 12.

[147]Leopold, A., *Report on a Game Survey of the North Central States*, p. 185.

[148]*Harpers Weekly, April 24, 1875*, p. 339.

Research and Management

Many of the earliest management measures originated to save wildlife populations were aimed at the pinnated grouse. Most of these early attempts were in the form of hunting regulations. Restrictions on market hunting, bag limits, closed seasons, and the various gun, dog, and trespass laws were just a few. These tangential attempts to aid the prairie chickens may have slowed up the decline but did not halt it or restore populations to former numbers.

Research, relatively new for prairie chickens in recent years, is being conducted in Wisconsin, Oklahoma, Kansas, Nebraska, and other states by state and federal biologists. A Prairie Grouse Technical Council was created in the early 1950's under the sponsorship of the National Wildlife Federation, and the annual or biennial meetings are attended by grouse technicians from approximately twenty states. There is considerable exchange of research information between the technicians who attend.

Following the first hunting regulations for the pinnated grouse in the 1800's, the next attempts to manage this species came when private, state, and federal refuges were set up in many parts of the United States. On these undisturbed lands, varying in size from a few to several thousand acres (see sharptail chapter, page 39-40), prairie chickens could theoretically reproduce unmolested by the hunter, plow and domestic livestock. Unfortunately, prairie chickens did not respond to any marked degree on these refuges; in most cases populations declined although many other wildlife species benefited considerably from the undisturbed habitat. The U. S. Fish and Wildlife Service has in the past few years begun an experimental program of trapping prairie chickens in South Dakota and releasing them on refuges (Example: Lower Souris Refuge in North Dakota) where the habitat appears suitable for reproduction.

An attempt to lease eighty-acre plots of land already inhabited by prairie chickens was started by the North Dakota State Game Department in 1955 but the program was short-lived. It was quickly realized that the project would be too costly and landowners were reluctant. Only eighty-seven acres from a proposed 1,500 acres were leased and the program was discontinued within three years.

One of the most successful projects has been carried out near Plainfield, Wisconsin, for the past five years. Encouraged by the Wisconsin Conservation Department, Dr. and Mrs. Fred Hamerstrom and approximately two hundred prairie chicken admirers, with considerable financial backing of their own, have spent nearly $200,000 in buying and leasing land occupied by prairie chickens.[149] This worthwhile project has attracted nationwide interest. Considerable biological research is being conducted on pinnate populations and the birds have increased in numbers.

First attempts at restocking began as early as the mid-1800's on the east coast of the United States where the birds were rapidly disappearing. Practically all of the eastern states stocked wild-trapped pinnates from 1870 to 1900, but the stockings all failed. A few of the releases succeeded for several years but gradually the birds died off. At one Maryland county it appeared the stockings were going to be a success when only two pairs were released in 1869 and, within five years, had multiplied to over two thousand pinnates. Hunting was restricted and the populations closely guarded by human protectors, but the populations gradually disappeared again. Thousands of wild-trapped prairie chickens and eggs were shipped overseas to England, Ireland, Germany, France and other foreign nations in the years between 1870-1900, but all the stockings failed. Judd was optimistic as late as 1905: "There is great probability of success in the restocking of much of the former range of the prairie hen if undertaken in the proper way and properly sustained by adequate protection laws."[150]

Unfortunately, little success has been achieved in the sixty years since Judd's statement. Many game breeders have attempted the propagation of the birds but have usually failed, and now that wild populations are down in most parts of the nation, the birds are difficult to obtain. Based on the failures of countless early stockings it is questionable whether stocked birds could maintain a foothold on the modern intensively farmed lands.

Management of the prairie chicken in North Dakota at the present time is confined to an annual booming ground census in the Sheyenne Grazing Unit (Ransom County), a township study area in Stutsman County, and scattered populations in Nelson, Griggs, Grand Forks, and Steele Counties. Additional data is often obtained during roadside and aerial counts for other wildlife species. The areas where most of the pinnates are found have been closed to all grouse hunting since 1945.

The Stutsman County spring booming ground counts since 1949 are shown in the following table:

---

[149]*Boom, (Quarterly Report of Soc. of Tympanuchus Cupido Pinnatus, Ltd.) Feb. 1964,* p. 7.

[150]Judd, S. D., op. cit., p. 13.

TABLE 10

PINNATED GROUSE COCKS OBSERVED ON BOOMING GROUNDS IN STUTSMAN COUNTY, 1949-62

Year	Number of Cocks Observed	Area Censused	Density of Cocks per Square Mile
1949	121		
1959	60		
1951	46		
1952	35		
1953	53		
1954	41		
1955	85	115 sq. mi.	.74
1956	44		
1957	64	114 sq. mi.	.56
1958	64		
1959	100	156 sq. mi.	.64
1960	60		
1961	21		
1962	31	90 sq. mi.	.34

5
Pheasant

Scientific name: *Phasianus colchicus*

Size:

Length, cocks 33-36 inches; hens 20-24 inches. Wingspan, cocks 32-34 inches; hens 24-29 inches. Weight, cocks up to 3½ lbs.; hens 2½ lbs. January-February (1962) weights of 210 cocks in North Dakota averaged 48.6 oz. The average weight for 618 hens during the same period was 35.9 oz.

Coloration:

Cocks are gaily colored with many irridescent brown, green, black, and white feathers; much red around the head. Hens are a drab brown. The long tail separates the hen from the grouse family.

Flight:

Strong flyers with an explosive takeoff. Cocks cackle loudly at takeoff; hens are generally silent. Both sexes often difficult to flush and will sneak rather than take to the air. Once airborne the birds may sail for considerable distance before landing.

Flock habits:

May be in singles or flocks of mixed sexes in fall and winter. Large flocks of 50 or more birds common in the years of high populations.

History

One would imagine the history of the pheasant in North Dakota to be relatively simple due to its short existence on the North American continent. Certainly the time of its introduction and growth as a species is easier to pinpoint than the native grouse family. Yet, when we pass out roses to those most deserving for pheasant stocking success in North Dakota, the direction in which to send the award is not clear-cut. Many large and small releases have been carried on by individuals or groups. Sportsmen, farmers, game breeders, the Game Department, and many others have contributed to the project. There have been planned pheasant releases and there have been indiscriminate releases. In some instances eggs were purchased and young birds hatched and released at various stages of growth. In other cases adult birds were literally "dumped" into the open. The time of release was often of little concern and some pheasants set foot on the Dakota prairie for the first time on top of a wintery blanket of snow. Still others made their initial appearance beneath a hot summer sun. Naturally, most releases were made in the periods between these extremes. Some of the releases were with pen-raised birds while others were

made with wild-trapped stock. To better appreciate the introduction of the pheasant in North Dakota we should briefly consider its early history in the United States.

Credit for the introduction of the pheasant is generally given to George Washington who liberated the English variety at Mount Vernon during his first term as president. Governor Wentworth of New Hampshire released English pheasants at his estate in 1793. Neither of these stockings was successful and it was ninety years before sportsmen were to see the first really successful establishment. Through the years, English, Chinese, Japanese, Mongolian Union. Success was achieved only in nineteen of these states.

First stocking at Kenmare. Spring of 1929. L. to R.: Ed Loader, Ike Lindberg, Frank Rundlett, and Dr. L. H. Burt.

The first successful stocking occurred in the Willamette Valley of Oregon when Judge O. N. Denny liberated the Chinese ring-neck variety in 1881. These birds multiplied rapidly, and the first open season was held for two and one-half months in 1892. Reports have it that over fifty thousand pheasants were killed on the first day of the season.

Earliest releases of importance to our state occurred at Sturgis, South Dakota, when N. L. Witcher imported Oregon pheasants and released them as early as 1891. The records are scanty on this, and Dr. A. Zetlitz of Sioux Falls received more attention with his Illinois game farm birds in South Dakota beginning in 1898. It is believed the first important stocking in our sister state was around 1909. The South Dakota Department of Game, Fish and Parks inaugurated pheasant releases in 1911 and liberated over seven thousand birds between 1914-17. The first Dakota season was one day, October 30, 1919, in Spink County, South Dakota. Approximately two hundred pheasants were killed with a two bird limit per hunter. Bad weather, characterized by a foot of snow, and followed by rain, took the luster off the hunt. There were fabulous hunts to follow, however, because by 1927 over two million pheasants were being killed annually in South Dakota.

The Minnesota Conservation Department attempted stocking with seventy pairs of birds in 1905. The first open season did not take place until the fall of 1924.

First attempts at stocking this bird in Montana were by "unknown persons prior to 1895"[151] and the 1895 game laws for Montana stated that it was unlawful to kill Chinese pheasants. The first open season in Montana was in 1928 and the state has had an open season every year since.

It is not believed stocking to the north of North Dakota has ever exerted any beneficial effects on this state's pheasant population. Success in the immediate Canadian provinces has been even more limited than it has in our own state. Saskatchewan did not have an open season until 1939 and the earliest stocking was around 1934. As early as 1912 five pairs were released west of Brandon, Manitoba. This stocking was rated unsuccessful, as was another in 1928. The Manitoba Game Branch released over one thousand birds in 1934, and still more in 1936, all with limited results. The province held open pheasant seasons in 1941 to 1945 but has held no open seasons since 1945. The largest harvest was six thousand birds in 1945.

North Dakota Game Department files show the earliest stockings were with seventy-five birds in 1910. These birds had been housed at the old St. John Hatchery in April of 1910 and at least some birds were raised from eggs produced by the adult hens. There were no important introductions again until 1915 when pheasant stocking operations were carried on by the Bottineau and Grafton State Game Farms. The 1909-10 Biennial Report of the Game and Fish Board of Control stated:

> After first being liberated there was at no time any effort made to restrain the birds; they would come and go at pleasure. For three months they ranged along and near the lake shore [at St. John]. Hundreds of people from all parts of the state visiting the fish hatchery, and frequenters of the Fish Lake summer resort, expressed themselves as pleased to note that the Game and Fish Board of Control was making practical demonstration in the introduction of this valuable, interesting and beautiful game bird.
>
> In July the old birds were liberated and up to the 10th of November they were reported nearly every day by someone.[152]

In 1911, forty pairs of pheasants were purchased at Grafton at $4.75 per pair. These were apparently some of the birds originating from a dozen eggs purchased by W. H. Williams of Grafton in 1904 from Oregon. Several years later in 1917, a well-publicized release was made with twenty-eight pheasants on the Kendall Farm near Oakes in Dickey County. Time and space does not permit listing all the persons instrumental in the pheasant's success in our state. Nearly all the older citizens can name one or more persons who played an important role in the stocking program. Sportsmen's clubs and individual sportsmen spent considerable money rearing and releasing the birds. Farmers often hatched eggs, released the pheasants, and protected them from hunting, inclement weather, predators, and the host of other pitfalls to the best of their ability. Long-term residents' efforts are typified by the following statements:

> A. J. Spire of Marmarth: (saw his first wild pheasant, at the Logging Camp Ranch sometime around 1930.) I didn't know there were such birds around and when we saw that pretty cock bird we all talked about it and wouldn't have thought of shooting it.

---

[151]Craig, V., *Letter*, March 22, 1961.
[152]*North Dakota State Game and Fish Dept., Biennial Report, 1909-10*, p. 88.

A. O. Odegard of Heimdal: The first pheasants around here were started between 1930-32.   Banker Sam Bye and I built a holding pen and handled the first 75-100 birds to be stocked in the area.

The first release to be made in the Kenmare area was in the spring of 1929 at Upper Des Lacs Lake and is illustrated on page 111.

Undoubtedly, the biggest stocking undertaken by farmers, sportsmen, and the Game Department was in the spring of 1932 when 15,460 wild birds were trapped in Dickey, Sargent and Richland Counties and released in forty-five counties across the state.   The estimated cost was .50¢ per bird and they were captured by the use of spotlights at night.

When the stocking picture is reviewed in North Dakota it is obvious that pheasants have taken hold and established themselves.   Just which stockings were of most importance is unknown.   As early as 1930 it was apparent that the first areas to experience rapid population increases were located in the south, especially in Dickey, Sargent and Richland Counties.   It was suggested that South Dakota's stocking program may have had more influence on North Dakota's population than any of the stockings in this state.   The 1930 Annual Report for the North Dakota Game and Fish Department said:

> Dickey, Ransom, Sargent and other counties along the South Dakota border have been well-stocked with the Chinese or Ringneck pheasant from birds which have drifted into North Dakota from its sister state to the south.   It was found that adult birds, for stocking purposes, could be trapped and distributed from the over-run in these counties cheaper and better than they could be propagated on our Game Farm.[153]

The total number released will never be known, but the Third Annual Report of the North Dakota Game and Fish Department issued the following statement in 1932:

> The pheasant has established itself in this state, something in excess of thirty thousand of these birds having been liberated in the last twenty years, and there is now no county but has numerous colonies of them scattered through it.[154]

[153]*North Dakota State Game and Fish Dept., First Annual Report, 1930,* p. 54.
[154]*North Dakota State Game and Fish Dept., Third Annual Report, 1932,* p. 13.

Soo line depot at Oakes, early 1940's.

Role

Like other introduced species of game the pheasant was imported and released to "fill a gap" or "fulfill a whimsey;" i.e., provide a bird to hunt. In North Dakota by the early 1900's the gap was being created when the prairie grouse habitat was damaged by farming. Many farmers and sportsmen wanted to see game birds again where they were on the decline. Still others were desirous of seeing something different and a bird such as the pheasant was a good subject on which to focus their attentions. The beautiful coloration, large size, excellent eating qualities, sporting behavior and generally innocuous feeding habits all were conducive to justify the pheasant's popularity. The bird had already exhibited the ability to reproduce in exorbitant numbers in other states such as Oregon and South Dakota. The pronounced differentiation in the sexes was in itself an answer to the question of overhunting that had puzzled the general public during those early years. In other words, it was easy to hold a "cock only" season on this species with the idea of saving the hen to reproduce more birds.

Looking back on those first attempts at pheasant stocking, one has a difficult time imagining why anyone would take offense at the program, but records indicate friction did exist. Some observers thought

the introductions may have been carried on before sufficient evidence was gathered concerning pheasant habits. It was believed the bird might, despite the claims, exhibit destructive feeding habits on certain agricultural crops. People were skeptical of its ability to withstand North Dakota's weather variables. And there was concern that pheasants would compete directly with native grouse to the point of exterminating them even in areas where grouse were relatively abundant. Unfortunately, many of these questions are still unanswered but it is a fact that the pheasant has become established.

The biennial report of the Game Department for 1919-20 gave the first indication of the dispute that was building up. Two pages were devoted to describing the virtues of the pheasant, especially in regard to feeding habits which exponents extolled as beneficial to mankind. The fact that the bird fed on clover, alfalfa, thistle, dandelion and a great variety of plants was in its favor. Many of the insects injurious to corn and wheat crops were reputedly eaten by the newcomer. It "ravenously destroys wire worms, potato bugs, squash bugs, tomato worms, grasshopper eggs and many other bad smelling bugs."[155] Further on:

> . . . The pheasant as it passes through the growing grain keeps its head near the ground and turns one eye up and down so it sees the larvae and eggs on the underside of the leaf.
>
> Among the people of an agricultural district the pheasant readily finds friends who will give it protection, as well as enemies who seek its destruction. To the farmer it is an eminently faithful and useful bird and in him it should find a true friend and a careful protector. As surely as he comes to understand their usefulness to him every farmer or landowner will desire as many of the birds about his farm as possible to protect his crops. . . .[156]

A few years later evidence of friction between the pro and con advocates of the pheasant was described in the 1925-26 Biennial Report:

> . . . the birds have obtained a foothold which is not at all likely to be broken.
> On the other hand a considerable number of our people feel that the Department in bringing these birds into North Dakota acted *not wisely*, but too well. That many are prejudiced against the Chinese pheasant is well known. This adverse sentiment inheres mainly in two more or less doubtful indictments against them.
>
> First, the Chinese pheasant is a great fighter — and he doesn't care who knows it. . . . Two or three well authenticated cases of the pheasant having attacked and killed prairie chickens have come to the attention of the Game and Fish Department; but these sporadic cases in themselves afford slight ground for the fear just mentioned. . . . The introduction of the Chinese pheasant undoubtedly adds a new element of danger, but we believe it is so slight as to be negligible.
>
> The second indictment against the pheasant has to do with his alleged extreme fondness for green corn — that is to say, for the tender blades of corn as they come peeping forth from the seed in May or June. Here, again, the human tendency to exaggerate has doubtless come into play. . . .
>
> The present purpose of the North Dakota Game and Fish Department is somewhat to slacken its program in respect to the importation and propagation of these birds. However, in spite of his militant nature and his penchant for growing corn, it is agreed by all who have tested the matter that the ringneck is mighty good eating![157]

[155]*North Dakota State Game and Fish Dept., Fifth Biennial Report, 1919-20,* p. 8.

[156]Ibid., p. 8.

[157]*North Dakota State Game and Fish Dept., Ninth Biennial Report, 1925-26,* p. 10.

As the pheasant populations built up during the late 1930's and early 1940's the criticism came almost entirely from the farmer. The first open season had been a one and one-half day in 1931 and both the hunting days and bag limits were increased in the late 1930's and early 1940's. The birds multiplied rapidly during these years and by 1942 only the northeastern corner of the state was without adequate or heavy pheasant populations. And, as is often the case with deer, quail and other game species elsewhere, this buildup was not only evident in North Dakota but in many other sections of the United States. The annual report for the State Game Department in 1942 stated:

> The fall of 1942 probably showed the largest population of ringneck pheasants ever to exist in North Dakota. Though the season was longer and the kill heavier than in 1941 many reports of crop damage were received from the southeast and western parts of the state. . . .

> The present pheasant population in North Dakota is so high that should there be no die-off from natural causes, and if there is a normal increase in 1943 the population will be so great that it will be imperative to reduce or control it throughout many areas in the state. Even now many farmers consider the pheasant a more serious threat to some of their crops than either grasshoppers or ground squirrels or both combined.[158]

[158]North Dakota State Game and Fish Dept., Annual Report, 1942-43, p. 5, 8.

Ellendale, Nov. 11, 1944. L. to R.: Jim Campbell, Ed Shave, Arnold Strand, Ted Kilby, unknown, and Jack Kramer.

By 1944 the pheasant population had reached its peak and letters to the Game Department asking for aid in control were commonplace. The following is a typical letter written during the peak period:

Richardton, North Dakota
February 6, 1945

Dear Sirs:

In regard to the pheasant situation I would like to call your attention. We have had at least $200 damage done to our haystacks, cornstalks and corn on the cob this winter. There are between 600 and 800 birds at our buildings continually and between 6,000 and 8,000 on our land. We have also had much crop damage the last few years.

The only means of scaring them is by shooting, although we are unable to get shells at the present time. We also have thought of poisoning them.

We have oats and barley but feel we cannot afford to feed them either. We understand that they may be of some value, but under such circumstances damage much more than their value. We would appreciate what you suggest we do. . . .

If you should like to verify any statements kindly send an agent out and see for yourselves.

Thanking you I am . . .

Sincerely,

Of course, there was the other side of the picture. Hunters were having a heyday. In the early 1940's everyone shot pheasants, ate pheasants, and enjoyed both. A wide variety of recipes was utilized by housewives and eating establishments. Some of the ladies went so far as to make pictures, fancy hats and clothing ornaments with pheasant feathers. Old-timer Arthur Anderson of Belfield just about sums it up for farmers and hunters all over the state when he says:

In those big pheasant years during the early 1940's including the year we had a winter season, [1944-45] several farmers around Belfield would practically beg us to come out and shoot pheasants. The birds were tearing down haystacks and when you get 300-400 in an area they can do a lot of damage. We'd go out and kill 10-15 in less than an hour's shooting and go back to Belfield and give most of them away — if we could get somebody to take them! Everybody ate pheasants at that time. One farmer I remember asking for hunters to come out to his farm was Peter Ebert.

Since the plush 1940's, pheasant numbers have declined considerably in most areas of the state. However, this still ranks as game bird number one in popularity.

Harvest

Once the pheasant became established it was a mere ten years before this new-comer replaced the grouse as the favorite upland game bird. Many hunters today prefer grouse over pheasant hunting but the general run-of-the-mill hunter quickly accepted the pheasant and this trend has continued down to the present time. In some respects this foreigner was easier to hunt than grouse. It reproduced at a faster rate than grouse, particularly in the 1930's and early 1940's when agriculture was booming and the grassland and grouse were diminishing. It was easier to hunt the pheasant from the road and many people preferred it on the dinner table. Finally, pheasants were conspicuously ostentatious in appearance — almost trophy-like when compared with the less colorful grouse.

Little has been written about the first open season on pheasants in North Dakota in 1931 except that it covered the three-county area of Richland, Sargent and

Dickey Counties and was in effect but one and one-half days. Everett Hyatt, lifelong resident of Ludden, wrote to the Department in 1961:

> We had no trouble getting our bag limit in the fall of 1931. Most of our hunting then was in corn fields and sweet clover patches. As I remember we had no trouble getting our limits during that first season.

Though the overall harvest the first few years was below that of present day those who hunted may well have experienced better individual success than the modern hunter. There were fewer hunters and probably more pheasants in the local areas then. Less than 35,000 resident licenses and one hundred nonresident licenses were sold in any one of those first eight seasons. The hunters had not, as yet, made the pheasant their solid number one upland game bird. Ducks and grouse were still more widespread and most popular. The methods of travel over unimproved roads to a relatively small open area was not as common as now when hunters from the northern part of the state may drive hundreds of miles for the opening. Those hunters living in close proximity to the pheasant range could take advantage of good hunting as well or better than now. Furthermore, hens were allowed in the bag as early as 1933 and this helped in "filling up" early. Seasons were short those first eight years, never over ten days, and this undoubtedly impeded and discouraged persons living at a distance who could hunt only one or two weekends. Economically speaking, hunting was more of a luxury and fewer hunters could afford the travel and equipment they now enjoy. Nevertheless, by 1936 *North Dakota Outdoors* stated: "Upland game bird surveys found the average number of pheasants bagged by each hunter reporting was about five times that of grouse."[159] Thus by 1936 the pheasant was rapidly gaining in popularity.

Unfortunately, the combination of drouth and depression in the 1930's created a decrease in the number of licenses sold as well as a decline in the harvest. An all-time low number of 14,500 upland game licenses was sold in 1937, and in 1938 it was estimated only 140,000 pheasants were harvested. This now seems strange in the face of the regulation that sanctioned the pheasant hen as legal game. Furthermore, the pheasant population was booming by 1938 as evidenced again by *North Dakota Outdoors*:

> According to Robert K. Ford, caretaker at the George Slade game farm located south of Dawson, they have had the largest increase of game birds this year than they have had for many years. Mr. Ford fed 3000 pheasants during the winter months, and he estimates that the increase was around 15,000.[160]

By 1940 the big harvest had commenced and for the first time exceeded 500,000 birds. The following year the number of upland game hunters passed the fifty thousand mark for the first time. The "Golden 40's" had begun for pheasant hunters. The harvest was estimated in the millions from 1940 to 1946, climaxed by 1944 and 1945 when nearly two and one-half million were taken each year. This harvest occurred despite the fact that a war was on, shotgun shells were scarce, gasoline was rationed, and many of the best hunters were away in the armed forces.

---

[159] *North Dakota Outdoors, Nov., 1936*, p. 3.
[160] *North Dakota Outdoors, Sept., 1938*, p. 29.

Three hundred pheasants taken west of Linton, fall of 1944.

. . . Pioneer hunters said, We have never seen so many upland game birds since we have been in the state! Due to pheasant and Huns, but not so true for grouse. Estimated bird populations are over 15,000,000 upland game birds, and over 7,500,000 can be harvested though there have never been over 1,500,000 ever taken in one year.[161]

Seasons were liberal, four hens were allowed in possession by 1945, and the hunter could hunt 136 days the same season. Hunting was so easy it was said by some to be merely "killing." The average hunter took over thirty-four pheasants per season for the four years 1942-45.[*]

The phenomenal increase of the bird was not strictly a local situation. During these years many species of game increased all over the United States.

In many sections of North Dakota the Chinese Ringneck pheasant has increased in such numbers that it has become a definite threat to farming operations. South Dakota is experiencing the same problem. . . . From different parts of the country come reports of both large and small game surpluses . . . on some National Forests and Parks reports come from government officials recommending that herds of big game be reduced to avert mass starvation and serious impairment of the range. . . .

Waterfowl has imposed a serious hardship on some farmers and partially destroyed important food crops the government has urged them to raise for the war effort . . . there is only one logical answer: reduce the surplus to the safe carrying capacity of the habitat — and if the sportsmen hunters are either unable or unwilling to do the job, game management agents should do it.[162]

[*]One must consider the different method of calculating game bird harvests in the 1940's as compared to the 1950's. Crippling loss was included in the 1940's and therefore might run 30% higher than the "bird in hand" figure used in the 1950's. Also, a small sample of hunters was used compared to the 1950's.

[161]*North Dakota Outdoors, Sept., 1942*, p. 5.

[162]*North Dakota Outdoors, Feb., 1943*, p. 2.

Golfer Sam Snead and Frank Cave, Bismarck, 1945.

In 1943 the State Game Department published a bulletin loaded with harvest pictures and statements from successful nonresident hunters and encouraging nonresidents to come to North Dakota for their hunting. Not only did the state have enormous numbers of upland game birds but the nonresident license sales had never exceeded four hundred in any season up to that time. Federal Aid Coordinator Roy Bach stated the feelings of the Department concerning the over-balance of game in this bulletin:

> There are several reasons perhaps for the remarkable increase in upland game bird populations during the past four or five years. No exception to drought conditions, upland game populations reached a low during the years '34 to '36. In 1936, too, a long time low was reached in economic conditions as far as agriculture and livestock was concerned. In the west and southwest the cattle production was reduced drastically. The Soil Conservation Service took over much of the land in the grazing section. Areas that had long been farmed intensively were let go back to nature and the AAA program was initiated. In other words, intensive utilization of land for agricultural or livestock raising purposes came to an end. Since 1937 the state has seen several wet and bountiful seasons. The past three years have been rather exceptional from the moisture viewpoint. Cover in the form of grasses and other plants has come back in an amazing way. Intensive land utilization has not kept pace with the amazing development of habitat. The west is not over-grazed and the agricultural regions are not, as yet over-farmed. In other words habitat from the birds' standpoint has kept ahead of land usage and the results of this are readily indicated . . . as far as habitat is concerned from a cover and food standpoint especially the summer of 1943 perhaps, represents the acme in North Dakota's game history.[163]

Gunners shot pheasants practically anywhere during these years of high populations. They could easily be shot from the road and walking was unnecessary. The birds "boiled out" of sweetclover patches for those who did get out and walk. Often the ground in the concentration areas had the appearance of being tramped down by cattle or other livestock and was littered with droppings and feathers. There were literally millions of pheasants, and hundreds on one section or one sweetclover patch. Nearly everyone enjoyed pheasants at the dinner table and servicemen traveling the railroads received free pheasant sandwiches served by the USO and other organizations at Mandan and other points where the troop trains stopped. It was natural that the hunters followed the birds and in the banner year of 1945, 62,000 resident and 4,800 nonresident license buyers enjoyed North Dakota hunting. The war had ended by this time and the birds were plentiful. Still the numbers of hunters must be considered small when compared with the numbers of pheasants that were in the field for the taking.

The boom years were coming to an end by 1946 and suddenly there was now the clamor for control in a different direction. The harvest of this bird fell off considerably in 1946. Instead of damage complaints from those directly dependent on the land for their income the pendulum swung in their direction; pheasant numbers were decreasing and it was now time for the hunters to complain. They wanted control of predators, the combining machine that was in widespread usage, the weather, and even the genes affecting the pheasants — or anything which would restore the bird to the bountiful numbers of a few years before. They wanted to go back to stocking and closing the seasons. In the 1946

[163]Anon., *North Dakota Offers Variety in Hunting*, p. 16.

Annual Report of the North Dakota Game and Fish Department, President Ira Gabrielson of the Wildlife Management Institute was quoted concerning the diminishing game numbers all over the United States. The decline was universal in this country just as the increase in game had been universal a few years before. Gabrielson remarked:

> 1946 produced the smallest stock of pheasants in the northern states, for many years. . . . The general effect has been to start the 'anvil chorus' going again blaming everything and everybody for these conditions. All the old nostrums have been trotted out. Every other suggestion will be made before the average gunner will face the fact that a combination of destruction of habitat, poor breeding conditions, and heavy gun pressure are the basic causes of this condition. Predators, the regulations, the weather during the hunting season and every other conceivable factor will be blamed before the average gunner will face the facts. This is natural but short sighted. . . .
>
> . . . From New York to the Dakotas the wails of the pheasant hunters have resounded from every angle. Pressure for bigger and better game farms, for control of predators, for this and that flew thick and fast following a rather disappointing pheasant season as measured against the very successful seasons of the past few years. If those who are crying would stop and think for a moment they should realize that it is not now, nor never will be possible for the land which must of necessity be primarily devoted to other purposes to produce continuously the maximum crops of pheasants that have been available in the past few years.[164]

During the eighteen years that have followed Mr. Gabrielson's statements there have been only minor population fluctuations and there have certainly been no population explosions except in small local areas. The number of upland game license buyers and pheasants harvested annually have not deviated far off the average for any one year. Unlike many of the eastern and lower midwestern states where human populations have increased rapidly since World War II, North Dakota has not yet felt the full impact of heavy human populations. Undoubtedly, there will be even more intensive use of Dakota land in the future.

A summary of pheasant harvests is shown in the following table.

TABLE 11   PHEASANT HARVESTS

Year	Pheasants Per Hunter During the Season	Estimated Pheasant Harvest	Year	Pheasants Per Hunter During the Season	Estimated Pheasant Harvest
1934	9.0	213,500	1948	6.2	460,000
1935	9.2	215,100	1949	5.6	410,000
1936	------	------------	1950	1.0	60,000
1937	------	------------	1951	2.9	193,000
1938	5.7	140,000	1952	2.6	175,000
1939	7.8	290,000	1953	Closed	
1940	13.1	510,700	1954	3.2	200,000
1941	16.7	840,000	1955	3.4	235,000
1942	34.1	1,770,000	1956	4.7	325,000
1943	37.2	1,510,000	1957	4.0	286,000
1944	48.9	2,450,000	1958	6.9	525,000
1945	35.7	2,400,000	1959	2.4	134,000
1946	8.4	590,000	1960	4.2	240,000
1947	4.5	283,800	1961	4.7	260,000
			1962	3.8	185,000

[164]North Dakota State Game and Fish Dept., Annual Report, 1946-47, p. 45.

Seasons and Regulations

Many sportsmen and farmers believe that the setting of seasons is one of the easiest problems of pheasant management. They presume that the Department makes pheasant population surveys, looks over the harvest and hunting pressure figures from previous years, adjusts bag limits and season lengths to coincide with the accumulated information, and then sets the dates. Unfortunately, it is not that simple. In fact, the biggest problem involved here seems to be not that of managing wildlife but that of managing people.

Final pheasant regulations each fall are generally drawn up on a conciliatory basis. Attention must be given the Department's recommendations, the varied desires of sportsmen and hunting clubs, the rights of farmers and ranchers, laws concerning game refuges in municipal, state and federal lands, and other groups with justified or unjustified reasons. Before the seasons are set there are considerations to be made which can generally be classified under four main headings:

(1) Regard for the game species in question and all game species.

(2) Personal or political grievances by individuals or groups.

(3) Traditions which have been built up over a period of years.

(4) Legislative restrictions.

These four main considerations and the minor reasons that come under them are discussed briefly here. Perhaps the reader will better appreciate the method of setting the seasons when he looks at the table and maps in this section. Sometimes the reasons given for wanting a season of one type or another overlap two of the main considerations. A good example of this is the setting of grouse or Hungarian partridge and pheasant seasons in recent years. The first two generally open in late September and the latter not until early or mid-October. The two different openings are biologically sound because grouse and partridge mature more quickly than pheasants and the hunting success is best on grouse somewhat earlier. Every year the Department receives pressure for a simultaneous opening of grouse, partridge and pheasants. Thus, the problem seems to be that of managing people and not the game. The main justification usually presented for the simultaneous opening is that hunters are killing off pheasants under the guise of hunting grouse or partridges. This would mean the reasoning must come under our number one consideration — *regard for all species.* But we cannot leave out consideration number two — *personal grievances* — because many pheasant hunters just don't want to see grouse or partridge hunters in the field ahead of them. Furthermore, the latter critics often have the farmer on their side because many farmers would just as soon see the seasons take place all at once so they won't be "bothered" long periods of time in the fall. The Department is criticized because it is said to be "creating law breakers" — hunters who will shoot pheasants during the grouse season because temptation is present. Here again enters the problem of human and not game management.

Sometimes the reasons given under consideration number three — that of *tradition* — can prove an aid or detriment. An example, again, is the early grouse season. From the earliest days of the white man in North Dakota it was acceptable and legal to hunt grouse in August. Old-timers preferred the meat of grouse killed in haying season to those killed in late October. "Shorty" Foreman of Marmarth says, "In the fall of 1911 four of us lived off grouse killed during the haying season. We ate grouse until October when the birds get 'flaky'." (Mr. Foreman explains this as splinters and tendons in the legs.)

Old-timer Glen Wood of Emmonsburg agrees, "We always enjoyed the haying season grouse as the best for eating."

"We always started hunting grouse in early September (often in hot weather) and flushed great numbers of birds," says Louis R. Nostdal of Rugby, who hunted the Smoky Lake area in 1902-05. "We customarily surrounded the thickets and really slaughtered them."

Not until 1930 was the season moved to late September or early October. The early grouse season has become such an accepted *tradition* that those who call for a simultaneous opening with pheasants often find many who will argue with them on the merits of such a late opening.

Another *tradition* worthy of mention is that of shooting cock pheasants. For many years hunters did not accept the idea that shooting only the cocks would not harm the pheasant population. As recently as 1953 the pheasant season was closed altogether because many sportsmen felt an open season would seriously damage the population. But as time has gone by it has become *traditional* to shoot cocks and the practice does not endanger the breeding stock.

There has been speculation as to what might happen if the Department and sportsmen's groups would recommend open seasons for both male and female pheasants. This type harvest is accepted for grouse, deer, partridge and other species and was accepted by nearly everyone during the boom pheasant years in the 1940's. It is practiced in other states where winterkill is of little consequence. But to make such a proposal at this time in North Dakota would certainly be against the *traditional* consideration of shooting nothing but cock pheasants for nearly twenty years and a hullabaloo would probably be raised.

The reasons under consideration number four — *legislative restrictions* — may also prove acceptable or unacceptable under certain conditions. A good example of a law which has affected the setting of game bird seasons in recent years has been the aggregate bird bag limit in effect until 1963. This stated that the daily bag limit could not exceed fifteen birds in the aggregate. It was conceivable that a hunter in an area where four game bird species could be taken might not take his daily limit as allowed. In a year when four pheasants, four sharptailed grouse, five Hungarian partridges and four ruffed grouse were legal the hunter could take seventeen birds daily if he followed the proclamation, but he would be over his limit under the aggregate bag law.

Another *legislative restriction* states that no season can be opened on any game bird before September 15th in any given year. In 1963 the first season was held on mourning doves in North Dakota. Since a large percentage of doves are on their migration, and south of North Dakota by September 15th, there must be a change in the aforementioned law before North Dakota hunters can expect to harvest many birds. To do this the season would have to be open in August or early September.

This is just a sampling of the many reasons offered under the four main considerations each fall when game seasons are set. Regulations over the years show the effects of these considerations. Daily shooting hours, bag limits, possession limits, season lengths, areas open and closed to hunting, types of weapons and transportation, use of dogs, killing one or both sexes, and opening dates are all subjects for controversy and concern before any pheasant season is decided. Sometimes changing conditions from one year to another have alleviated or created problems before the dates are set. Until 1963 there was a 9:00 a.m. daily opening for shooting upland game birds. It was a compromise between the sportsmen desiring to hunt in the morning hours and landowners not wanting to be roused out of bed before sunrise. For many years the question of sunrise or noon shooting was kicked back and forth. The regulation for the particular period was dependent on the political pressure bearing the most weight.

Probably the biggest problem in setting the pheasant season has been the designation of open and closed areas. Since the range has stabilized somewhat the past fifteen years, and North Dakota is on the northern extremities of prime pheasant range, it is taken for granted that many northern areas in the state will not legally have open seasons. The Department attempts to set dates based on the census figures for the current year. But usually the public will not have it so "cut and dried." There is considerable hassling over the open units. *Personal grievances* rate as the most important consideration. One group of sportsmen may be pushing for one regulation and another group in the same area, or one nearby, may be arguing against the proposal. The census data indicating the pheasant population may be important but takes a back seat to the existent public relations problem already created. It is ironical that sportsmen will hire professional game managers and then relegate them to a secondary role by demanding management based on personal feelings.

The regulations listed in this section are self-explanatory in most instances. Maps are shown for each fifth or sixth year throughout the thirty years of open seasons for pheasants.

TABLE 12   PHEASANT REGULATIONS THROUGH THE YEARS

Year	Season Length	Daily Shooting Hours	Total Days of Hunting*	Day of Week Season Opened	Daily Limit	Possession Limit	Open Area
1925-1927	Closed						Short season recommended by the Department for the first time in 1925 and again in 1927
1931	Oct. 17 (noon) - Oct. 18	½ hr. before sunrise to sunset after first day	1½	Saturday	3 cocks	6 cocks	Open only in Richland, Sargent and Dickey Counties
1932	Oct. 15 (noon) - Oct. 19	Sunrise to sunset	4½	Saturday	4 (1 hen)	8 (2 hens)	Open in Ransom, Richland, Sargent, Dickey, and a portion of LaMoure Counties
1933	Unit 1: Oct. 15 (noon) - Oct. 24 Unit 2: Oct. 15 (noon) - Oct. 17	Sunrise to sunset	9½	Sunday	Oct. 15-17, (3 cocks) After Oct. 17 5 (1 hen)	Oct. 20-26 6 cocks After Oct. 17 10 (2 hens)	See map, p. 134.
1934	Unit 1: Oct. 20 (noon) - Nov. 2 Unit 2: Oct. 20 - Oct. 26	Noon to sunset but no Mon. and Tues. hunting. After Oct. 26 sunrise to sunset except no Mon. or Tues. hunting	7½	Saturday	Oct. 20-26, 3 cocks After Oct. 27 5 (2 hens)	Oct. 15-17 6 cocks After Oct. 27 10 (4 hens)	Open in the southern half of state.
1935	Oct. 12 (noon) - Oct. 20	Sunrise to sunset after first day	8½	Saturday	Unit 1: 5 cocks Unit 2: 3 cocks Unit 3: 2 cocks Unit 4: 1 cock	Unit 1: 5 cocks Unit 2: 3 cocks Unit 3: 2 cocks Unit 4: 1 cock	Open statewide

PHEASANT REGULATIONS (Continued)

Year	Season Length	Total Days of Hunting*	Day of Week	Daily Limit	Possession Limit	Open Area
1936	Oct. 10 (noon) - Oct. 20 Unit 1: 2nd season Nov. 3 (noon) - Nov. 12	10½	Saturday	Unit 1: 5 (1 hen) Unit 2: 5 (1 hen) Unit 3: 3 cocks Unit 4: 3 cocks	Unit 1: 5 (1 hen) Unit 2: 5 (1 hen) Unit 3: 3 cocks Unit 4: 3 cocks	Southern half of state open
1937	Oct. 9 - Oct. 18	10	Saturday	Unit 1: 4 cocks Unit 2: 3 cocks	Unit 1: 4 cocks Unit 2: 3 cocks	State open except for eight counties in the southwest corner
1938	Oct. 1 - Oct. 10	10	Saturday	Unit 1: 6 (1 hen) Unit 2: 3 cocks	Unit 1: 6 (1 hen) Unit 2: 3 cocks	See map, page 134.
1939	Oct. 1 - Oct. 15	15	Sunday	Unit 1: 5 (1 hen) Unit 2: 3 cocks	Unit 1: 5 (1 hen) Unit 2: 3 cocks	See map, page 134.
1940	Oct. 1 - Oct. 21	21	Tuesday	Unit 1: 5 (1 hen) Unit 2: 3 (1 hen) Unit 3: 2 (1 hen)	Unit 1: 5 (1 hen) Unit 2: 3 (1 hen) Unit 3: 2 (1 hen)	Open statewide
1941	Sept. 28 - Oct. 26	29	Sunday	Unit 1: 5 (1 hen) Unit 2: 3 (1 hen)	Unit 1: 10 (2 hens) Unit 2: 6 (2 hens)	Open statewide except five northeast counties
1942	Unit 1: Sept. 26 - Nov. 1 Late: Nov. 10 - Nov. 30 Unit 2: Sept. 26 - Nov. 30 Unit 3: Sept. 26 - Nov. 1	57	Saturday	5 (2 hens)	10 (4 hens)	Open statewide except five northeast counties

PHEASANT REGULATIONS (Continued)

Year	Season Length	Daily Shooting Hours	Total Days of Hunting*	Day of Week Season Opened	Daily Limit	Possession Limit	Open Area
1943	Units 1 and 3: Sept. 25-Dec. 3 Unit 2: Sept. 25 - Dec. 31	Sunrise to sunset	98	Saturday	Units 1 and 2: 7 (2 hens) Unit 3: 5 (1 hen)	Units 1 and 2: 14 (4 hens) Unit 3: 5 (2 hens)	Open statewide except for four northeast corner counties
1944	Unit 1: Sept. 20 - Dec. 31 Late: Jan. 27 - Feb. 28 Unit 2: Sept. 20 - Dec. 31 Unit 3: Sept. 20 - Dec. 8	½ hour before sunrise to sunset	136	1st - Wednesday 2nd - Saturday	Units 1 and 2: 8 (2 hens) Unit 3: 5 (1 hen) Unit 1 (late): 5 cocks	Units 1 and 2: 16 (4 hens) Unit 3: 10 (2 hens) Unit 1 (late): 10 cocks	See map, page 135
1945	Unit 1: Sept. 30 - Dec. 31 Units 2, 3, and 4: Sept. 30 - Dec. 8	½ hour before sunrise to sunset	93	Sunday	Units 1 and 2: 7 (2 hens) Unit 3: 5 (1 hen) Unit 4: 3 cocks	Units 1 and 2: 14 (2 hens) Unit 3: 10 (1 hen) Unit 4: 6 cocks	Open statewide except for four northeast corner counties
1946	Unit 1: Oct. 5 - Nov. 30 Unit 2: Oct. 13 - Nov. 18	½ hour before sunrise to sunset	57	Unit 1 – Saturday Unit 2 – Sunday	Unit 1: 4 cocks Unit 2: 3 cocks	Unit 1: 8 cocks Unit 2: 6 cocks	Closed in all or parts of 11 northeast counties
1947	Unit 1: Oct. 17 - Nov. 15 Unit 2: Oct. 17 - Oct. 26	½ hour before sunrise to sunset	30	Friday	Unit 1: 3 cocks Unit 2: 2 cocks	Unit 1: 6 cocks Unit 2: 4 cocks	Open in southern one-third of state
1948	Unit 1: Oct. 8 (noon) - Nov. 20 Unit 2: Oct. 8 (noon) - Nov. 7	½ hour before sunrise to sunset except opening day	43½	Friday	Unit 1: 4 cocks Unit 2: 3 cocks	Unit 1: 8 cocks Unit 2: 6 cocks	Open in southern one-third of state

PHEASANT REGULATIONS (Continued)

Year	Season Length	Daily Shooting Hours	Total Days of Hunting*	Day of Week Season Opened	Daily Limit	Possession Limit	Open Area
1949	Oct. 7 (noon) - Nov. 5	Noon to sunset	16	Friday	3 cocks	6 cocks	Open in southern half of state (approx.)
1950	Oct. 27 (noon) - Nov. 5	Noon to sunset	5	Friday	2 cocks	2 cocks	See map, page 135
1951	Unit 1: Oct. 5 (noon) - Nov. 4 Unit 2: Oct. 24 (noon) - Nov. 4	Noon to sunset except ½ hour before sunrise to 1 hour before sunset on Sat. and Sun.	20½	Unit 1: Friday Unit 2: Wednesday	Unit 1: 3 cocks Unit 2: 2 cocks	Unit 1: 6 cocks Unit 2: 2 cocks	Open west of Missouri River and five southeast counties
1952	Unit 1: Sept. 26 (noon) - Nov. 2 Unit 2: Sept. 26 (noon) - Oct. 12	Noon to sunset except ½ hour before sunrise to sunset on Sat. and Sun.	25	Friday	Unit 1: 4 cocks Unit 2: 3 cocks	Unit 1: 8 cocks Unit 2: 6 cocks	Open west of Missouri River and along Missouri River on east side plus six southeast counties
1953	Closed statewide						
1954	Unit 1: Oct. 30 (noon) - Nov. 7 Late Season: Nov. 20 (noon) - Nov. 28 Units 2 and 3: Oct. 30 (noon) - Nov. 7	Noon to sunset except ½ hour before sunrise to sunset on Sun.	12	Saturday	Units 1 and 2: 3 cocks Unit 3: 2 cocks	Units 1 and 2: 6 cocks Unit 3: 4 cocks	Open west of Missouri River and four southeast counties
1955	Unit 1: Oct. 14 (noon) - Nov. 6 Units 2, 3, and 4: Oct. 21 (noon) - Nov. 6 Unit 5: Oct. 21 (noon) - Nov. 23 Late Season, Units 1 and 3: Nov. 18 (noon) - Nov. 27	Noon to sunset except ½ hour before sunrise to sunset on Sat. and Sun.	23	Friday	Unit 1: 4 cocks Units 2 and 4: 2 cocks Unit 3: 3 cocks Unit 5: 2 cocks Late season, Units 1 and 3: 3 cocks	Unit 1: 8 cocks Units 2 and 4: 4 cocks Unit 3: 6 cocks Unit 5: 2 cocks Late season, Units 1 and 3: 6 cocks	See map, page 136

PHEASANT REGULATIONS (Continued)

Year	Season Length	Daily Shooting Hours	Total Days of Hunting*	Day of Week Season Opened	Daily Limit	Possession Limit	Open Area
1956	Units 1 and 2: Oct. 12 (noon) - Nov. 4 Unit 3: Oct. 12 (noon) - Oct. 21 Unit 1, Late Season, S&W of Missouri River only: Nov. 16 - Nov. 25	9:00 a.m. to sunset except noon opening on opening day	43½	Friday	Unit 1: 3 cocks Unit 2: 2 cocks Unit 3: 2 cocks	Unit 1: 6 cocks Unit 2: 4 cocks Unit 3: 2 cocks	Similar to 1955 but larger area open
1957	Units 1 and 5: Oct. 12 - Nov. 7 Unit 2: Oct. 12 - Oct. 31 Units 3 and 4: Oct. 12 - Oct. 20 Late Season, Units 1, 2, and 5: Nov. 16 - Nov. 24	9:00 a.m. to sunset	36	Saturday	Unit 1: 4 cocks Units 2 and 5: 3 cocks Units 1 and 5: 3 cocks	Unit 1: 8 cocks Units 2 and 5: 6 cocks Units 3 and 4: 2 cocks	Closed generally over eastern half of state except southeast corner counties
1958	Units 1 and 2: Oct. 4 - Nov. 6 Late Season: Nov. 12 - Dec. 7 Unit 3: Oct. 4 - Oct. 12	9:00 a.m. to sunset	60	Saturday	Unit 1: 4 cocks Unit 2: 3 cocks Unit 3: 2 cocks Late season: Unit 1: 4 cocks Unit 2: 3 cocks	Unit 1: 8 cocks Unit 2: 6 cocks Unit 3: 2 cocks Late season: Unit 1: 8 cocks Unit 2: 6 cocks	Closed in all of parts of 22 eastern counties except southeast corner counties
1959	Units 1 and 2: Oct. 17 - Nov. 8 Unit 3: Oct. 17 - Oct. 25	9:00 a.m. to sunset	23	Saturday	Units 1 and 2: 3 cocks Unit 3: 2 cocks	Units 1 and 2: 6 cocks Unit 3: 2 cocks	Closed in all or parts of 21 eastern counties except southeast counties

Examples of Pheasant Hunting Seasons
1944

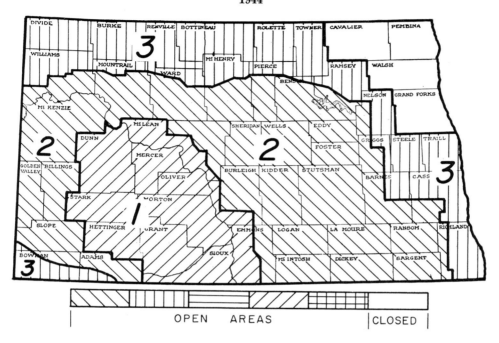

1950

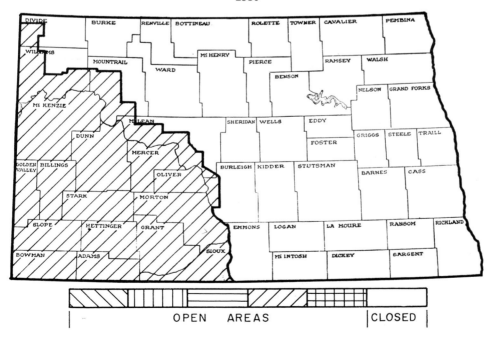

Examples of Pheasant Hunting Seasons

1955

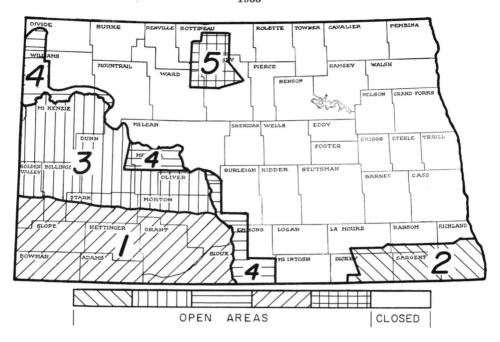

1960

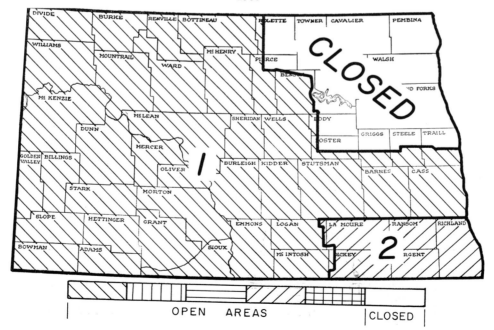

Limiting Factors

Before anyone can pass judgment on the long list of limiting factors affecting a pheasant population the *productivity* of the species should be considered. Leopold defined *productivity* as the "rate at which mature breeding stock produces other mature stock, or mature removable stock."[165] Figures should be used to illustrate *productivity* rather than simply *rate of increase*. For example, an ideal environment for pheasants living in an entirely unmolested area would show a *rate of increase* somewhat similar to this:

End of	Young	+	Adults	=	Total
1st year	10	+	2	=	12
2nd year ($12 \div 2$) $10 =$ 60	+	12	=	72
3rd year ($72 \div 2$) $10 =$ 360	+	72	=	432

The above idealistic situation has been visualized with a 50:50 ratio of cocks and hens with all hens successfully rearing ten young. This, of course, would never happen because there are many things which directly and indirectly kill pheasants. The above set of figures shows strictly *rate of increase* and not *productivity*. *Productivity* in terms of game management includes only the removable stock taken by hunters plus that which has been gained in the breeding stock. Thus, there would be *rate of increase*

[165]Leopold, A., *Game Management*, p. 22.

TED CORNEHH
(63)

but unless harvested by hunters it cannot be regarded as *productivity*. The average person often confuses the two terms.

A more realistic set of figures for pheasants might look something like this:

End of	Young	+	Adults	=	Total	Taken by Hunters	Taken by Other Enemies		Birds Left
1st year		10	+	2	=	12	− 3	− 3	=	6
2nd year (6÷2) 10 =	30	+	6	=	36	− 9	− 9	=	18
3rd year (18÷2) 10 =	90	+	18	=	108	−27	−27	=	54

The hypothetical figures show one-fourth of the population removed by hunting and another one-fourth removed by weather, predators, roadkill, mowing and other enemies. Now, if more pheasants were removed by hunters and less by the other enemies — for example, one-third by hunters and one-sixth by enemies — the *rate of increase* would be the same as the above figures but the *productivity* (crop removed by hunters plus increase in breeding stock) would be considerably larger:

End of	Young	+	Adults	=	Total	Taken by Hunters	Taken by Other Enemies		Birds Left
1st year		10	+	2	=	12	− 4	− 2	=	6
2nd year (6÷2) 10 =	30	+	6	=	36	−12	− 6	=	18
3nd year (18÷2) 10 =	90	+	18	=	108	−36	−18	=	54

So *productivity* is something taken away from "other enemies" of game — a transfer of mortality from natural enemies to the human hunter. It's more than this, however, because environment must be considered before breeding potential can be realized.

Since a game species never attains the idealistic population increase we must consider the factors that limit the increase. First, we have those things that directly kill game and are called *decimating factors*.[166] Secondly, where the loss of a game population is through an indirect method it can be classified under *welfare factors*. The main groupings are:

Decimating Factors	*Welfare Factors*
(1) Hunting	(6) Food supply
(2) Predators	(7) Water supply
(3) Starvation	(8) Coverts (cover)
(4) Disease and parasites	(9) Special factors
(5) Accidents	

There are many subfactors for each group. In other words to say "predators" means not just one but perhaps fifty predators. "Accidents" could mean roadkill, flying into a telephone wire, or a long list of variables. Furthermore, the *decimating factors* often overlap with the *welfare factors*. For example, a direct factor like starvation or drouth is merely an acute stage of a lack of food or water. In some cases the *decimating factors* predation or hunting might actually prove

[166]Ibid., p. 29.

beneficial in removing weak, diseased birds — the result being a healthier population and the potential created for a larger future population. It should be kept in mind that both groups of *decimating* and *welfare factors* are not necessarily detrimental to the population. But when any one, or combination, of these factors limits *productivity* and retards population increases, it is then known as a *limiting factor*. The aim of game management is to spot the *limiting factor* and correct it so that *productivity* is regained. Too often this cannot be accomplished because (1) more than one factor is in effect at the same time and (2) the scope of control for the factor is so broad that it cannot be checked. To go even further, many times when a limiting factor is checked another one reappears. This is often true in predation. When one population such as coyotes is removed, there is usually an increase in foxes or some other predator.

The human race has become more efficient in the manner and methods of changing the landscape and this has not generally benefited wildlife. The chances of the nine major factors (listed as *decimating* or *welfare*) for becoming *limiting* have become more of a reality as time has gone by. A seemingly unimportant minor factor such as roadkill has become more important the past ten years than it was in the 1930's because there are many more cars, roads, and a faster rate of travel involved.

The change in environment the past twenty years is almost beyond comprehension and must be considered a major *limiting factor* as far as pheasants are concerned. In the 1930's a peak of thirteen million acres of idle land was reached. This was nearly half of the 27.5 million acres of cropland in North Dakota and much of it was sweet clover, a crop considered to be almost ideal for pheasants. Through the years this ideal land was gradually utilized for crops or grazing. In 1956 the Soil Bank Program of the Federal Government was inaugurated and land was again being retired, but by 1961 only 2.7 million acres were "rested" — a mere 10 percent as compared with the thirteen million acres of a quarter of a century earlier. This was still a boost for wildlife as was evidenced by a sixty-eight broods per twenty mile roadside count made in July of 1961 — the highest count made in North Dakota in many years. But the drouth struck in the summer of 1961 and over 80 percent of the idle land, which was mainly in hay and sweet clover, was cut. This meant the loss of winter cover and food for wildlife. The Game Department had no alternative but to recommend liberal seasons in the fall of 1961 in order to channel the game into the hunter's bag rather than into winter loss, possible starvation, predation, or some other factor helped out by lack of cover. The well-meaning public, unwilling to accept the losses, is more apt to call for stepped-up predator control programs, winter feeding, and closed hunting seasons in the belief that these will save wildlife. The obstacles are too great, too many *limiting factors* have been created with such a loss of food and habitat, and it would appear inevitable that the pheasant (or other) populations will decline. The uncontrollable factor of a winter blizzard alone, paired with the deficiency of cover, would prove destructive enough in one short two day period to prove that money was wasted on predator control, winter feeding and other well-meaning human activities.

The history of practically all state game departments across the nation has included the problem of how to reduce the *limiting factors* so that particular game populations are productive. Most of the states had to give up early on pheasants because these factors were either too numerous or too severe. Only nineteen of the fifty states have passed the stocking stage thus far. Here in North Dakota, except for a few plush years in the 1940's, there has been a general desire and endeavor to produce more pheasants. Many things have been attempted by both the Department and interested groups of farmers and sportsmen. Part of the programs have been attempted because of public demand and many have been tried because they seemed logical and proper.

As early as the territorial year of 1875 hunting regulations and seasons were set up in an effort to allow certain big game and grouse time in which to raise their young. Consequently, it was believed that hunting was a major *limiting factor* on some species and that controlled hunting would stop the killing during reproduction periods. It should be added that regulation changes did not stop once they were inaugurated. As several sportsmen put it recently, "I need

Car-killed hen and orphaned brood.

a lawyer just to read the proclamation for me!" Hunting has been a *limiting factor* for some species such as the slow reproducers like buffalo or bear, but its degree of importance to pheasants is not nearly so great.

As recently as 1953 there was a closed pheasant season statewide because of public demand. The belief was that it would result in better reproduction in the years to follow. The Department has not favored closed seasons for pheasants because (1) with a "cocks only" season there should be no harm to the breeding stock, (2) hunting pressure has never been heavy enough to endanger the population, (3) hunting has not been the most important limiting factor and to recess it would not alleviate the major factors, and (4) it has been the Department's job to provide recreation which closed seasons would curtail.

The second step, after the introduction of many regulations, was control of predation. As early as the Biennial Report of the North Dakota State Game and Fish Board of Control for 1909-10, a section was devoted to the problem of what should be done to rid the country of sharp-shinned and Cooper's hawks, great horned owls, stray cats and dogs, and crows. Department literature suggested the use of pole traps in ridding the country of pests and providing protection for game. This was many years before the first pheasant season, but predation was even then regarded as a *limiting factor* on other game.

One of the predators to receive early attention was the crow. Before 1910 the Game Department and others had condemned this bird as one of the worst, if not the worst, nest destroyer in the business. Part of the Game and Fish Department 1915-16 Biennial Report reads as follows:

> One of the greatest pests we have in relation to increased propagation of prairie chickens is the crow. I have made a sufficient investigation to personally substantiate the statement. An effort should be made to set apart the last week of May, of each year, for special efforts, not only by the wardens, but by the sportsmen and the public in general, to shoot or kill these birds and to destroy their nests, and thus head off the terrific toll they are taking each season from our game birds. These pirates seem to have increased due to the past few years of protection of birds in general. [Report of Chief Game Warden.][167]

In the 1923-24 Biennial Report, the Game and Fish Department estimated over 100,000 crows were killed during the year 1924 in the state. By the time the pheasant population began to blossom in the early 1930's the crow campaign was in full swing. The 1930 Annual Report for the Department (and several other later years) devoted many words to the crow:

> SWAT THE CROW should continue to be the war-cry of the farmers and sportsmen. The very evident loss suffered by the farmer is apparent, because of depredations in the poultry yard. The destruction of the nests of our song-birds, causes an indirect loss to the farmer; the song-birds depend on weed seeds and insects for their sustenance; the sportsman suffers a loss, because of the breaking up of the early nests of ducks and grouse. Second broods are never as numerous or so large, when the hunting season opens. Not much that is really new can be stated on the crow question; the old bears repeating, for the need is great.[168]

---

[167]*North Dakota State Game and Fish Dept., Fourth Biennial Report, 1915-16*, p. 14.

[168]*North Dakota State Game and Fish Dept., First Annual Report*, 1930, p. 27.

Two counties (Rolette and Towner) had started paying bounties on the bird at this time and by 1932 three counties and many sportsmen's clubs around the state were paying from .10¢ to .15¢ per dead crow. The Department's annual report for 1963 stated:

> Another year has passed since last we called your attention in our annual report, to the predators of our state. We are sorry to say that our arch enemy, the crows, seemed to be calling just a little louder over their depredations as they were congregating, just prior to leaving our bleak and lonely prairies this fall for greener fields, where they might continue to carry on their devastating work amongst our feathered friends.[169]

Trapping crows, 1940's.

The campaign was reaching its peak by this time and the reward posters were out aplenty for old "Blacky." By 1935 the State Junior Warden's League (founded in 1934), sponsored by the North Dakota Game and Fish Department, included in its spring work program, "Destroy ten or more crows, also crow's nests and eggs." The annual report for the Department the same year stated: "Of these natural enemies the crow heads the list! — the greatest winged enemy of game birds in North Dakota."[170] Nearly five full pages with pictures were devoted to the campaign against the bird. One issue of *North Dakota Outdoors* encouraged crow hunting by including one-half dozen choice recipes for the dinner table. The campaign continued until 1949. As recently as 1949, an appropriated bounty (.20¢ per crow) fund was still being operated, but for the past fifteen years there has been little publicity and interest concerning this bird.

Other predators, of course, have had their share of publicity too. The 1930 Annual Report for the Department read: "A dead coyote is no longer a menace to our game birds, especially the Chinese Pheasants which are an easy prey."[171]

Hawks, eagles, raccoons, badgers, weasels, skunks, horned owls, snowy owls, roving cats and dogs, and many others had their share of publicity. The 1934 Annual Report appealed to the sportsmen and public to control wild cats. "Remember that each cat or kitten kept out of fields and woods will mean more birds in North Dakota."[172]

[169]*North Dakota State Game and Fish Dept., Fifth Annual Report*, 1934, p. 21.
[170]*North Dakota State Game and Fish Dept., Sixth Annual Report*, 1935, p. 71.
[171]*North Dakota State Game and Fish Dept., First Annual Report*, 1930, p. 27.
[172]*North Dakota State Game and Fish Dept., Fifth Annual Report*, 1934, p. 25.

Surprisingly enough that modern "culprit" the red fox did not receive much adverse publicity until the early 1940's when it started to become numerous. The fox was on the list of protected furbearers from November 1st to late February or March (depending on the year) from 1927 to 1943. In 1943 it was placed on the state bounty list and since that time has had the biggest share of predator publicity. The pros and cons about foxes written just in North Dakota in recent years would fill a bookcase as full as a set of encyclopedias. There are many people in 1964 who rate the fox the number one *limiting factor* on pheasant populations. In fact there are many who claim the Department is unaware that foxes eat pheasants. The Department is, of course, aware of this just as it is aware that storms, hunters, mowers, automobiles and 40 or 50 other predators kill pheasants. The primary reason the Department has not favored the bounty system for any predator population is that it has failed to slow up the population increase; it has failed in its intended purpose. Secondly, there has been no evidence that any one predator has been anything more than a *decimating factor,* no more *limiting* than the other factors discussed in this section.

Winter mortality has received considerable attention from the Department and public. Blizzards and starvation are generally linked together in the minds of most people, but the former rates by far the more important. Thousands of North Dakotans have witnessed the effects of a northern blizzard with its below zero temperatures and blinding snow on the pheasant population. Many farmers and sportsmen have picked up frozen and dying pheasants during a blizzard and harbored them in poultry houses, livestock buildings and even the family kitchen until the storm subsided. In recent years people have begun to realize the pheasant is not as well-adapted to winter storms as grouse and partridges. Furthermore, many times during the last twenty-five years the Department has examined frozen pheasants and found their crops filled with wheat and other food — solid evidence that starvation played little part in the mortality. However, during long periods of snow cover, starvation has been found to be a factor in pheasant losses. Even in these unusual cases where starvation was a factor, feeding is a prohibitive project because of the cost involved. The Department's annual report for 1936 contained a lengthy answer to this problem. It was estimated that feed priced at .60¢ per bushel would cost over $50,000 before all of the statewide populations of pheasants could be taken care of. This figure was more than the annual revenue of the Department at the time. The statement emphasized that most of the birds picked up after a storm in 1935 had full crops.[173] In 1937 *North Dakota Outdoors* summed up the Department's attitude on winter feeding:

> With an open bird season this fall that was supposed to annihilate all the pheasants in North Dakota surely the Game and Fish Department will not have to spend any money buying bird feed. Thanks fellows, it's an ill wind that blows no good.[174]

It is notable that this concern is still prevalent, and as recently as 1959-60 the Department was contacted by many persons who wanted feed to save pheasants after a local storm.

[173]*North Dakota State Game and Fish Dept., Seventh Annual Report, 1935-36,* p. 17.
[174]*North Dakota Outdoors, Dec., 1937,* p. 20.

Sudden snowstorms occasionally cut back pheasant populations.

In 1950 it was estimated ten million pounds of grain would be necessary to provide for an estimated two and one-half million birds for a ten day period. This would require over $16,000 per day. At this rate the complete annual income from license sales would have been expended in only six days.[175]

In 1937 *North Dakota Outdoors* carried a lengthy article concerning the publicity regarding pheasant starvation. An examination of seventy-seven birds picked up after a winter storm (1936-37) showed that only four birds had died from lack of food. Most of the deaths were apparently birds weakened by gunshot wounds, accidents or disease.[176]

Heavy storms in February and March of 1943 received much publicity. A severe blizzard occurred March 13-17 and pheasant losses ran from 20 to 25 percent in the southeast to 50 percent in the Bottineau area. This storm dropped from 6 to 35 inches of snow across the state and wind velocities were in excess of twenty-five miles per hour throughout the period. The Department was flooded with correspondence regarding the situation. Surveys indicated largest losses were in those areas of sparse winter cover and generally on the smaller flocks. As in the case of previous years most of the birds perished because of suffocation and other factors, not starvation. Despite these spectacular losses North Dakotans experienced their best all-time pheasant hunting within two years after these storms. If the population had been low, however, as in 1959 this increase might not have occurred.

[175]*North Dakota Outdoors, May, 1950,* p. 15.
[176]*North Dakota Outdoors, June, 1937,* p. 6.

Winter mortality was back in the picture by the late 1940's and early 1950's. The following was included in the 1950-51 Annual Report for the Department:

> After the big decline beginning in the early 40's and ending about 1946, pheasants were generally on the increase in nearly all sections of the state until the severe winters of 1949-1950. Mortality from storms was high in most areas, including the southwest after the March blizzard of 1950 — Severe winters and loss of natural habitat have been two important factors in the pheasant picture for the last ten years.[177]

Though there have been local blizzards which have affected pheasants in the past ten years, they have not been as damaging and widespread as those of earlier years. Sometimes starvation must actually be considered because drouth may curtail the food supply to the point that little is available to the birds when only moderate snows do come in the winter.

There is little doubt that the summer drouths of the mid-1930's had some affect on the birds. Many people attribute the big pheasant populations to the drouth but, in reality, the boom did not take place until the early 1940's when more moisture was found everyplace. *North Dakota Outdoors* again commented:

> Perhaps nothing else could have done as much to awaken the people to the needs of wildlife, more, or as much, as has the drouth. When crop conditions are good and prosperity is flourishing, human nature seems to take wildlife for granted, scarcely giving it a thought of appreciation, to say nothing about conserving it, and far less building or propagating.
>
> Now, in this desolate picture which we have in the state today, with dust storms sweeping our prairies, surface water vanished, wells gone dry and farmers' fields and meadows turned brown, people are uniting in one thought to take such action, as will save the state from further destruction. No more is there indifference of minds about the need of conserving water. . . .
>
> Out of it all will come a greater North Dakota — out of it will come an increase in all forms of wildlife — out of it all will come a greater understanding by the people of the needs of wildlife, a heightened reward for its presence among us, and a stronger will in all of us to unite in its propagation and protection.[178]

A few years after this statement the pheasant population reached its largest numbers, but then farmers swung gradually back to the intensive agriculture that preceded the drouth. Pheasants have declined in many areas. The utilization of the land by mankind has brought to light other decimating factors which are more important than those of earlier years. Many of these factors have been publicized from time to time and in some instances have been regarded as important to the pheasant's welfare. Recently, loss of habitat has received the greatest amount of publicity by the Department and other groups. Many farmers have taken advantage of the tree planting program offered by the Department since 1951 and the Department has experimented with various cover types on state-owned game management areas.

As early as 1937 *North Dakota Outdoors* was stressing a "tread easy" attitude in the spreading of poisons for grasshoppers because of the possible harmful effects on pheasants.[179] Spraying with powerful chemicals has now become more of a problem. Experiments carried on at the Spiritwood Game Field

---

[177]*North Dakota State Game and Fish Dept., Annual Report, 1950-51*, p. 46.
[178]*North Dakota Outdoors*, Aug., 1936, p. 2.
[179]*North Dakota Outdoors*, May, 1937, p. 4.

Station in the summer of 1950 with aldrin, chlordane, DDT, and toxaphene insecticides showed that the killing of insects indirectly affected young ducks and coots because it reduced the food supply, and directly affected them when the dead insects were eaten. Young pheasants were fed poisoned grasshoppers in the laboratory and considerable mortality was observed.

The problem of burning roadside ditches, thickets, slough bottoms and other cover has long been discussed and publicized. In 1949 *North Dakota Outdoors* devoted considerable space to the harmful effects of burning on wildlife, especially in regard to nest destruction, loss of food, and loss of escape and protective cover.[180]

Many of our long-term residents will testify that pheasants began their biggest decline when strawstacks disappeared from the prairie scene. The stacks were an excellent source of food and cover in the winter and many have felt that both pheasants and grouse benefited from their presence.

Time and space does not permit a listing of all the *decimating* and *welfare* factors. Many conscientious farmers have honestly and apologetically reported to the Department the numbers of birds and nests destroyed while mowing fields and roadsides. Motorists have blamed themselves for killing pheasants with their cars. Hunters have apologized for killing "too many" birds simply because the opportunity presented itself in some bygone year. Still other unusual situations have received publicity:

> A drouth condition affecting young birds in the Red River Valley in areas where there is considerable gumbo is the cracking of the soil, which traps the young birds as they travel through the fields seeking food. Some of the crevices opened in the soil were several feet deep, and spell sure death to the little birds falling into them. To anyone not walking into the fields this might be news, but we venture to say that several thousand birds are swallowed by the earth in this manner every year when there is a shortage of moisture.[181]

No doubt pheasant chicks could be lost in the described manner, and it is conceivable that many sportsmen, farmers, and small boys were inclined to peer down into the crevices in the ground for these unfortunates in the years that followed this publicity. Crevices have been just one of many "special factors" considered when the pheasant population ups and downs are discussed.

[18] *North Dakota Outdoors, Jan., 1949*, p. 4.
[181] *North Dakota Outdoors, Aug., 1936*, p. 3.

Research and Management

In the preceding section many possible limiting factors were discussed chronologically as the public took interest in them. Since these factors received publicity and pheasant populations declined after the 1940's, the people most interested in hunting demanded that something be done to save the bird. This desire to "save" the species had originated for native wildlife before the turn of the century in the more heavily populated areas of the United States. As mentioned previously, the attempts occurred with (1) restrictions on hunting, (2) a bounty system to encourage the removal of predators, (3) the establishment of refuges, (4) stocking or restocking of game species, and (5) an attempt to control the environment.

In recent years game departments across the nation have been concerned with the last of these five ideas — environmental control. They have concentrated on this because little success had been achieved in restoring game populations with the first four ideas. On the other hand, it is distressing that a large segment of the public is still dwelling on the first four as cure-alls. Accumulative research by game departments has shown that hunting restrictions have not been the answer for the pinnated grouse, sage grouse, and other species. Seasons have been closed on these

for many years in North Dakota and their numbers have not increased. A bounty system dating back to 1900 has neither increased the game nor decreased the predation to any noticeable extent. There have been many refuges and rest areas in the state but game populations have not steadily increased and overflowed to surrounding areas as hoped. Stocking was responsible for the pheasant's success in the Dakotas in the 1920's, but restocking attempts have resulted in more failures than successes in recent years. Finally, there have been many failures experienced with the attempts to control the environment, but this idea still appears to have the greatest chance of maintaining and increasing wildlife populations. Most persons have recognized the fundamental fact that wildlife must have a place to feed, live, and reproduce. Game managers across the nation are concentrating their efforts along this line at the present time.

The major step in expanding game management and research work in the United States came when the Pittman-Robertson Act was signed into federal law by President Franklin Roosevelt on September 2, 1937. The act set aside a special fund from money collected on an 11 percent excise tax on the sale of sporting arms and ammunition. The fund is allocated to the states for the development of wildlife restoration projects with the U. S. Government providing 75 percent of the total cost and the individual state furnishing the remaining 25 percent. From this source of financial aid many states initiated their first work on research and management. Actually, the act went further than this because it was permissible to use the money in four ways: (1) land acquisition, (2) development or restoration, (3) investigational or survey work, and (4) coordination projects. The first money was made available on July 1, 1938, on the federal level, and North Dakota legislators approved the plan and legalized it in North Dakota in March of 1939. Some of the first money on research in the state was received in February of 1940 and some of the first spent on land acquisition was received in March of the same year.

The Game Department is often criticized for not knowing more about the factors that limit pheasant populations. The public should realize that the Department is handicapped by being in a position where it cannot remedy a situation even though the problem is understood. Control of the weather or man's activities is out of the game manager's hands. Secondly, the scope of some problems is so great that efforts to alleviate them are next to impossible. A good example is the case of pheasants in the Red River Valley, an area low in most wildlife species. An effort to restore the necessary habitat for pheasants would be expensive and unacceptable to the landowners in this fertile agricultural area. Finally, there is much yet to be learned about the physical and social requirements of many wildlife species before progressive steps can be made under current land use practices. Present research and management is aimed at managing wildlife populations on lands under "multiple use," a term almost as ugly as the word "progress" to the professional wildlifer at the present time. It is up to wise management and continued research to prove that wildlife can survive on lands used intensively for other purposes. Whether this can ever be accomplished remains to be seen.

Obviously, the states with large game departments and income will perform the best wildlife research. Some states (California and Michigan) often employ

Biologists Adams, Schroeder, and Oldenburg spotlight pheasants for banding
at Oakes, fall of 1961.

as many as one hundred biologists, some of whom can do full-time work on one game species. They are performing research in the true sense of the word. Other states, such as North Dakota, may have less than twenty biologists who are occupied with many projects relative to several game species. Under this setup more game management work is conducted than research. Research suffers from a lack of manpower and finances and, in the long run, little new is learned about the game birds and animals.

Since 1940 there have been several management projects conducted on the pheasant in North Dakota. Most of them are carried on to "keep a finger" on populations and are often censuses. And, although there have been some good research projects completed since 1940, most of the work is management. Sometimes management and research projects are combined as illustrated by the pheasant roadside counts inaugurated in 1940. This was research when started because it was not tested and proven accurate. But after twenty years of modification it has developed into a game survey and must be classed as management.

Other early research in North Dakota originated in 1940 with a series of nesting studies. Nesting success, predation data, and other pertinent information was discovered.

Although the list of management and research projects for the pheasant may change from year to year in North Dakota, the following list shows the Pittman-Robertson jobs which are currently conducted by the Game Department each year. Since space is limited each project cannot be fully explained in this book, but readers who are interested in learning more about North Dakota pheasants from information in the technical P-R reports may write the Department and request individual reports. The same holds true for all other game birds written up in this book:

ANNUAL PHEASANT P-R REPORTS

Roadside Counts (crowing counts)   Roadside Brood Counts
Hunter Questionnaires   Incidence of Lead Shot
Winter Sex Ratios   Disease and Parasites
Aerial Township Counts   Nesting Studies
Harvest Studies   Trapping and Marking Techniques
Pheasant Age Ratios   Insecticide and Herbicide Studies
Various Game Management Study Areas   Land Use Studies
Rural Mail Carriers Reports

The results of four major P-R pheasant projects are shown in the following tables.

TABLE 13

DEPARTMENT PHEASANT BROOD COUNTS OVER THREE MAJOR DISTRICTS, 1956-63
Number of Broods per One Hundred Miles Driving
(One route per district)

Dist.	General Area	1956	1957	1958	1959	1960	1961	1962	1963
9	SW corner	21	48	43	28	55	40	25	48
10	S. Central	20	35	28	3	23	8	5	18
12	SE corner	3	30	48	55	15	18	60	113

TABLE 14   DEPARTMENT PHEASANT CROWING COUNTS OVER 11 MAJOR DISTRICTS, 1949-63

Number of Calls Per Two Minute Stop (one route per district)

Dist.	General Area	1949	1950	1951	1952	1953	1954	1955	1956	1957	1958	1959	1960	1961	1962	1963
1	NW corner	----	3.4	4.3	1.4	1.8	3.1	4.2	5.4	2.5	----	0.9	1.6	3.7	2.3	1.0
2	N. central	----	4.6	1.9	21.8	14.0	10.8	----	9.9	3.4	4.3	2.5	2.0	2.9	2.2	2.5
3	N. central	1.5	1.6	3.8	----	----	----	0.3	0.0	----	----	----	----	----	0.7	1.7
5	W. central	2.3	2.0	2.8	2.7	4.7	5.3	16.4	6.3	----	----	3.2	1.0	1.7	0.8	0.7
6	Central	13.6	7.6	12.5	18.5	13.6	25.0	23.7	19.5	20.2	25.3	6.3	4.8	2.5	1.9	1.4
7	Central	2.6	----	0.7	----	0.9	----	----	5.8	3.5	3.3	2.7	1.6	1.6	0.9	0.7
8	E. central	----	1.2	0.4	----	1.8	----	2.4	2.2	1.8	----	----	7.6	1.3	1.1	----
9	SW corner	9.3	7.4	7.7	1.2	3.4	----	5.4	6.7	4.8	12.0	16.0	8.0	10.9	5.1	10.9
10	S. central	24.1	7.7	24.5	41.0	15.0	29.5	68.5	42.9	25.7	21.2	17.7	4.5	8.4	2.1	8.2
11	S. central	21.2	9.2	0.5	7.7	7.9	----	11.1	13.8	----	12.6	9.8	4.6	4.3	2.0	----
12	SE corner	4.3	0.8	0.3	0.3	1.2	1.8	2.6	1.2	----	6.2	20.1	15.1	14.6	9.0	18.4

Table 15

PHEASANT AGE RATIOS TAKEN FROM CHECKING STATION COLLECTIONS DURING THE HUNTING SEASONS, 1955-63

Year	Southwestern North Dakota		Southeastern North Dakota	
	No. Birds	Immatures/Ad. Hen	No. Birds	Immatures/Ad. Hen
1955	5178	4.54	1306	2.93
1956	7143	3.17	2581	3.99
1957	7348	7.74	1260	5.09
1958	8005	3.46	1970	4.26
1959	1966	2.09	1083	2.38
1960	1125	6.09	1338	6.25
1961	888	3.08	1862	6.17
1962	497	6.94	2046	4.56
1963	802	8.46	2470	4.84

Table 16

NUMBERS OF PHEASANTS REPORTED BY RURAL CARRIERS IN NORTH DAKOTA, 1946-63

Year	Max. No. of Carriers Reporting	April Count Pheas./Mi.	July Count Pheas./Mi.	September Count Pheas./Mi.
1946	465	_____	.187	.116
1947	335	.152	.127	.141
1948	329	.131	.214	.131
1949	368	.115	.150	.098
1950	334	.089	.062	.075
1951	375	.102	.096	.094
1952	353	.108	.076	.054
1953	380	.052	.048	.043
1954	375	.083	.109	.097
1955	392	.082	.084	.086
1956	388	.067	.047	.073
1957	355	.085	.060	.085
1958	338	.106	.089	.086
1959	328	.109	.054	.032
1960	348	.038	.030	.037
1961	313	.043	.053	.046
1962	345	.039	.036	.028
1963	326	.053		
10 year avg.		.070	.066	.064

6

Hungarian Partridge

Scientific name: *Perdix perdix perdix*

Size:

Length, 12-13 inches. Wingspan, 15-17 inches. Weight, 14-18 oz. Average weight of fifty-one North Dakota birds, including forty immatures, in 1963 was 13.0 oz. The largest bird weighed 17.3 oz.

Coloration:

A reddish-brown bird with a gray breast. Difficult to determine sex except when held in hand or during breeding season when cocks have red around eyes and dark horseshoe marking on breast. Old hens sometimes have the horseshoe. The bright rusty-red tail is conspicuous in the air.

Flight:

Strong, rapid, short distance flyer. The explosive takeoff is accompanied by a strident shriek or whistle. Flight is characterized by quick turns and wing beats. The covey generally takes off all at once.

Flock habits:

The adult cock and hen remain together throughout the reproductive period. The family group remains together until the following spring and may be joined by other birds who have been unsuccessful in mating. Sometimes more than one covey will band together.

History

The second exotic game bird to be successfully introduced to the farmlands and prairies of North Dakota was the Hungarian partridge, or just plain "Hun". The bird goes under the more proper names of European partridge, Grey partridge, or Common partridge in other parts of the world. It holds the distinction of being one of the most widespread game bird species in the world, being found throughout Europe, Asia, the British Isles, and the Scandinavian countries. It has been introduced successfully into many other countries around the globe.

First introduction of the Hun in North America came about the same time as the first pheasant stocking. Richard Bache, a son-in-law of Benjamin Franklin, transplanted Huns to his estate near Beverly, New Jersey, about 1790. But, as with the pheasant, these initial stockings were unsuccessful and over a century passed before Huns became established anywhere on this continent. Well-publicized releases were made in California in 1877, Washington in 1897 and Oregon in 1900. Over 150,000 partridges were released in the United States up until 1940. Before the campaign was over no less than twenty-nine states and several Canadian provinces had par-

A Covey of Partridges in Europe, 1870's.

ticipated. To this can be added the probability of many private stockings in the remaining twenty-one states.

Success of stocking was even more limited with Huns than it was with pheasants in the United States. As of 1964 only nineteen states had wild Huns within their borders and at least half of them had only small, local isolated colonies.

North Dakota was most fortunate in having partridge populations established in every county of the state by the early 1940's. However, the highest densities of partridges in North America are found in some of the Canadian provinces.

By far the most successful stocking of Huns in North America took place near Calgary, Alberta, in 1908-09. There were 180 pairs in the original release but within five years the birds had multiplied and spread over southern Alberta and into Saskatchewan at a rate of twenty-eight miles per year. The first Alberta season was in 1913 with a daily bag limit of five birds and twenty-five for the season. By 1942 Alberta hunters were permitted a bag of twenty Huns per day and 250 for the season. Roadside counts in 1950 showed as many as twenty-five coveys in two miles of driving by Department personnel in the province. It is an accepted fact that Alberta has been the heart of the Hun range just as South Dakota has been the center of the pheasant range in North America.

Saskatchewan benefited by Alberta's program and never found it necessary to stock partridges. Wild birds moved into the province voluntarily. The first open season in Saskatchewan was held in 1927.

Manitoba stocked Huns in 1925 but, like Saskatchewan, the partridge's success in Manitoba was attributed to the famous Alberta releases. The first open season on the Hun in Manitoba was in 1931.

Minnesota introduced Huns as early as 1926 (some private stockings had been made in the early 1920's). The first season was held in 1939.

Private parties first released partridges in South Dakota in 1923, but the first Department stockings came in 1924-25 when eighty-three pairs were liberated in Brown and Roberts Counties. The first open season was in the two extreme northeastern counties (Roberts and Marshall) in 1937.

Montana purchased six hundred partridges direct from Europe in 1921 and from 1921-29 liberated over 6,600 birds. The first open season in Montana took place in 1929 and encompassed eight counties.

First reports of wild Huns being observed in North Dakota came from residents of the northwestern counties in 1923. It is believed that these birds originated from the Alberta stockings and spread to North Dakota by way of Saskatchewan or Montana. First mention of Hungarian partridges in North Dakota game laws appeared in March, 1909, when it was emphasized that no one could have Hungarian partridges in possession at any time. It has been assumed that there were no Huns in the state in 1909, but state officials were aware of the bird's success in Canada and possibly wanted to protect it should it make an appearance in this state.

There is mention of fifty pairs of Hungarian partridges being stocked in North Dakota in 1915 but details of who stocked them and where they were released are lacking. It must be assumed that these were released by private parties since Department records carry no detailed reports on this.

Approximately one hundred pairs of Huns were purchased by the North Dakota Game Department directly from Czechoslovakia in 1923. The birds cost $9.00 per pair and were housed at the old Grafton Game Farm. First releases from these were made in 1924.

During the years 1924-34 more than 7,500 Huns were introduced into various sections of North Dakota. Quite a number of birds were purchased overseas from an outlet in New York City and costs ran as high as $14.85 per pair in 1930. These releases were written up in great detail by the Department in the First Annual Report of 1930 and a complete listing of clubs receiving birds was included. Various sportsmen clubs and Izaak Walton groups received shipments of 50 to 85 Huns each. Additional Huns were obtained from Saskatchewan in 1936 in exchange for 1,100 pheasants.

Stocking success of the Hun was similar to that of the pheasant. The Department will probably never know which of the many liberations proved of most value. Perhaps the immigrations from the north were the most important. Then again, some local stockings undoubtedly speeded up the rapid spread of the birds across North Dakota. One thing is certain, they did succeed and as early as 1926 the Department was thinking about opening the season on this newcomer. The Ninth Biennial Report of the Game Department for 1925-26 read as follows:

> This department has received favorable reports from those sections in which Hungarian partridges were liberated, showing that these birds are rapidly increasing in number. They appear to be highly favored by the sportsmen, and no doubt before long the gunners will have a chance to try their luck in shooting at them.[182]

Obviously, the Hungarian partridge had become established in the state; this statement was made only three years after the first partridge releases.

---

[182]*North Dakota State Game and Fish Dept., Ninth Biennial Report, 1925-26, p. 15.*

TED CORNELL

Role

The role of the Hungarian partridge in North Dakota's history has been a complacent one. Everyone likes the partridge so it has never been the object of criticism that the pheasant has from time to time. The species has only slightly objectionable habits where economic interests are concerned so the public has always favored it. Evidently, there were not two sides to the issue when a Hun stocking program was initiated. Public sentiment was comparable to today when there is a chance a new species might succeed — "it will be something new and different to hunt and have around!" North Dakota was fortunate with Huns just as it had been with pheasants a few short years before.

Although the partridge reached high state populations in the 1940's and local highs at other times, farmers never complained about crop damage as they did with pheasants. Because of their size and habits Huns can become abundant without being conspicuous and therefore are not considered a nuisance. The annual reports of the Game Department have never carried derogatory remarks or debates

about Huns.   The birds hang around farm buildings, feedlots, and shelterbelts in compact little coveys of 6 to 15 and feed on waste grains and weed seeds.   These habits put them on friendly terms with the farmer.   Mr. Leslie W. Johnson of Cooperstown wrote the Department in May of 1946 and described this relationship, "The Hun is a nice bird to have around.   They don't gather in huge flocks like the pheasants and, to the best of my knowledge, do very little damage to the grain fields.   I have yet to hear of any farmer complain of them."

One of the chief reasons Huns have never been criticized is probably that they seldom ever build up in the large numbers which commonly occur in Europe. Densities as high as one bird per acre are common in Czechoslovakia and other European countries but one bird per six to eight acres is about the limit in the United States.   During the 1940's, when pheasants and Huns were both abundant, farmer complaints always concerned the pheasants which sometimes congregated into flocks of 200 to 300 and more. Occasionally, Huns are sighted in flocks of fifty birds but are usually welcomed by everyone. Here it should be pointed out that the pheasant is blessed with a pugnacious nature which does not add to his popularity. This "mean streak" is sometimes exhibited on the grouse and Huns, and even on other pheasants, in nest destroying, chasing or fighting. People are quick to condemn him for it.

Hunters will readily admit that Huns are more difficult to hunt than grouse and pheasants.   The bird is hard to find, is an elusive target, and is difficult to "flock shoot."   The hunter quickly realizes the advantage of using a good dog. Sometimes the birds hold so well there is trouble flushing them even when the covey has been "marked down."   Cripples, too, are frequently lost when a good dog is not employed.

It has been stated many times in North Dakota, and other states and provinces, that partridges are taken "incidentally to other game."   It is a secondary or "filler" species for most hunters.   Even in Alberta Huns generally take a backseat to ruffed grouse or pheasants on the hunter's popularity list despite the fact they are more abundant than the other two species.   In North Dakota the Hun is rated behind pheasants and grouse as an upland gunner's choice and must be ranked below waterfowl in the overall popularity.   The bird is a tough target; difficult to find, and its size does not fulfill the requirements for the hunter who desires meat on the table.   The quality of the meat is tops, but pheasants and grouse again rate priority over the smaller Huns.   In Europe the partridge is the best known, most popular game bird, and the favorite of sportsmen.   Oven ten million partridges are killed each year there.[183]

The Hun in North Dakota has become slightly more popular in recent years because of its widespread distribution.   It also becomes more popular when other species are low in numbers.   Apparently at this time the future of the partridge is as bright as that of any upland game bird.   Perhaps the species will eventually show a greater role of importance than either grouse or waterfowl in this state.

[183]Westerskov, K., *The Partridge as a Game Bird*, p. 1.

Harvest

It is generally agreed that the Hungarian partridge has been the most underharvested of the three major upland game bird species in this state. Several reasons have been mentioned in the preceding section but, more specifically, the Hun is underharvested because: (1) It is hunted incidentally to other game; the percentage of hunters who concentrate on partridge hunting is small compared to the numbers that hunt pheasants or ducks. There is a limited number of hunters who live in the Red River Valley and other areas who list the partridge as their favorite species, but in many cases they have learned to accept it because their area has few ducks, pheasants, and grouse. (2) The Hun is not large enough to attract many North Dakota hunters. (3) Huns are difficult to hunt or shoot. (4) The species seldom reaches the densities necessary to attract full-time partridge hunters. (5) Partridges are usually present around shelterbelts in close proximity to farm buildings; most people realize the shooting is restricted on this part of the average farm and hesitate to ask permission to hunt.

Since the first pheasant season opened in 1931, hunters were already enjoying that spectacular bird before the Hun was well-dispersed across the state.

Mixed Bag with Huns on the Model A Hood. Pleasant Lake, 1939.

The southern half of North Dakota was open to pheasant hunting in 1934 and by 1935 the entire state was open. It was apparent from the beginning that the Hun would probably not be the favorite of hunters. The 1932 Third Annual Report of the Department, mentioned this partridge:

> The introduction of the Hungarian partridge is of more recent note, about thirty-five hundred of them having been brought into the state since 1926. In some respects they have proved themselves more hardy than the pheasant, as well as more inclined to increase and spread themselves after being released. As they are imported from Europe the first cost of distribution is many times that of the pheasant and it has not been possible to distribute in numbers comparable with those in which the latter species of bird has been handled.[184]

The first open season for Huns was held in 1934 and, as for the first pheasant season, few records were kept to indicate the harvest, hunter success, and other details. The first season took place in the opposite corner of the state from the first pheasant season. Ten counties were opened in the northwestern section of the state in 1934 (see map, page 168) and by 1935 all but nine southeastern counties were open to partridge hunting, indicating that the birds had spread rapidly in a relatively short time. Despite the fact that 1934 was a drought year, a condition not considered beneficial to game bird reproduction, the first open season was held and the 1934 Annual Report of the Department stated:

> For the first time in the history of our state, we had an open season on the Hungarian partridge. Although the season was of but two days' duration, many of our sportsmen enjoyed the speed of these birds, as well as their first Hungarian partridge "feed." These birds are very prolific, and bid fair to become the "Ace" of propagated birds in North Dakota.[185]

To better appreciate the harvest of partridges we should digress from the North Dakota harvest for a brief period and scan the earlier history. Often heard today are market hunting stories of buffalo, deer, waterfowl, and prairie chickens in North Dakota during the early settlement period. This was quite common in the 1880's and 1890's, but was ended before the pheasant and Hun became established. Laws were quickly introduced which practically eliminated this commercialism of wild game. European histories are loaded with references to the poaching and selling of partridges. The earliest method was the use of nets, viz. "yarn hand nets," and many other types that could be used for daytime or night-time trapping. The use of falcons and hawks was also common practice in the 1700's, and Frederick William I of Bavaria supposedly took 1,500 partridges during one autumn season hunting with this method. The comprehensive Czech account, *Koroptev*, stated, "For a long time partridges were only trapped in nets or hunted with the aid of falcons or hawks, rather than shot.[186]

When the gun began to be employed in hunting, wealthy sportsmen staged some spectacular partridge shooting on the densely populated areas of Bohemia and Moravia. Beaters were used to flush birds and, on one Bohemian hunt in 1755, twenty-three shooters took 19,543 partridges in eighteen days. Another

[184]*North Dakota State Game and Fish Dept., Third Annual Report, 1932*, p. 13.

[185]*North Dakota State Game and Fish Dept., Fifth Annual Report, 1934*, p. 25.

[186]Kokes, O. and Knobloch, E., *Koroptev, The Partridge, its Life History, Propagation and Hunting*, p. 7.

Jack Samuelson, A. T. Klett, and Smitty with a Limit for Four, Bottineau County, October, 1959.

eighteen day shoot staged by Emperor Francis I and his court at Opocno in 1758 produced a kill of 63,250 game birds and animals of which 29,545 were partridges. More than 116,000 shots were fired.[187]

American millionaire, James Gordon Bennett, owner of the New York Daily Herald, hunted at Zelena Hora (Bohemia) in 1904 under terms for a guaranteed bag of ten thousand partridges.[188]

Partridge meat is considered such a delicacy that it has been sold for several centuries on the market. As early as 1509, the birds sold for the equivalent of .10¢ each in Czechoslovakia and in 1619 for .50¢ each.[189]

Largest harvests of Huns in North America have probably taken place in Alberta, North Dakota, and Washington. The estimate in Alberta in 1950 was 105,000 Huns. The harvest estimate for Washington in 1950 was 82,000. However, records are scanty for most provinces and states that have the species and the actual harvests are unknown. An example of this was Minnesota. Hunters reporting on the annual hunter questionnaire confused Hungarian partridge with ruffed grouse and the estimated Hun harvests of over fifty thousand in 1955 and 1956 were probably nearer twenty thousand.

[187]Ibid., p. 9.
[188]Ibid., p. 10.
[189]Ibid., p. 8.

Recent history of Hun hunting in North Dakota has not been nearly so spectacular as the early European accounts. Following the first season in 1934 the population multiplied rapidly and actually "peaked out" before the pheasant as far as harvest was concerned. By 1939 the partridge harvest had surpassed the grouse and the trend continued through 1944. Biggest harvests occurred in 1941 and 1942 while the biggest pheasant harvests did not arrive until 1944 and 1945. Table 17 indicates hunters were taking over seven Huns apiece in the period 1940-42.

Further evidence that the partridge was not as important to the hunter as grouse or pheasants was provided by the closed seasons during the five year period 1945-49. The Hun population began declining by 1943 and there was little consternation on the part of the public demanding open seasons. This has not been the case with grouse, pheasants, or waterfowl. Occasionally, there are short seasons with reduced bag limits, but seldom have there been completely closed seasons for these latter species.

Population decline is evidenced by Department roadside counts which showed a statewide average of 1.68 Huns-per-mile in 1941 as compared with .15 in 1946. The 1946 Annual Roadside Census Report stated:

> It will be noted that this bird which reached its high point in the state in 1941, has suffered a continual drop each year for six years. In fact our indices show that we now have about 12 percent as many birds in the state today as in 1941.[190]

Low populations persisted until the early 1950's. Though open seasons were held from 1950 through 1952 only mediocre harvests were realized. The season was closed again in 1953. It was not until 1955 that the populations began a comeback which resulted in good hunting in the late 1950's and early 1960's in most sections of the state. Roadside counts in 1958 showed .85 to 1.00 Huns-per-mile and indicated above average populations.

---

[190]*North Dakota State Game and Fish Dept., P-R Report No. 242, Feb., 1946,* p. 7.

TABLE 17   HUNGARIAN PARTRIDGE HARVESTS

Year	Huns per Hunter during the Season	Estimated Hun Harvest	Year	Huns per Hunter during the Season	Estimated Hun Harvest
1934	No information		1949	Closed	
1935	2.6	61,000	1950		4,000
1936	No information		1951	0.7	48,000
1937	No information		1952	0.8	53,000
1938	2.8	70,000	1953	Closed	
1939	4.4	160,000	1954	0.5	30,000
1940	7.1	280,000	1955	0.9	64,000
1941	7.7	390,000	1956	1.8	126,000
1942	7.2	370,000	1957	1.2	86,000
1943	4.9	200,000	1958	2.0	152,000
1944	2.9	150,000	1959	1.4	76,000
1945	Closed		1960	2.4	139,000
1946	Closed		1961	2.0	108,000
1947	Closed		1962	2.4	118,000
1948	Closed				

Seasons and Regulations

There are few dyed-in-the-wool partridge hunters and the setting of seasons for Huns has become more routine than for grouse or pheasants. The partridge is the "bonus" or "extra" parcel of the hunt. Realizing this fact, sportsmen and farmers are less inclined to quibble over the welfare of the partridge except when the population is drastically low — a condition sometimes difficult to ascertain because of the bird's habits. Consequently, the four main considerations discussed in the pheasant chapter prevail to a lesser degree when the Hun seasons are set. If these considerations are broached they are usually applied to other species before Huns. Literally speaking, the Hun is often "carried along" with the grouse or pheasants.

As evidence of the lackadaisical interest in Huns, the five year period 1945-49 was entirely closed to partridge hunting. The September 1945 issue of *North Dakota Outdoors* stated:

> Hungarian partridges showed a pleasing and readily noted increase over last year. In fact, this is the second consecutive year our Huns have enjoyed a comeback. The first [1944] was slight. This year it was greater.[191]

Despite the small increases mentioned, the population was considered low and it was five years before the season was reopened.

Following the first season in 1934, it was common practice to open Hun and pheasant seasons at the same time. Not until 1950

---

[191]*North Dakota Outdoors, Sept., 1945, p. 8.*

did the Hun season open ahead of the pheasant, and since 1956 this procedure has been followed. If it were not for the sharptail grouse it is questionable whether the Hun season would ever have been opened before the pheasant. But with sufficient numbers of sportsmen favoring an early grouse season, and with the realization that the best grouse hunting is in September, the seasons of these two birds have been opened at the same time in recent years. There has been some political pressure from farmers and hunters, particularly in the eastern sections of the state, requesting that Huns be opened with the pheasants. These requests have come from areas that have had closed grouse seasons for twenty years and thereby emphasize that the primary interest is in pheasants and not Huns. Biologically speaking, the early Hun seasons are sound recommendations because, like grouse, the Huns are ready for an early harvest and the sportsman benefits by receiving more hunting days for his license money. Seldom does the advocate of the simultaneous opening show any regard for the Hun in this argument — his main concern is for the other major species.

A controversy that occasionally arises when the Hun and grouse seasons are proposed concerns the harvest of both male and female birds. The public has come to realize that the harvest of cocks exerts little influence on pheasant reproduction. But what happens to grouse and Hun populations when both cocks and hens are killed? Here we are killing the bird that lays the "Golden egg." This point is often brought up and used as a reason for shortening or closing the season to protect the breeding stock. Certainly the reasoning may have some merit. But other factors must also be considered. Since the pheasant cannot withstand a severe winter as well as grouse or Huns, the weather may have far more bearing on the populations than the question of whether to harvest one or both sexes. Secondly, the Hun is a monogamous species on which the harvest, if made at all, should probably be made on both cocks and hens. Saving 50 percent more hens probably adds little or nothing to the reproduction. This is not true for pheasants or grouse because both species are polygamous and one cock may serve many hens.

It has become customary the past few years to add extra hunting days through the use of split seasons — a second coming after the closing of the deer season in November. It permits the ardent hunter to get into the field during colder weather, sometimes with snow, and experience has shown this second season effects no damage to the populations.

Bag limits of five birds daily and ten in possession in recent years have been accepted as a happy medium by the average hunter. Seldom does he get the chance to take five Huns in one day, but when the opportunity presents itself this number gives him a good bag without annihilating the average covey. If a party of hunters is engaged in the kill it becomes a different situation. Even then, however, most modern hunters will say, "I just cannot hit partridges" or "We all shot at the same bird." These suggest that Huns are not being overharvested.

Many of the questions that come to mind when one looks at the Hun regulations were discussed in the pheasant chapter and need not be repeated here. These include such topics as daily shooting hours, opening day of the week, what areas to open, and many others.

TABLE 18

HUNGARIAN PARTRIDGE REGULATIONS

Year	Season Length	Daily Shooting Hours	Total Days of Hunting*	Day of Week Season Opened	Daily Limit	Possession Limit	Open Area
1934	Oct. 6 (noon) - Oct. 7	Sunrise to sunset after first day	1½	Saturday	3	6	Ten northwest counties in the state. See map, page 168
1935	Oct. 12 (noon) - Oct. 20	Sunrise to sunset after first day	8½	Saturday	Unit 1: 1 Unit 2: 3 Unit 3: 2	Unit 1: 1 Unit 2: 3 Unit 3: 2	All except ten southeast counties
1936	Oct. 10 - Oct. 11	Noon to sunset both days	1	Saturday	3	3	All except eight southeast counties
1937	Oct. 9 - Oct. 11	7:00 a.m. - 4:00 p.m.	3	Saturday	3	3	All except five southeast and eight southwest counties
1938	Oct. 1 - Oct. 10	7:00 a.m. - 4:00 p.m.	10	Saturday	3	3	All except five southeast and eight southwest counties. See map, page 168
1939	Oct. 1 - Oct. 15	7:00 a.m. - 4:00 p.m.	15	Sunday	Unit 1: 3 Unit 2: 2	Unit 1: 3 Unit 2: 2	All except eight southwest counties
1940	Oct. 1 - Oct. 21	Sunrise to 5:00 p.m.	21	Tuesday	5	5	Statewide
1941	Sept. 28 - Oct. 26	Sunrise to 6:00 p.m.	29	Sunday	6	12	Statewide
1942	Unit 1: Sept. 26 - Nov. 30 Unit 2: Sept. 26 - Nov. 1	Sunrise to sunset	57	Saturday	8	16	Statewide. See map, page 169
1943	Sept. 25 - Dec. 3	Sunrise to sunset	70	Saturday	5	10	Statewide
1944	Sept. 20 - Oct. 15	½ hour before sunrise to sunset	26	Wednesday	5	10	Statewide

HUNGARIAN PARTRIDGE REGULATIONS (Continued)

Year	Season Length	Daily Shooting Hours	Total Days of Hunting*	Day of Week Season Opened	Daily Limit	Possession Limit	Open Area
1945 thru 1949	Closed seasons						
1950	Oct. 6 - Nov. 5	Noon to sunset	15½	Saturday	2	4	Open generally over western half of state. See map, page 169
1951	Sept. 28 - Nov. 4	Noon to sunset except full day Sat. and Sun.	25	Friday	3	3	Statewide
1952	Sept. 26 - Nov. 2	Noon to sunset except full day Sat. and Sun.	25	Friday	5	10	Statewide
1953	Closed season						
1954	Oct. 1 - Oct. 17	Noon to sunset except full day on Sun.	10	Friday	3	6	All counties closed southwest of Missouri River. See map, page 170
1955	Oct. 1 - Nov. 6	Noon to sunset except full day Sat. and Sun.	24½	Saturday	4	8	All open except five complete and parts of four other southwest corner counties of state.
1956	Sept. 28 - Nov. 4	9:00 a.m. to sunset	38	Saturday	Unit 1: 5 Unit 2: 3	Unit 1: 10 Unit 2: 6	All open except parts of Bowman, Slope, Billings and Golden Valley Counties.
1957	Sept. 28 - Nov. 7	9:00 a.m. to sunset	41	Saturday	Unit 1: 5 Unit 2: 3	Unit 1: 10 Unit 2: 6	All open except parts of Bowman, Slope, Billings and Golden Valley Counties. See map, page 170
1958	Unit 1: Sept.27 - Nov. 6 Units 2 and 3: Oct. 4 - Nov. 6	9:00 a.m. to sunset	41	Saturday	5	10	Statewide

HUNGARIAN PARTRIDGE REGULATIONS (Continued)

Year	Season Length	Daily Shooting Hours	Total Days of Hunting*	Day of Week Season Opened	Daily Limit	Possession Limit	Open Area
1959	Sept. 26 - Nov. 8	9:00 a.m. to sunset	44	Saturday	5	10	Statewide
1960	Oct. 1 - Nov. 10	9:00 a.m. to sunset	41	Saturday	5	10	Statewide
1961	Unit 1: Sept. 30 - Nov. 9 Unit 2: Oct. 14 - Nov. 9	9:00 a.m. to sunset	41	Saturday	5	10	Statewide
1962	Sept. 15 - Nov. 18	9:00 a.m. to sunset	65	Saturday	5	10	Statewide
1963	Sept. 21 - Nov. 7 and Nov. 18 - Dec. 15	Sunrise to sunset	76	Saturday	5	10	Statewide

*Based on eight hours per day of hunting. (For exp., two half days = one day of hunting.)

Examples of Hungarian Partridge Hunting Seasons

1934

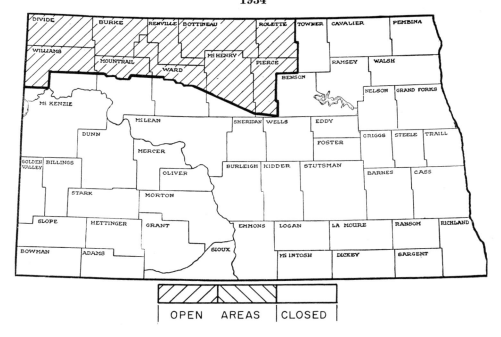

1938

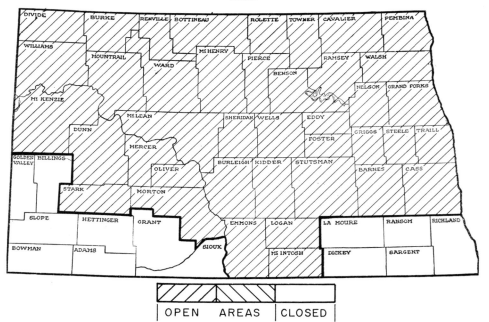

Examples of Hungarian Partridge Hunting Seasons

1942

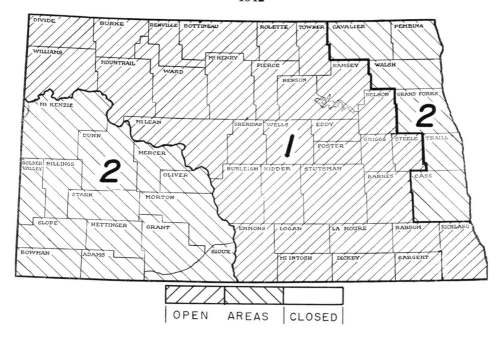

1950

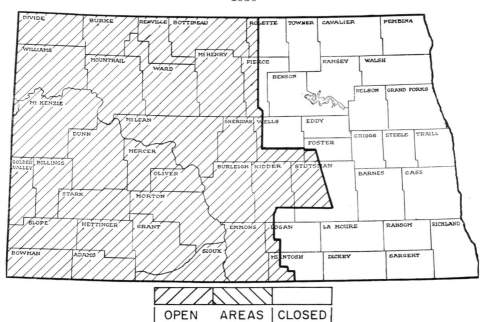

Examples of Hungarian Partridge Hunting Seasons

1954

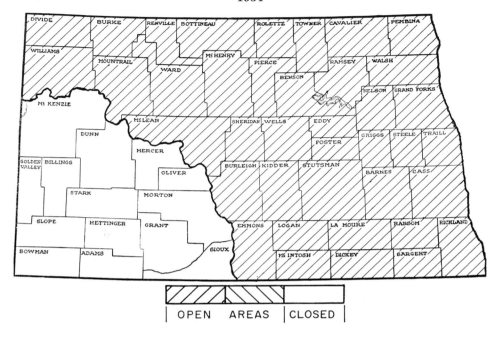

1957

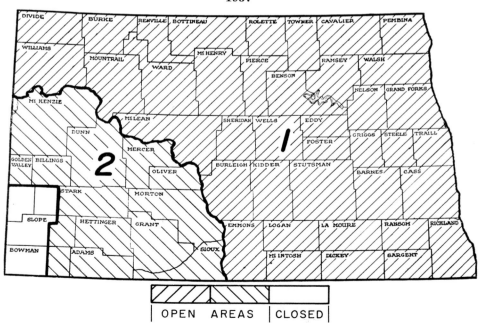

Limiting Factors

Although the Hungarian partridge is present in every county of the state it is not always abundant in every county from year to year. The Department frequently hears comments such as this: "We had several Huns around here last winter and early this spring. I thought there would be lots more this year but they seem to stay about the same — we never have more than two or three coveys. Why?" The answer is not completely known. Experience has shown that the farmer who allows hunting on the coveys around his farm has about the same number of Huns each year as the farmer who does not allow hunting. Even when a covey is almost completely destroyed by hunters, inclement weather, or predators, it is usually not long before another covey or pair moves in to replace the original stock. Naturally, if there is destruction of the habitat either by the activities of man or nature there may be no reappearance of the birds.

The breeding potential of the partridge is the highest of the three major upland game birds in North Dakota and the general public often wonders why populations do not explode as they did in the early 1940's. The Hun female lays from 15 to 20 eggs at her

first nesting and this is well above the 9 to 12 egg average per clutch for grouse and pheasant hens. Broods of 18 to 20 young Huns are a common sight in August and September. Thus, the productivity tables presented in the pheasant chapter indicate that we should expect larger populations of Huns than the other species. But the partridge is shorter-lived than the pheasant and has a population turnover of 80 to 85 percent each year compared with about 75 percent turnover for pheasants. The Hun must have a higher breeding potential to keep pace with such a die-off. Obviously, the Hun population is subject to more rapid population changes than grouse and pheasants, and that *decimating* and *welfare factors* that limit populations are in more critical balance. Added to this is the realization that the bird is a monogamous species, so the picture is further complicated.

Considerably more research has been conducted on pheasants than Huns in the United States. Most states spend their research money on the species that are most important to hunters. Consequently, pheasants, quail, deer, cottontail rabbits, doves and others rate priority across the nation. Deer, pheasants, and waterfowl rank ahead of the Hun in North Dakota. The "whys" and "whats" regarding North Dakota Huns are many.

The partridge is a bird of the agricultural regions. It has been most successful in the northern plains of the United States where rainfall is normally 15 to 25 inches per year with moderate humidity. Best soil types for Huns are the highly fertile, sandy and clay loams where the topography is level or gently rolling and well-drained. The species thrives with agriculture as long as the *decimating* and *welfare factors* do not become insurmountable. Some practices such as the planting of shelterbelts and strip cropping are beneficial to Huns while necessary evils like mowing and grazing are detrimental. Most investigations have shown that agricultural practices and weather are the two major influences.

Mowing has received the sharpest criticism both in the United States and abroad. In Europe there is far less loss of Hun hens and nests because farmers have handed down a tradition of flushing out nesting game birds ahead of the mower. When nests are destroyed the eggs are often saved and incubated. Brushy fence rows and small fields are the custom in Europe and many observers believe this type of farming benefits Huns. Agricultural practices received blame for 85 percent of the nesting losses in the state of Washington and 72 percent of the destroyed nests were by mowing machines.[192] Similar results were noted in Michigan and Wisconsin studies where approximately 50 percent of the unsuccessful nests fell victim to the same machine.[193] It is noted in the next section of this chapter (Research and Management) that the peak of hatching for North Dakota Huns is in mid to late June. This is the period of extensive mowing of hay crops in the state and could conceivably be a major limiting factor. Other such practices are grazing, burning, and plowing, to name just a few.

Most investigators have shown that Huns are not as vulnerable to snowstorms as pheasants. The habit of "coveying up" protects them from cold. By

---

[192]Yocum, C. F., *The Hungarian Partridge in the Palouse Region, Washington*, p. 186.

[193]Westerskov, K., *Management Practices for the European Partridge in Ohio and Denmark and Remarks on General Decline Factors*, p. 2.

burrowing into the snow they use it as insulation. Ice storms, particularly on top of snow, can prove a lethal killer by smothering. Although they are not as "winter-hardy" as grouse they are more so than pheasants. When snow depths exceed six inches for more than one month Hun mortality increases.[194] The fact that Huns can survive on a smaller food supply consisting of weed seeds and small grains is to their advantage.

Weather may become a decimating factor in spring or summer during the early weeks of the Hun chick's life. Heavy rainfall combined with cold temperatures apparently takes heavy toll on the young of practically all upland game birds. Losses may result directly from chilling and exposure and may indirectly lead to disease.

The effect of drouth on partridges is not completely understood, but census records indicate low reproduction during years of summer drouth on pheasants, grouse, and partridges. Studies in Utah showed that Huns were never found more than one-half mile from water at any season of the year.[195] Whether water, other than dew, is a necessity in North Dakota is unknown. Perhaps it is fortunate that North Dakota does have an abundance of potholes — there has been considerable concern over their disappearance by drainage and drouth in recent years.

Many of the statements regarding predation in the pheasant chapter apply to Huns. Most reports from the general public at the present time condemn the red fox as the number one predator on practically all game in North Dakota. Observers with a broader viewpoint are cognizant of the many other predators, some of which are troublesome for relatively short periods during the year. Crow, skunk, badger, and raccoon are nest destroyers and most detrimental during the important reproductive period. Northern snowy owls visit the state when snow is on the ground and are often observed making Hun kills. Certain hawks and eagles harass juvenile and adult Huns from spring until fall. And finally, resident predators such as mink, weasels, foxes, coyotes bobcats, horned owls, and vagrant cats and dogs may take Huns at any season. To pick any one predator species and prove that its elimination benefited the Hun population without removing all the other predators is a virtual impossibility. When those "would be" predators of Huns are considered there is a long list of species to eliminate. In Europe, where there have been more extensive studies, foxes, badgers, owls and certain hawks are considered less harmful to Hun populations than skunks, weasels, crows and stray cats.[196] In North Dakota, as was mentioned earlier, the red fox and crow have received much blame for pheasant population decreases. Farmer and hunter questionnaires often comment on the damage of these but surprisingly, when Hun losses are concerned, many of the complaints are directed towards snowy owls and stray cats.

The importance of automobile mortality on Hun populations is always open for speculation. These losses are particularly noticeable during the summer and winter months when it is common to pick up four or five birds all killed at one time, probably from one covey. One of the few studies made in North Dakota

[194]Silvonen, L., *The Fluctuations of Partridge and European Hare Populations in Southwest Finland*, p. 8-10.

[195]Porter, R. D., *The Hungarian Partridge in Utah*, p. 100.

[196]Kokes and Knobloch, op. cit., p. 94.

was conducted by Merrill Hammond at Lower Souris Refuge in 1938-41 and highway mortality was found to average about one bird per covey for the period.[197] In recent years, with more cars traveling more roads, this figure may be higher over a larger area of the state.

Population cycles which affect game birds and animals have been much discussed for many years. Many competent observers have accepted the ten year cycle for snowshoe rabbits and ruffed grouse, the four year cycle for lemmings and mice, and less noticeable ones for other birds and animals.[198] A questionnaire sent out by the North Dakota Game and Fish Department in 1951 to other states and provinces indicated that Huns were cyclic in one out of every five states. As in many other phases of partridge management, data has not been kept long enough to make predictions in North Dakota. Based on sex and age information taken from wing samples since 1951, it would appear that any population reductions attributable to cycles occurred in 1952 or 1953 and in 1959. However, there was a drouth which affected all upland game bird reproduction in 1959.

A minor subject that arises when discussing the limiting factors of Hun populations is that of competition between upland game bird species. Conflicts between adult grouse and pheasants have been mentioned on page 104. How important this interspecies strife is to game bird reproduction is relatively unknown. In the case of Huns there is considerable evidence of "parasitism" by pheasant hens laying eggs in Hun nests. Early studies in Iowa in 1930 showed 7 of 26 Hun nests "parasitized" by pheasants.[199] Similar studies showed over seven percent of the Hun nests contained pheasant eggs in the state of Washington.[200] In North Dakota in 1942 eight Hun nests were found with pheasant eggs in them.[201] This "parasitism" may be relatively unimportant to the overall production of game birds but competition between adult birds may have more significance. It has been particularly noticeable in North Dakota that areas of highest Hun production are not the same areas where pheasant populations are high. This has been evident in the north-central and Red River Valley areas of the state the past seven years. Large populations of Huns may be found in Bottineau, McHenry and other counties where few pheasants are to be found. Likewise, in the period 1955-58 good populations of Huns were present in southeastern North Dakota (Dickey, Sargent, Richland Counties) where the pheasant population was mediocre. In 1960 and 1961, when the pheasant experienced substantial increases in the southeast the Hun declined. Similar increases occurred in southwestern North Dakota in 1960 and 1961 when the pheasant population dipped downward.

In the face of all these possible limiting factors the influence of weather and habitat changes appear to have the most bearing on the success of Hun reproduction.

---

[197]Hammond, M. C., *Fall and Winter Mortality Among Hungarian Partridges in Bottineau and McHenry Counties, North Dakota*, p. 382.

[198]Webb, R., Letter, Nov. 14, 1961.

[199]Errington, P. L. and Hamerstrom, F. N., *Observations on the Effect of a Spring Drought on Reproduction in the Hungarian Partridge*, p. 71.

[200]Yocum, op. cit., p. 183.

[201]*North Dakota State Game and Fish Dept., Upland Game Nesting Studies, 1942, P-R Report No. 278*, p. 51.

Research and Management

As mentioned in the section on "Research and Management" in the pheasant chapter, intensive research on most of the game species in North Dakota is limited by expenses and personnel. It is little wonder then that scanty research has been conducted on the Hungarian partridge. Data collected is largely census information. The emphasis is placed on management rather than research. This is unfortunate because (1) North Dakota has sufficient numbers of Huns for research work, and (2) comparatively few Hun studies have been conducted in North America and much could be learned about them.

One of the Hun projects carried on in the state has been a sex and age study. Information for this work is obtained from wings sent in by hunters. Like the roadside and rural carrier counts the project has value through its use over a period of several years. For example, the study shows that hunting success declined during the years when there were less than two and one-half juveniles per adult in the bag. This is illustrated in Table 19 for the years 1951-54. Though the information is obtained after the hunting season has ended each year it is valuable in making long-range population estimates. When used in con-

junction with breeding pair counts the following spring, or brood counts the next summer, the information has additional value.

Wing studies also furnish important information concerning the hatching dates of the partridge. All juvenile birds can be aged within a couple of days of their hatching date by measurement of the moult on the primary feathers.[202] Table 20 shows that in a normal year between 40 and 45 percent of the hatch is completed by June 30. With this information in mind it may be possible to reduce nesting losses by delaying mowing operations until after July 1st when economically possible.

Some of the earliest census work on Huns in North Dakota was initiated in 1940 with the use of roadside counts of upland game birds. After an experimentation period this method was proved reliable for determining population trends. Approximately 350 rural mail carriers from all parts of the state have cooperated in making the counts. Because they drive 40,000 to 50,000 miles four times during the year these men report valuable data that would be impossible to obtain under present funds and manpower of the Game Department. Although the figures in Table 21 may not appear to have value for the average person at first glance, they show definite population increases and decreases. When tabulated by districts these figures show population changes for specific areas. January counts are not included in the table because they have been proven the least reliable of the four made during the year.

Roadside counts carried on by Department personnel usually parallel the figures showing up on the rural carrier reports. In addition to roadside brood counts, Department personnel report random covey and brood counts of Huns all during the year. Some of this information is shown in Table 22 along with covey counts made by Merrill Hammond of the U. S. Fish and Wildlife Service at Lower Souris Refuge in the period 1938-41.[203] These random tallies have some value in estimating population trends. Summer counts are important because they indicate reproductive success when the juvenile:adult ratio figures are used.

---

[202]Petrides, G. A., *Notes on Age Determination in Juvenal European Quail,* p. 116.

[203]Hammond, op. cit., p. 377.

There have been several other game management and research studies made of North Dakota Huns but space does not allow full reporting on the results of all these projects. Examples of these studies are: nesting information obtained from pheasant nesting work and predator studies, lead shot incidence information, parasite and disease data, and census and food information obtained by habitat biologists on tree planting study plots.

Aerial census work often provides information on Huns. Trapping and banding for pheasants has provided information on the partridge in the past. Although Huns are more difficult to trap than grouse or pheasants, a trapping and banding project may rate top priority for Hun research in the future when, and if, funds are made available.

Table 19

SEX AND AGE RATIOS FOR HUNGARIAN PARTRIDGE IN NORTH DAKOTA, 1950-63

Year	Adult:Juvenile Ratio	Male:Female Ratio	No. of Birds in Sample
1950	1:3.27	1.54:1	94
1951	1:2.28	0.88:1	92
1952	1:1.44	1.05:1	83
1953	Closed season		
1954	Insufficient data		
1955	1:3.07	1.10:1	497
1956	1:4.35	1.20:1	624
1957	1:3.78	1.00:1	1254
1958	1:2.97	1.11:1	1965
1959	1:2.41	1.13:1	1160
1960	1:3.72	1.05:1	1019
1961	1:4.21	0.96:1	1927
1962	1:3.81	1.04:1	2390
1963	1:4.05	0.98:1	3062

Table 20

HATCHING DATES FOR THE HUNGARIAN PARTRIDGE IN NORTH DAKOTA, 1955-63

Period Hatched	Number of Juvenile Birds									9 Yr. %'s
	1955	1956	1957	1958	1959	1960	1961	1962	1963	
Before June 8	15	9	14	21	0	0	1	12	38	1.3
June 9-15	24	8	50	111	12	10	112	87	228	7.7
June 16-22	45	28	180	198	73	100	347	279	438	20.3
June 23-29	32	102	118	114	117	175	247	266	321	18.0
June 30 - July 6	24	59	84	117	109	74	141	172	211	11.9
July 7-13	25	29	81	136	82	65	104	156	163	10.1
July 14-20	21	42	98	118	95	52	78	170	170	10.2
July 21-27	16	27	40	90	92	43	79	137	127	7.8
July 28 - Aug. 3	8	33	55	95	51	33	29	102	95	6.0
Aug. 4-10	8	18	25	63	35	39	33	55	57	4.0
Aug. 11-17	1	6	15	17	8	6	13	42	45	1.9
Aug. 18-24	1	0	2	12	1	6	4	20	9	0.7
After Aug. 25	0	3	0	2	3	0	0	4	0	0.1
No. of Juveniles in Sample	220	364	762	1094	678	603	1188	1502	1902	100.0 (8313 wings)

Table 21

NUMBERS OF HUNGARIAN PARTRIDGE REPORTED BY
RURAL CARRIERS IN NORTH DAKOTA 1946-63

Year	Max. No. Carriers Reporting During the Year	April Count Huns/Mile	July Count Huns/Mile	September Count Huns/Mile
1946	465	-------	.059	.065
1947	335	.047	.059	.057
1948	329	.050	.091	.115
1949	368	.071	.092	.103
1950	334	.060	.044	.036
1951	375	.053	.069	.082
1952	353	.063	.062	.061
1953	380	.027	.047	.065
1954	375	.042	.093	.071
1955	392	.042	.079	.112
1956	388	.046	.040	.089
1957	355	.026	.080	.118
1958	338	.051	.103	.107
1959	328	.039	.043	.045
1960	348	.036	.034	.072
1961	313	.031	.035	.064
1962	345	.036	.053	.064
1963	326	.028		
Avg. Huns/Mi. 1953-63		.038	.062	.080

Table 22

AVERAGE COVEY SIZE FOR HUNGARIAN PARTRIDGES
IN NORTH DAKOTA RECORDED BY MONTH

Year	Total Coveys (broods) Observed	Area	Jan.	Feb.	Mar.	Apr. May	June
1938-39	143	(Bott.-McHenry)	10.5	10.1	-------	-------	-------
1940-41	382	(Bott.-McHenry)	8.6	8.2	-------	-------	-------
1958	365	(Statewide)	-------	-------	-------	-------	
1959	618	(Statewide)	8.2	7.0	3.3	-------	17.5
1960	1032	(Statewide)	8.0	7.4	5.9	-------	-------
1961	230	(Statewide)	10.4	4.6	4.8	-------	-------
1962	498	(Statewide)	8.5	8.4	6.7	-------	-------
1963	31	(Statewide)	8.6	6.3	2.8	-------	-------

AVERAGE COVEY SIZE FOR HUNGARIAN PARTRIDGES
IN NORTH DAKOTA RECORDED BY MONTH — (Continued)

Year	Total Coveys (broods) Observed	Area	July	Aug.	Sept.	Oct.	Nov.	Dec.
1938-39	143	(Bott.-McHenry)	-------	-------	12.6	12.5	12.7	10.9
1940-41	382	(Bott.-McHenry)	-------	-------	10.1	10.2	9.4	9.9
1958	365	(Statewide)	13.2	13.6	12.9	9.2	8.7	8.3
1959	618	(Statewide)	8.5	10.5	8.4	8.3	8.4	-------
1960	1032	(Statewide)	11.1	13.2	11.9	12.3	9.8	7.6
1961	230	(Statewide)	13.1	14.2	14.7	11.2	11.2	9.3
1962	498	(Statewide)	11.6	12.2	11.1	8.1	9.0	10.4
1963	31	(Statewide)	-------	-------	-------	-------	-------	-------

7

Wild Turkey

Scientific name: *Meleagris gallopavo sp.*

Size:
Gobblers larger than hens.   Length, 36-48 inches.   Wingspan, 50-60 inches.   Weight, gobblers up to 30 lbs.; hens 6-10 lbs.

Coloration:
Gobblers are dark with many gaily colored irridescent feathers. Hens are drab, dark brown.   The wattles on the throat of the gobbler are a striking red and blue.   Gobblers have a long tuft up to ten inches in length on the breast.   Old hens have short tufts.

Flight:
Although large, the turkey is a strong, rapid flyer.   When hunted the bird may run rather than fly.   Like pheasants, they are excellent runners.

Flock habits:
Dominant gobblers are accompanied by 5-6 hens in the spring. Unsuccessful gobblers may travel alone or in small groups. Large mixed flocks are common from late summer until the following spring.

History

Another game bird introduced into North Dakota in recent years is the wild turkey. Contrary to the beliefs of many sportsmen the wild turkey was not found in North Dakota during ancient times. The northern limit of the range at the time of the first white explorers was about two hundred miles south of the state.

One main reason that wild turkeys were believed native to North Dakota was that sandhill cranes were often called "wild turkeys." Several old-timers interviewed for this book the past three years stated that they often heard this misnomer applied to cranes. According to Taverner the misnomer is also true in Canada:

> The bird so commonly called "Wild Turkey" in the Prairie Provinces is not a turkey at all, but a crane of the order Cruiformes and an entirely different bird. The true wild turkey has never been recorded in Canada west of southern Ontario.[204]

Some of the earliest human inhabitants of North Dakota, the Mandan Indians, considered the wild turkey one of the "Greatest curiosities."[205] When some of their members visited Washington in the early 1840's

[204]Taverner, P. A., *Birds of Canada*, p. 167.

[205]Sears, R., *Information for the People, or Treasury of Useful Knowledge*, p. 60.

they took home a wild turkey to show their tribe. Certainly the Mandans were not living in wild turkey range during the eighteenth and nineteenth centuries or they would not have gone to the trouble of carrying the turkey skin halfway across the continent.

Alexander Henry traveled from his fur post at Pembina to visit the Mandans on the Missouri River. On July 21, 1806, he wrote:

> One of the natives had a turkey-cock's tail, great numbers of which they got from the Schians [Cheyennes]; and which serve them as fans; this was a new and fresh one, of beautiful hue. I gave him five rounds of ammunition for it, with which he appeared well satisfied, and left me, but soon returned with the ammunition, and demanded the tail.[206]

Apparently, this particular Indian considered the turkey tail a prize and rarity or he would have been satisfied with his trade.

A review of the accounts of the early explorers and naturalists soon convinces the researcher that the wild turkey was not native here. Lewis and Clark witnessed the bird only as far north as the "extrance of the Tylors River [Dry Creek 40 miles south of Pierre, S. D.] above the Big Bend in the Missouri River" in southern South Dakota.[207] Other early adventurers who saw the turkey only in southern South Dakota were Maximilian (1833), Loisel (1803-05), and Audubon (1843). J. H. Taylor noted that the turkey was absent from North Dakota on his trip to Ft. Berthold in 1869. And Coues (1874) reported the turkey absent in northern Dakota and noted he'd only seen one turkey record for Minnesota. Roosevelt (1885) and Larson (1928) stressed the fact that the turkey was not a resident of the state. Over and Thomas (1946) stated that the wild turkey was missing in South Dakota after 1875 and was common only in the two southeastern counties (Union and Clay) before that date.

Besides the Big Missouri River Bottoms the other most logical spots for turkeys in North Dakota would have been the Turtle Mountains, Pembina Hills, and bottomlands of the Yellowstone, Red, Sheyenne, and James Rivers. These regions were not as extensively traveled by the early white explorers but none of these men left accounts of turkeys being present. Hatch stated that the wild turkey was not a rare bird in southwestern Minnesota around 1860 and was seen as late as 1871 in Minnesota. He believed it had disappeared from that state by 1890, however. It is not beyond the realm of possibility that an occasional flock or straggler wandered into North Dakota during the historic past but in these instances the bird was roaming outside of the range specified by the early observers. Martin Almquist of Fullerton, North Dakota, was the only old-timer interviewed for this book who states that he shot wild turkeys in the state. His comments of October 11, 1962, were verified by his brother, Elmer, who was on hand for the turkey kill made by Martin back in 1906. Martin says:

> In the fall of 1906 I was hunting hawks in a large grove of trees near our house (Sec. 2, T. 131N, R. 62W, Dickey Co.) when 5 or 6 wild turkeys flew into the grove. I shot one with the 10 gauge muzzle-loading shotgun. At first I thought it was a domestic bird belonging to Van Garvan's, our neighbors to the south. They raised turkeys. Hoffer's, our neighbors to the north had no turkeys. A later check with

---

[206]Coues, op. cit., p. 355.

[207]Burroughs, op. cit., p. 222.

Van Garvan's showed that the 6 to 8 pound bird I had killed was not like their birds and was a wild bird. Our family ate it a couple of days later. The only thing we could guess was that it had come into our area from the Sheyenne River Bottoms some distance away.

The range of the wild turkey in North America during historic times included thirty-nine states, southern Ontario, and parts of Mexico and Yucatan. The birds have now disappeared from nineteen of these states, plus Ontario, and in some other sections still within the turkey range. There has been considerable restocking with varying success.

Domestic turkeys originated from wild birds that were domesticated around 1500, or earlier. The early Spanish explorers in North America noted that the natives of Yucatan had already domesticated turkeys by 1517. The Spaniards took birds to Spain and by 1524 the turkey was taken to England. The first domestic birds came from the Mexican subspecies but in modern times there has been a great variety of crosses. The main difference between the wild

Wild-trapped Merriam's Turkeys Delivered to the Dickinson Airport by Colorado State Game Officials, for Release in the Killdeer Mountains, March, 1964.

birds and the domestic is in the coloration of the feathers. Most noticeable is the tail coloration where the tips of the feathers are nearly white in the domestic birds and wood brown in wild birds. Even this characteristic is not reliable in modern times because of the extensive crossbreeding of the subspecies.

Turkey stocking in North Dakota was attempted in the 1930's and 1940's but the most earnest and successful stocking was initiated by the Izaak Walton League, Missouri Slope Chapter, in the early 1950's. In 1951 this organization purchased turkey eggs at $1.75 each and adult birds at an average of $25.00 each and began pen-raising turkeys with cooperative farmers. First significant releases of this Eastern wild turkey (*Meleagris gallopavo sylvestris*) were made in 1952 along the Heart River, Missouri River, and in southwestern counties. Approximately 58 birds were released in 1952, 301 in 1953, 412 in 1954, 349 in 1955 and 211 in 1956. By 1957 a total of 1,331 had been released in North Dakota. By 1963 over 2,000 turkeys had been stocked here.

On January 18, 1953, six hens and two gobblers of the Merriam's subspecies of wild turkey (*M. g. merriami*) were released in the Pine Forest region of Slope County. These were adult wild-trapped birds obtained by the Izaak Walton League and the North Dakota Game and Fish Department in a trade that sent twenty-three North Dakota sharp-tailed grouse to the State Game Department of New Mexico. These Merriam's wild turkeys have done well in North Dakota and, during the years 1954-58, the annual population was estimated at about three hundred birds in the Pine Forest area. In March of 1964 fourteen additional wild-trapped Merriam's turkeys from Colorado were released at the northwest corner of the Killdeer Mountains in Dunn County.

A third subspecies to be brought into the state was the Rio Grande (*M. g. intermedia*). Fifty-three of these adult wild-trapped birds were obtained by the Izaak Walton League in a three-way trade involving a California ranch, the Izaak Walton League, the King Ranch, and the Texas Game Department. The Izaak Walton League had purchased some Barbary sheep from the Hearst Ranch in California but shuttled them on to Texas in exchange for the turkeys. Thirty-one of these Rio Grande turkeys were released along the Little Missouri River north of Medora (Grassy Butte area) and the remaining twenty-two turned loose along the Big Missouri River between Washburn and the Garrison Dam in February, 1955. The only population of true Rio Grandes remaining in North Dakota at the present time is the flock near Grassy Butte. The Big Missouri River stocking has undoubtedly crossed with the Eastern wild turkeys released in the same areas.

The Izaak Walton League estimated in early 1955 that there were about one thousand wild turkeys in the state. In the fall of 1956 they estimated 2,500 to 3,000. The Game Department estimates since that time, based on landowner questionnaires sent out annually, showed approximately 1,500 in 1960-61 and 1,800 in the winter of 1962-63. Department estimates would be conservative since the questionnaires were sent to only the prime turkey areas and do not include many small stocked areas in the state. Furthermore, not all landowners return the annual questionnaires although they may have turkeys on their land. On the other hand, there has been so much crossbreeding of the wild turkeys with domestic flocks that an accurate count of the wild flock is difficult.

Role

Since the wild turkey has been in North Dakota but a short period of time, it has not earned an important role among sportsmen, landowners, and the Game Department. Its numbers in the future will determine the role it will assume.

As a general rule the turkey has been accepted with open arms by most hunters and landowners. In the past the pheasant was a relatively easy game bird to sell the public; the turkey has been even more readily accepted. Large size and excellent eating qualities, combined with a reputation for being an outstanding sporting bird, have been strong selling points.

The Indians, in areas where the bird existed, did not hunt it as intensively as did the white settlers. Indians ate the meat, and decorated their clothes and weapons with the feathers, but to some tribes it was a taboo to kill the turkey. To the white man turkeys were a choice item on the table and he killed them at every opportunity. Early in the nineteenth century, the birds sold from .06¢ to .25¢ each but by the end of the century they were selling for about $5.00 apiece.[208]

---

[208]Edminster, op. cit., p. 59.

From the standpoint of sport the turkey was easy to hunt and trap when the white man first arrived in North America. Like most game birds it did not become wild until it had been hunted by man. Irving (1832) was one of the early travelers who spoke of the turkey as a "stupid" bird that could be easily killed.

At the present time the turkey is considered by many people the most difficult game bird to hunt. And for the same reason it is appreciated for its sporting qualities. Examples of the favorable comments on the 1963 turkey hunting questionnaires in North Dakota are as follows:

> *Dickinson hunter* — This is my second turkey hunt but the first time I have been successful in getting a turkey. I am convinced the turkey is one of the most elusive and evasive of game birds and therefore one of the sportiest to hunt.
>
> *Belfield hunter* — Great sport. Saw only two birds but it would not hurt me if I did not get a bird.
>
> *Bismarck hunter* — They were wild this year and that is the way we want them. Three of us hunted, one got his. This is a fair percent. Great fun!
>
> *Bismarck hunter* — On December 1st I spent the morning only in the Wildwood Lake and Painted Woods area near Washburn. I saw three turkeys, each of which flushed wildly before even a rifle shot could be attempted. Please don't think I'm disgusted — far be it! I enjoy my North Dakota hunting.

The past has shown that the Eastern wild turkey is dependent on timberland for its survival, the southwestern turkeys favoring arid brushlands. During the stocking period around 1950 many persons felt that the river bottoms and other wooded sections of North Dakota would support the bird. Although the state has few of the choice, mast-producing trees important to turkeys in the historic eastern range, it was believed the birds would survive on the available plants and waste products of agriculture. Pheasant and grouse populations in 1950 had been on a noticeable decline since the epochal populations of the mid-1940's, and the turkey could supplement the fall game bird harvests.

Izaak Walton League Turkey Releases, Blackburn Ranch, North of Bismarck, December, 1961.

Many landowners along the Big Missouri Bottoms, and other areas, actively participated in establishing the wild turkey in North Dakota. In many cases they cooperated with the Izaak Walton League by propagating birds in specially constructed pens and releasing them in suitable areas. They posted their land and kept an eye on the birds. Unhappily, by 1957 the Game Department had received damage complaints from landowners. These complaints were based on flocks of turkeys, numbering from 30 to 300, that tore apart strawstacks or came into feedlots and stole grain from hogs, cattle, and other livestock. Oddly enough the complaints were not confined to one area but came from widely separated points on the Missouri and Heart Rivers and the Pine Forest in Slope County. In an effort to reduce the complaints the Game Department inaugurated a program (see Research and Management section) whereby turkeys were trapped in complaint areas and moved to areas where the public was asking for stocking. As a second step the Department, along with the cooperation of the Izaak Walton League, recommended an open season. This would disperse the birds over a larger area, reduce complaints, and provide sport for a limited number of hunters. Although at this date there are more sportsmen and landowners asking for wild turkey stocking than there are complaints, landowner questionnaires show a greater diversity of opinion on wild turkeys than was displayed in the early 1950's. Many people have come to realize that the turkeys are in many places dependent on the gratuity of the landowner. Secondly, the birds have not always gone as wild as desired. Examples of the landowner questionnaires in recent years show some of the feelings prevalent:

1958   (Pine Forest, Slope County):
They do spread out in the summer months but move back in the winter. This is when they do most of the damage, though there are a few at the stacks in summer.
1960   (Stanton):
We did not see them after November. They cause silage spoilage by scratching off the seal on the surface of the pile.
1960   (Flasher):
I do not have any turkeys on my place nor do I want any. If they come here, or are planted, I plan to have them moved out or disposed of. They are just going to cause damage to my crops and livestock feed and attract hunters that will cause still more damage.

Landowners were cognizant of the fact that wild turkeys often crossbreed with domestic turkeys as shown by the following statements:

1958   (Judson):
Three or four years ago I was raising turkeys. First my turkey hens and 12 young left with the wild turkeys. One year later the tame gobbler joined them and they are still with them. I can't get them home; what can I do about it? Give me advice.
1960   (Carson):
They (wild turkeys) crossed with a tame gobbler. There were six young from one of the hens and we never did see the others again. Five of the young disappeared last fall. The old hen and a young hen winter here. They are mating with the tame gobbler again.
1962   (Amidon):
We had more turkeys around our place this summer but they were a mixed up mess. Apparently there was some crossbreeding with domestic white turkeys because quite a few of them had lots of white in them.

As a result of landowner complaints there have been several instances when the Game Department trapped and moved turkeys since 1958. All too often, the public sees the newspaper story which expounds on the turkey trapping as a great benefit to the area that will receive the birds. The story does not speak of the home area of the birds; in reality someone is anxious to get rid of them or they would not have been trapped in the first place. The following are examples of wild turkeys moved by the Department at the request of landowners:

  1958 (February) — 25 wild-trapped birds moved from Hensler to points south of Mandan near the Missouri River.

  1958 (April) — 32 birds moved from the Sanger area north of Mandan to the Cannonball River.

  1960 (December) — 25 birds moved from the Heart River south of Judson to the Riverdale Game Management Area.

  1961 (December) — 21 turkeys moved from the Turtle Mountains north of Bottineau to the mouth of White Earth River southwest of Stanley.

  1963 (March) — 25 turkeys moved from the Heart River south of Judson to the Beach area.

Fortunately, in these cases and others, there have been willing recipients for the birds that were trapped. And there is no question that the wild turkey is being distributed over a wide area in the state. It should make better hunting; it could also make more landowner complaints.

The North Dakota Game Department was not enthusiastic about the stocking of wild turkeys in the early 1950's. The Department pointed out that the bird would be stocked out of its historic range and either food or weather could prove a limiting factor. There were few mast trees so necessary in recognized turkey ranges. Cover was sparse for this woodland species. North Dakota winters could reduce turkey populations as they had cut back pheasants in the past. The cost of $1.75 per egg and $25.00 per adult bird was prohibitive from the standpoint of a statewide stocking program. And, after contacting other states who were attempting to restock, it was learned that these attempts were usually unsuccessful, even with favorable habitat. There was the perennial problem of wild turkeys crossbreeding with domestic flocks and the results producing birds that were not of a sporting type. Finally, there was always the problem of the turkey competing with the native wildlife and domestic livestock.

The future of the wild turkey is still in doubt. The role it has played thus far is a minor one because only a proportionately few hunters have sought the bird; most landowners have appreciated the turkey's presence in its current numbers, and the Department has not been overburdened with stocking and trapping expenses. It is hoped that this will become an important game bird of the future in North Dakota.

Harvest

The wild turkey is a good example of a game species noted for quality rather than quantity. The number harvested is not so important to the hunter as the opportunity to kill one in a season or, perhaps in a lifetime. It is paralleled by the Canada goose in being a premium game bird.

The annual harvest in the United States is less than thirty thousand. This figure is far below the nationwide harvests of the six major species reported in this book. Since 1958, the first of four open seasons, the total legal harvest in North Dakota has been slightly over seven hundred birds. Results of the four open seasons are on page 90.

TABLE 23   WILD TURKEY HARVESTS

Year	Estimated Harvest	Number of Permits	Method of Harvest by Successful Turkey Hunters
1958	97	376	C. F. rifles only. (1 bow kill)
1959-60	Closed seasons		
1961	195	309	60% by shotguns, 40% by rifles
1962	241	399	73% by shotguns, 27% by rifles (1 bow kill)
1963	171	306	72% by shotguns, 28% by rifles

The methods of harvesting wild turkeys during the historic past have been many. Some of the most sporting and satisfying methods are legal in the present day (viz: calling, driving, tracking).

It has been stated that this was considered a "stupid" bird easily killed by hunters in sections of the continent where it has not been previously hunted by man. Once they were hunted for a period of time they acquired a fear of man and his weapons. This "streak of wildness" was appreciated by most modern hunters, but they often had to vary their techniques in killing the bird or they would too often have come in from the fields empty-handed.

During the days of the Indians, turkey hunting was easy. They were often lured in with calls and stuffed decoys. Sometimes they were caught bare-handed. Calls, which are still common, were frequently made from the wing bone of the turkey hen. Log traps and snares baited with grain were used. Buffalo Bill Cody and a group of army troopers in southwestern United States once surrounded and killed five hundred turkeys with guns, clubs, and stones — the birds were that tame. As time passed the birds became more wary, and dogs, horses, and guns were used. Chasing turkeys with greyhounds and horses was popular at one time in the southwest. The birds were tired out by continual chasing and could be caught by dogs or shot by men on horseback. Pointer and setter dogs are used today in finding and flushing turkeys in southeastern United States but many of the old methods of chasing, snaring, and trapping are outlawed in all sections of the country.

Tracking turkeys after a fresh snow and making the kill when the birds are flushed has been a popular method of harvesting them for many years. Drive hunting, similar to deer drives, has also been used. And finally, no matter what methods or weapons are employed in modern times, most experienced turkey hunters agree that the most successful hunter is the one who is familiar with the habits of the bird. Experience and knowing the habits of the turkey are more important than the method the hunter uses.

Choice of firearms for turkeys today is generally governed by habitat and the number of hunters. In open country of the southwestern United States the rifle is a preferred weapon while in the heavily timbered areas of the south the shotgun is considered best. During the first open season (1958) in North Dakota center-fire rifles were specified. Several hunters complained that the choice meat was damaged by bullets of big bore rifles so the past three seasons hunters have been permitted the use of either rifles or shotguns. The smaller .22 caliber rifle is now legal along with larger rifles. Shotguns under 10 gauge generally with number 2 or 4 shot, have been gaining in popularity as shown in the

Merriam's Turkeys Taken at the Jacobson Ranch, Pine Forest Area of Slope County, November 26, 1961. Left to Right: Joe Kytoichuk, Joe Zilkowski, Allan Buckman, and Andy Lindlo, all of Belfield.

harvest table listed in this section. A hunter's degree of skill should determine his best weapon. The turkey is a durable bird, difficult to kill, and this is often frustrating. Because of this, the inexperienced sportsman may change his weapon or technique. William Webb hunted the southlands in the 1870's when weapons and ammunition were not as efficient as they are today, but he probably speaks for many hunters in the past and present:

> For this shooting, a shotgun is, of course, the best, although I have had fine sport among the birds with the rifle. When using shot at one on the wing, the hunter must not conclude his aim is bad, if no immediate effect is observed. The flying turkey will not shrink, as the prairie chicken does, when receiving and carrying off lead. I have frequently heard shot rattle upon a gobbler's stout feathers without any apparent effect, and found him afterward, fluttering helpless, a mile away.[209]

There will probably never be great numbers of wild turkeys harvested in North Dakota. But it should be kept in mind that nearly all of the several hundred persons who have pursued the birds these first four seasons have spoken highly of turkey hunting. The bird may have its drawbacks in being semi-domesticated and tame to some, but its size and excellent eating qualities are evidently all that are needed to arouse the interest of the majority of the hunters at the present time.

---

[209]Webb, op. cit., p. 460.

Seasons and Regulations

The North Dakota Game Department, and participating sportsmen, did not have a set of traditions to overcome when the first wild turkey season was proposed in 1958. The turkey was a new species and few residents had ever hunted it before. Consequently, there was little argument between different groups of people regarding the proposed seasons and regulations. The Game Department briefed itself on the regulations in other states. Then a rather "hurry-up" set of regulations was drawn up and the first open season took place in November, 1958.

There were few laws relating to the wild turkey prior to 1955. It was listed as a game bird in the Game and Fish Code but it was not until 1955 that a supplement to the Code specifically stated (Sect. 20-0803):

The Governor, in his order or proclamation, may provide for the number of big game and wild turkey permits or licenses to be issued for the taking of each species and the manner in which such permits or licenses shall be issued for big game and wild turkeys only.

Most persons realized that a wide open season patterned after the pheasant, grouse, or Hun seasons would be impossible for the turkey because it was not present in sufficient numbers. It was a premium bird that could be hunted in a similar manner to big game under a lottery or permit system. The Izaak Walton League, the group most responsible for the turkey's introduction, recommended that the turkey be hunted under a lottery with the cost of the permit set at $6.00, the same as for big game. It was not necessary to purchase a small game license for turkeys that first season. All hunters who applied received a permit. Four hundred and seventy-five permits were made available to the public but only 390 hunters applied. The high cost of the license, plus the fact that the turkey was a new species, held down the number of applications.

During the 1959 Legislative Session in North Dakota, a new, and more specific law (H. B. 561), relative to wild turkeys was introduced, passed, and written into the Game and Fish Code (Chapt. 20-0807):

> The governor may by proclamation provide for a permit season to take wild turkeys in such manner, number, places and times as shall be deemed to be in the best interests of the state. The fee for a wild turkey permit shall be three dollars, provided, however, that all applicants must have a resident hunting license.

This law currently governs the cost and manner of distributing turkey licenses. The number of permits issued during the open season is based on the estimated turkey population. Landowner questionnaires and Game Department census figures provide the information needed in this estimate. Landowners currently receive gratis permits to hunt on their own land.

As mentioned earlier, the 1958 turkey regulations stipulated that legal firearms for the taking of wild turkeys had to be center-fire rifles. After 1961 the .22 caliber rifle and shotguns were declared legal. The latter have gained rapidly in popularity the past two seasons, and by 1962 three out of four successful turkey hunters reported that they had made their kill with a shotgun.

The bow and arrow has been a legal weapon for turkeys since 1958. A "bow only" open area in McLean County was permitted in 1958 and met with considerable disapproval on the part of landowners and gun hunters. As a result practically all of the "bow only" area was closed to hunting by the landowners.

November turkey seasons in North Dakota have been well-accepted. Those hunters obtaining permits appreciate this season that is opened later than other game bird hunting seasons. The turkey, being a traditional Thanksgiving trophy, is appealing to the hunter and his family in November. Visibility in the woods is better for late fall hunters. The tracking hunter may receive the necessary snow. In 1962 the turkey season opened simultaneously with the deer season and met with considerable discord. Neither turkey nor deer hunters appreciated the other group in the field at the same time. There were many complaints that turkeys were being shot illegally without the required permit. Landowners too, were critical of the simultaneous seasons, and in many instances closed their land to hunting one, or both species.

Although the November turkey season has been fairly well-accepted by North Dakotans there is the possibility of spring seasons in the not too distant future, providing they meet with public approval. Virginia, Florida, and South Dakota hold spring seasons on the wild turkey. The main purpose in holding the spring hunt is to facilitate a better harvest of male birds. Like pheasants, too many turkey gobblers are surplus birds that should be removed from the population. Gobblers are easier to hunt in the spring than in the fall. They are in breeding plumage, exhibit considerable strutting, and respond to the turkey (hen) call in the spring. From sunrise to late morning the hunter can selectively hunt the gobblers. The spring gobbler season, strongly advocated by the states who hold it, is a good method of harvesting surplus birds without harming the overall population. It also permits the dyed-in-the-wool hunter a bonus period of hunting.

Turkey seasons in North Dakota will undoubtedly be conducted on a limited basis for quite a few years to come. Unless the population multiplies many times its present size a closely regulated permit type season will be held. Turkey seasons and regulations since the first open season in 1958 are as follows:

Izaak Walton League Pen-raised Turkeys, Missiouri River Bottoms, Early 1950's.

TABLE 24

WILD TURKEY SEASONS AND REGULATIONS

Year	Season Length	Daily Shooting Hours	Total Days of Hunting	Day of Week Season Opened	Season Limit	No. Hunting Permits	Open Areas
1958	Nov. 14 (noon) – Nov. 23	Sunrise to 4:00 p.m. after first day	9½	Friday	1 male	376	Big Mo. River: Garrison Dam – S. D. State line. Heart River: Mouth to Heart Butte Dam. Pine Forest: Slope and Bowman Counties. Four townships in McKenzie County.
1959-60	Closed seasons						
1961	Nov. 25 - Dec. 3	9:00 a.m.-4:00 p.m.	9	Saturday	1 (either sex)	309	Nine counties: Burleigh, Emmons, Grant, McKenzie, McLean, Mercer, Oliver, Morton, Slope.
1962	Nov. 20 - Dec. 2	9:00 a.m. - 4:00 p.m.	13	Tuesday	1 (either sex)	399	Same nine counties as 1961.
1963	Nov. 22 - Nov. 27	9:00 a.m. - 4:00 p.m.	6	Friday	1 (either sex)	306	Seven counties: Burleigh, Emmons, Morton, Mercer, Grant, McLean, Oliver.

Limiting Factors

The wild turkey was one of the first game birds hunted persistently for food by the Pilgrims on the Atlantic coast. Forests were natural areas for the birds but settlers cleared the land and killed turkeys at every opportunity. Therefore, the loss of habitat and overhunting are credited as the two greatest factors in drastically reducing turkey populations. Their present range represents only a fraction of the original and in recent years habitat restoration has been realized as the most important step in reestablishing the wild bird in the United States. Restocking and controlled hunting have further benefited the populations. These combined management practices have paid off in substantial population increases in Pennsylvania where the harvest of 3,800 turkeys in 1930 increased to a harvest of seventeen thousand birds in 1961. Similar, but less spectacular increases have been noted in other states.

Land clearing that began in the 1600's in eastern United States was achieved in many ways. Cutting of the forests was necessary in the building of homes, factories, ships, and the many smaller items essential to daily living. Wood was the number one fuel for the period. After the trees were cut down the land

Deer and Turkey Habitat Inundated by the Waters of Oahe Reservoir Near the North Dakota-South Dakota Line, 1962.

Timber Clearing on the Missouri River Bottoms West of Wilton, 1962.

was further cleared by burning, the soil cultivated, and crops planted. Early observers watched the wild turkey disappear from these regions and pointed the accusing finger at hunters, lumbermen, industrialists, farmers and other groups of individuals. In reality, the reduction in turkey populations and other game was the result of the combined forces of mankind. One group was as responsible as the next. Some observers realized the situation and lumped the blame onto "man" in general. Sears wrote, ". . . This bird was formerly very abundant; but the progress and aggressions of man have compelled them to seek refuge in the remote interior."[210]   One hundred years later in 1947, Glover and Bailey stated: "Man is the wild turkey's worst enemy . . . the turkey population . . . is inversely proportional to the number of people living in an area."[211]

Man was not thinking strongly about turkeys or game one way or another as he built his cities and farms and reduced the habitat. He enjoyed hunting and the aesthetic values of the game and he did not purposely kill it off. But he went about the business of building a more comfortable living for himself and the turkey suffered by his actions. As Edminster explained, "Chopping down trees and plowing up soil did not kill turkeys; it just prevented any more from being produced. The result is the same . . ."[212]

Promiscuous hunting was considered a limiting factor on turkey populations as early as 1708 when they were protected by closed seasons in New York State. The condemnation of overhunting has persisted to the present time. Henshaw said:

> It is the gun that has been the chief cause of the destruction of our game, large and small. Whatever weight may be attached to other causes, these fade into insignificance when compared with the effect of firearms.[213]

[210]Sears, op. cit., p. 60.

[211]Edminster, op. cit., p. 95.

[212]Ibid., p. 93.

[213]Henshaw, H. W., *The Book of Birds, Common Birds of Town and Country and American Game Birds*, p. 107.

Hornaday, long a critic of overhunting, stated, "Let no man be so rash as to conclude that armies of hunters . . . cannot easily and quickly wipe out all the turkeys that remain. They will not last long."[214]

In a strict sense, the overhunting of the past described by these observers cannot be compared with the controlled hunting of today. At the present time there are comparatively few persons who blame legal hunting as a major limiting factor. The poacher is still considered a problem, however.

One of the few cases of overhunting in recent years occurred in the 1940's at Rainy Buttes in Hettinger County. A man named Anderson raised Eastern wild turkeys for a few years and released them. The population built up to about seventy-five birds and was observed by the present Game Commissioner, Russell Stuart, in 1947. There was little interest and few regulations governing the wild turkey at the time, and by 1948 the wild flock had disappeared. Promiscuous hunting was believed to have been largely responsible for the flock's disappearance.

Because the wild turkey has been recently stocked in North Dakota, and was not native to the state in the past, it is difficult to judge the factors which might be considered limiting. Since the native turkey range was located a considerable distance south of the state line, one immediately thinks that North Dakota weather was not suitable for them. Over long periods of time it could

[214]Hornaday, op. cit., p. 37.

Bottomland Inundation from the Waters of Garrison Reservoir Between New Town and Williston, 1962.

have been a limiting factor on the populations. There have been relatively mild winters the past ten years and turkeys undoubtedly benefited from agricultural crops which provided food in winter. In many states, where the true wild birds are to be found, up to 65 percent of the turkey's food supply comes from mast crops such as acorn. This is not possible in North Dakota but the bird has survived on waste products and handouts from the farmer. Although the turkey consumes large quantities of food it feeds on many items and, in winter, can survive up to two or three weeks with no food whatsoever.

It has been stressed repeatedly that woodlands are required by the Eastern wild turkey. The range is being expanded in several southern states through proper forest management and controlled hunting. In North Dakota the main wooded areas along the Missouri River are being inundated by the backwaters of Garrison and Oahe Dams. Wild turkey populations will undoubtedly take a setback in these areas. On the other hand, populations in the wooded sections of the western Badlands may increase in years to come. Overall turkey populations may not drop as much as might be expected. Present interest in stocking and restocking may also tend to hold up populations in many areas of the state.

Man has been accused of being the most serious predator on this bird. Less than 50 percent of all wild turkey nests are successful each year even in the states where true native birds are still found. Most of the nesting failures are due to molestation by man. Mowing of small grain crops and merely "looking at" nests are the main causes of nest desertion.

Among the leading predators blamed for nesting losses are raccoons, skunks, dogs, cats, hogs, cattle, and crows. Those most often blamed for killing poults and adult birds are bobcats, dogs, domestic cats, foxes, horned owls, eagles, hawks, and the human poacher. Landowner questionnaires in North Dakota since 1958 have mentioned most of these. The human poacher and bobcat have been mentioned most often.

Back in the period 1940-42 the North Dakota Game Department received numerous complaints from domestic turkey raisers who condemned the ring-necked pheasant as a "predator" on turkey eggs and poults. Two letters complained that over two hundred young turkeys had been killed by cock pheasants during 1940-41. A third letter claimed that pheasants killed thirty-five young turkeys. Game Department personnel visited the damage areas but "seriously doubted" that pheasants were responsible.

The Department has received few reports of disease or starvation affecting wild turkey flocks. Both, or either, could become important under particular weather conditions. They have not yet been blamed for reducing populations.

A determination of the limiting factors on wild turkey populations is difficult at this time. In view of the fact that they were not native to North Dakota during the historic past it is entirely possible that these wild birds can exist in the state only because of agricultural activities. They depend on the landowner for food, particularly in winter. In fact, it is many times impossible to determine whether the turkeys found in North Dakota are wild or domesticated.

Research and Management

The main concern of the Game Department during the first ten years of wild turkeys in North Dakota has been to estimate population trends. This has not been an easy task because of the numbers of individuals and groups that have indiscriminately stocked birds into all parts of the state. In a majority of the cases accurate records have not been kept by the parties who did the stocking. There is a definite paucity of information on the number of birds released and on the location and success of releases.

The first attempt at management was the stocking which began in the early 1950's. Turkeys were introduced into all parts of the state by interested participants who spent varying sums of money for several subspecies. Most of the birds were of a semidomesticated character. All too often they were released into areas of questionable habitat. Success of the stockings varied from dismal failures to surprising successes.

When the Department was unable to obtain reliable information on the numbers of turkeys stocked an effort was made to obtain a count of the birds that had survived in the wild. Landowners living in known turkey range were personally interviewed and their names placed on a list for future write-in ques-

tionnaires. The first questionnaires were mailed in 1958 and at the present time there are about 450 landowners participating in the survey.

In addition to landowner questionnaires the Department obtains census data on the turkey while making aerial counts on other wildlife. During periods of adequate snowfall, flocks are counted in areas that are inaccessible to ground travel or where questionable ground counts have been made. Aerial counts of turkeys, however, are not conducted on a systematic basis as in the case with deer, antelope, waterfowl and other game species.

The next step in the management of this bird occurred in the winter of 1957-58 when several landowners complained of turkey damage on strawstacks, corn piles, and grain intended for domestic livestock in winter feedlots. The Department was committed to the task of reducing the size of flocks, keeping them out of the damage areas, or eliminating them completely. Between seventy-five and one hundred birds were trapped that first year and turned over to the Missouri Slope Chapter of the Izaak Walton League. Club members then banded and released the birds in new areas where landowners were asking for wild turkeys. Although trapping success has been definitely limited, the project has served to reduce many landowner damage complaints by removing birds or scaring them out of an area for a considerable period of time.

A second attempt at reducing landowner complaints occurred in the fall of 1958 when an open season was recommended for the first time. The recommendation met with the approval of the public and a season was held that fall. Although only about one hundred wild turkeys were harvested the flocks were scattered and many landowners expressed satisfaction with the open season. It offered sportsmen their first opportunity to hunt the birds.

Another aid has been the information received from questionnaires sent out to the hunters who obtain a turkey permit each fall. One of the main values of this information is to determine the harvest. As an example, the 1962 hunter returns showed that nearly half of the turkey populations in the Pine Forest Area of Slope-Bowman Counties had been legally harvested and a closed season in 1963 would, in all probability, benefit populations in that area.

Although the North Dakota Game Department has conducted little research and management on wild turkeys, there has been a considerable amount of money and time spent since the 1930's in the states located in native wild turkey range. Much has been learned about the bird's requirements but little has been done to restore the large populations of the past. Most of the action programs have been minor steps of little consequence. Winter feeding, restocking, predator control, and increased restrictions on hunting are just a few of the "sniper" programs aimed at conserving or restoring the wild bird. A large-scale management plan in North Dakota is improbable in this state where the turkey is out of its native range.

8

Rare Upland Game Birds

When the native grouse populations began to decline shortly after 1900, North Dakota sportsmen and landowners started looking for other game species as replacements. Some persons wanted to restock with grouse and other native game birds of the United States, but earlier attempts with grouse in the eastern parts of the nation had resulted in dismal failures. Many persons, encouraged by the successful stocking of the foreign pheasant in Oregon (1881), looked overseas for species that might succeed here.

It has been long recognized that stocking at best is a hit-and-miss method of restoring game bird populations in a given area. First of all, for every successful attempt since the earliest in the 1700's, there have been more than one hundred failures. This fact has been realized with both native and exotic species. Only four kinds of foreign bird colonists have succeeded: the house sparrow, the starling, the Hungarian partridge, and the pheasant.[215] Ironically, the first two (sparrow and starling) have been declared pests in most sections of the country while the native species have suffered by their presence. This brings the second realization that if the one in a hundred stockings does succeed, it may turn out later that the species stocked was desirable in its native range but an economic pest in new range.

Among the many foreign gallinaceous birds that were brought into the United States before 1900 and failed to make the grade were European quail, bamboo quail, capercaillie, peacock and guinea fowl. In the past fifty years many other species have been stocked and have failed.

Persons interested in introducing new species in North Dakota should check thoroughly with the State Game and Fish Commissioner before releasing either foreign or native species here. Present state laws prohibit the indiscriminate releasing of birds, animals, and fish into the wild without the approval of the Commissioner. The law is designed to protect against the release of undesirable species and the diseases and parasites they might bring with them.

Some of the native and foreign upland game birds which have been stocked by private parties and the Game Department in the past are as follows:

[215]Elton, C. S., *The Ecology of Invasions by Animals and Plants*, p. 75.

Bobwhite Quail

The bobwhite was at one time native to thirty-five states. It was not, however, observed in historic times in North Dakota. According to early observers the quail was found only as close to North Dakota as southern Minnesota and southern South Dakota.

Because the quail has long been accepted as an excellent sporting bird with no objectionable habits, and was a native within 200 or 300 miles of North Dakota, it is understandable that it was one of the first game birds to be brought here. Old newspapers and Game Department files are loaded with accounts of quail stocking in many parts of the state before 1900. As early as 1877, seasons were closed to quail hunting and stockings were being made. In fact, during most of the years between the 1880's and the 1920's the laws specifically stated quail hunting was prohibited. Some examples and results of the early stockings are as listed below:

Bismarck Tribune Files:

April 24, 1897 — The six dozen quail brought recently from the east by the sportsmen have been turned out and are expected to thrive.

July 14, 1897 — The quail that were recently turned out are thriving and several flocks of young ones have been seen.

January 12, 1906 — A couple of years ago J. S. Werner of Dawson planted 50 quail on his place and they did fairly well the first year. Now he has only four left and offers a reward of $25.00 for the conviction of the party who supposedly shot them.

August 23, 1908 — A few years ago the Bismarck Gun Club turned loose about a hundred quail in the bottoms north and south of the city and their welfare has been closely watched by club members since. That the quail have thrived is evidenced by the fact that this summer large flocks of them have been seen at various points, and it is hoped that by closely protecting them for a few years longer the woods will be full of them, so to speak.

There is hearsay evidence that a flock of a dozen quail, presumably shipped in and released, were sighted near Grand Harbor northwest of Devils Lake in 1894-95.[216] An earlier source reported two of the birds at Ft. Berthold in 1882. It was believed that these birds had come from Ft. Sully, South Dakota, where quail had been liberated four years earlier.[217]

North Dakota Game and Fish Files:

1923-24 Eighth Biennial Report — The quail has been shipped in by Sportsmen's Clubs and individuals and released in several localities in the state, apparently thriving for a year or two, but sooner or later disappearing again, presumably because of heavy drifting snow storms. Have some reports of their being seen or heard the past season in several localities, apparently authentic but not always confirmed.[218]

1925-26 Ninth Biennial Report — Ten dozen Bobwhite quail were imported from Kansas by the Department (at a cost of $36.00 per doz.) and distributed in the western and southwestern portions of the state.[219]

1931 Second Annual Report — Quail — owing to the climatic conditions of last winter, and the wonderful season this spring and summer, a good many coveys of quail have been reported to this Department.[220]

---

[216]Judd, E. T., op. cit., p. 15.
[217]Wood, op. cit., p. 81.
[218]*North Dakota State Game and Fish Dept., Eighth Biennial Report, 1923-24,* p. 13
[219]*North Dakota State Game and Fish Dept., Ninth Biennial Report, 1925-26,* p. 15.
[220]*North Dakota State Game and Fish Dept., Second Annual Report, 1931,* p. 6.

It would be impossible to estimate the number of quail that have been stocked in North Dakota the past eighty years, but it would probably run well into the thousands. Why the quail did not succeed is not known but the most repeated reason offered is that the weather is too severe for them. Winter weather probably restricted their range. Crops of a dozen North Dakota quail were examined in the early 1900's; nine-tenths of their December food supply consisted of sumac berries.[221]

The North Dakota Game Department still receives an occasional inquiry on the possibilities of quail stocking in the state. As recently as the late 1950's a landowner from Bowman reported that he was interested. Whether the bobwhite ever succeeds in becoming established in the state is highly doubtful, particularly when one looks at the record of quail stocking the past eighty years.

Chukar Partridge

A foreign (India) game bird that has been stocked in practically every state of the Union since 1893 is the chukar partridge. This bird, halfway between the Hun and the sharptail in size, was a stocking failure until the early 1940's when it became established in states west of the Rocky Mountains. Highest populations of chukars are presently found in Nevada, California, Oregon, and Washington but several other states hold open seasons on the species and populations are increasing. Since the chukar has done so well the past twenty years there has been renewed interest in stocking it.

First attempts with chukar partridges by the North Dakota Game Department came in 1937 although other private stockings may have been made earlier. During the period 1937-53 chukars were placed in all corners of the state by the Department, sportsmen's clubs, and private parties. Approximately 2,300 chukars were raised and released by the Department during this period. From 1953 to 1956 the Department stocked another group of 3,300 chukars at twelve, or more, release sites in the Badlands of southwestern North Dakota.

Success with chukars in the state, particularly the releases around 1940, paralleled that of many of the pheasant and quail stockings of the past. The birds thrived a year or two, some reproduction was observed, and then the populations dwindled away to nothing. Since stocking was terminated in 1956 there has been little increase noted in the populations. On the other hand, the birds did not completely die out in a couple years as happened with the 1940 plantings. In fact at two ranches, Vanvig's and Ripley's, chukars have hung on for nearly ten years. At these two places, fifteen miles south of Medora, the birds spend most of their time close to the buildings, feed with the ranchers' livestock, and when flushed, fly readily to the nearby buttes overlooking the

[221]Judd, S. D., op. cit., p. 25.

Little Missouri River. The wintering flock at the Ripley Ranch generally numbers from 100 to 200 birds. During spring and summer, pairs and broods are often observed some distance from the ranch but when winter arrives they are back at the ranch buildings. There is always the possibility that these populations will explode and spread out but there is no evidence that this will occur.

The chukar partridge in North Dakota, at least, is hanging on. What is holding back an increase in the populations is not known. Weather and habitat have been mentioned as possible limiting factors but one can only speculate on the real factors at this time. In the meantime, there is sufficient breeding stock of chukars in the Badlands to discourage any further stockings until the birds show signs of adapting to the state.

The Outsiders

There is no question that other exotic and native gallinacious birds have been stocked in North Dakota at some time in the past. As an example, a few years ago (1958) a member of a sportsmen's club in north-central North Dakota, while talking about pheasant stockings in his area, hastened to add that the club had also released a couple dozen coturnix quail. Club members were anxiously awaiting the outcome of the releases of this small migratory bird that has been introduced into so many places in the United States since World War II. No further word was ever heard from the project in North Dakota.

Another example of exotic stocking that did not materialize was mentioned in a short history of the North Dakota Wildlife Federation in 1945:

> Had it not been for the war the Federation would have tried planting the cock-of-the-north (Capercaillie) in the northern part of the state. This bird is the largest of the grouse family. The cock-of-the-north, a native of Norway, may do well in the Turtle and Pembina Mountain areas.[222]

Occasionally, a native or exotic bird from a nearby province or state is sighted in North Dakota. An example of these rare visitors was described by Wood in 1923:

> Willow Ptarmigan: Mr. Russell Reid reports that a poorly mounted specimen taken October, 1909, in the Killdeer Mountains, Dunn County, was sent to J. D. Allen at Mandan.
> The species is a straggler or accidental winter visitant in the state . . . . .[223]

There is considerable research and experimentation being conducted on many foreign game birds at the present time. Many species have been introduced and some have succeeded. These experiments should be continued. After all, the habitat and weather are subject to change and certain new species might fill in a gap left by a resident species that is on the decline. We must recognize that the two most common upland game birds in North Dakota at the present time, the pheasant and the Hun, are introduced species and, in the future, new species might fit into North Dakota's wildlife picture. The most important thing to remember is that the introduction should be made only after careful research and experimentation has been conducted. This is no time nor place for "dump and hope" fiascos.

---

[222]Stone, H., A Letter to the Lover of the Outdoors, A History of the North Dakota Wildlife Federation, p. 3.
[223]Wood, op. cit., p. 35.

9

Licenses and Administration

The question is often asked, "When was a hunting license first required in North Dakota?" The answer is not clear-cut, but it appears the first hunting license covered by state law was sold in 1897. In 1896 a license was required if the hunter was going to hunt with a dog, and at least two sources indicate that hunting licenses were sold by the Game Department as early as 1895.

First mention in state laws appeared in the First Biennial Report of the State Fish and Game Commissioner (W. W. Barrett) in 1893-94, in which he recommended that people from "outside the state" should pay "a reasonable license fee" to hunt and fish in North Dakota.[224] There was no further mention of this until 1897 when both resident and nonresident hunting licenses were authorized and put into law by the legislature. Whether the resident hunting license sold in 1895 was legal under state law is not known. Perhaps it was sold on a voluntary basis. According to Joseph H. Taylor, "revenue was raised from a license or hunting permit fund" in 1895.[225] He did not mention the cost, but *Outdoor Life Magazine* published the following: "North Dakota — 1895, $25.00 nonresident license and 50 cents resident license . . . 1897, resident license fee increased to 75 cents . . ."[226]

Few records exist of the numbers sold prior to 1909. (See Table 25). A. O. Odegard of Heimdal loaned this Department a complete set of hunting licenses, purchased and used by himself from 1896 to 1962, but he is probably one of the few persons who purchased the special "dog hunting permit" in 1896 (See page 207). Many persons hunted without a license prior to 1910 because they were unaware that they needed one. Certainly there were few game wardens to enforce the requirement.

The cost has changed little the past sixty years. It is interesting, and ironic, that when the cost was

---

[224]*North Dakota State Game and Fish Dept., First Biennial Report, 1893-94*, p. 337.
[225]Taylor, op. cit., p. 112.
[226]*Outdoor Life Magazine*, Jan., 1905, p. 55.

increased twice during this period, the extra income was obligated to a bounty fund, something not recognized as an aid to wildlife populations. Neither is it considered a wise financial expenditure. In 1919 the $1.00 license was increased to $1.50 and the additional .50¢ placed in a crow bounty fund; in 1957 it was raised to $2.00 and .50¢ directed to a fox bounty fund.

Many hunters rate the value of their hunting license strictly on the amount of game they kill. Certain hunters who averaged a kill of forty-nine pheasants in the 1944 season and four pheasants during the 1962 season can see no reason why they should pay more for a hunting license in 1965. In fact, this type of hunter may be the one who says, "I don't hunt in North Dakota anymore. I go to South Dakota and Canada!" This is the easy way of getting what this hunter considers his "money's worth," but he is certainly not aiding the game species where they need the most help. Much more respect should go to the license buyer who closely follows the functions of his Game Department and then insists that the Department income be spent for the welfare of the birds and animals. This long-range outlook is needed to preserve hunting for the future.

All too often in the past, politics have been confused with Game Department policies. As early as the 1911-12 Game and Fish Board of Control Report, outside pressure groups were accused by board members of tampering with the hunters' license fund:

> . . . they want at least half of the money paid into a special fund for a specific purpose by the sportsmen, to use for the improvement of the roads, for building bridges or for draining some piece of swampland, so that this work can be done without a special tax being levied to raise the funds necessary for the work.
>
> The sportsmen have received no financial help whatever from the state in the matter of game protection or game propagation, and now that they have, by paying one dollar each on a license to shoot game during the open season, created a handsome fund, the school districts or the county commissioners want them to divide this fund with the people and let them use it for some purpose foreign to that for which the fund was created.[227]

There have been few attempts in recent years to divert the license money to funds outside the Game and Fish Department. This does not mean, however, that all the funds within the Department have been wisely spent. Bounty expenditures are one example. So are game bird stockings which have been made in areas that were devoid of food and cover. By and large, however, the hunter buying the North Dakota license can be sure he is personally contributing to wise game management in the state.

Occasionally, a local resident will claim that the nonresident hunter is killing all the game. The fallacy of this statement may be noticed when one looks at the following table. There may be a few nonresident hunters each year who kill and transport more game than specified by law, but it is a mistake to say that the number of nonresidents hunting the state is excessive. As the table shows, the most nonresidents ever hunting North Dakota was in 1945 when 4,877 purchased the special license. This is a low figure, particularly when compared with the number of nonresidents hunting nearby states. (Exp. South Dakota, 70,000 nonresident pheasant hunters in 1963). The nonresident license fee of $25.00 was inaugurated in 1897 and has been in effect to 1964.

---

[227]*North Dakota State Game and Fish Dept., Second Biennial Report, 1911-12*, p. 32.

All game hunting was legal under the $1.50 license until 1931 when a special $5.00 license was legalized for big game. At the present time, deer, antelope and turkey require separate licenses.

Finally, it should be realized that the "upland game hunting license" has gone under several different titles since 1896 when it was legalized. In 1896 the license was a permit to hunt with a dog. From 1897 to the present time a license has been required to hunt upland game with or without a dog.

The numbers and costs of hunting licenses from 1896 to 1963 are shown in Table 25.

The first hunting license, 1896. The cost was .75¢.

TABLE 25   NORTH DAKOTA HUNTING LICENSES, 1896-1963

Year	Resident	Nonresident	Cost of License Resident	Nonresident
1896-97	No information	--------	$ .75	$25.00
1898	5,469	131	.75	25.00
1899-1908	No information	--------	.75	25.00
1909	23,712	143	1.00	25.00
1910	26,542	97	1.00	25.00
1911	25,506	63	1.00	25.00
1912	25,683	60	1.00	25.00
1913	33,354	101	1.00	25.00
1914	38,945	52	1.00	25.00
1915	36,383	107	1.00	25.00
1916	39,540	160	1.00	25.00
1917	No information	--------	1.00	25.00
1918	No information	--------	1.00	25.00
1919	32,771	82	1.50	25.00
1920	32,622	114	1.50	25.00
1921	No information	--------	1.50	25.00
1922	32,928	102	1.50	25.00
1923	37,190	133	1.50	25.00
1924	34,784	277	1.50	25.00
1925	35,983	178	1.50	25.00
1926	33,879	153	1.50	25.00
1927	33,108	163	1.50	25.00
1928	41,432	263	1.50	25.00
1929	39,232	233	1.50	25.00
1930	34,385	167	1.50	25.00
1931	24,251	65	1.50	25.00
1932	28,654	66	1.50	25.00
1933	34,223	57	1.50	25.00
1934	23,606	6	1.50	25.00
1935	23,383	15	1.50	25.00
1936	24,714	9	1.50	25.00
1937	14,532	15	1.50	25.00
1938	24,000	19	1.50	25.00
1939	36,900	45	1.50	25.00
1940	39,500	86	1.50	25.00
1941	54,800	280	1.50	25.00
1942	54,200	403	1.50	25.00
1943	40,424	898	1.50	25.00
1944	56,986	1968	1.50	25.00
1945	62,167	4877	1.50	25.00
1946	67,622	2407	1.50	25.00
1947	60,080	1900	1.50	25.00
1948	70,714	3213	1.50	25.00
1949	71,098	2078	1.50	25.00
1950	57,481	1484	1.50	25.00
1951	63,997	2105	1.50	25.00
1952	65,877	1981	1.50	25.00
1953	48,218	1423	1.50	25.00
1954	60,328	2018	1.50	25.00
1955	66,533	3315	1.50	25.00
1956	66,122	3395	1.50	25.00
1957	68,278	3514	2.00	25.00
1958	72,546	3523	2.00	25.00
1959	54,125	1353	2.00	25.00
1960	61,473	1928	2.00	25.00
1961	60,243	1192	1.50	25.00
1962	56,091	1390	1.50	25.00
1963	71,480	2493	2.00	25.00

Table 26

NORTH DAKOTA STATE GAME AND FISH ADMINISTRATORS
THROUGH THE YEARS (By Governor's Appointment)

1884	Territorial governor authorized to appoint a fish commissioner but no record of appointment made. This act was repealed in 1885.
1891-92	Superintendent of irrigation and forestry designated as head of game and fish functions. W. W. Barrett of Church's Ferry was the superintendent. No other game and fish personnel.
1893-96	Superintendent of Irrigation and Forestry, W. W. Barrett, operated game and fish functions with the aid of forty-eight protectors. By the legislation of 1895 Mr. Barrett's title was changed to fish commissioner.
1897-98	Superintendent of Irrigation and Forestry, W. W. Barrett, conducted game and fish operations with the aid of protectors and the first State Warden, George E. Bowers. The state warden appointed the protectors and conducted first hunting license sales.
1899-1902	Superintendent of Irrigation and Forestry, W. W. Barrett, acted as game and fish commissioner with the aid of protectors and two State Wardens, George E. Bowers and Ever Wagness.
1903-04	Two state wardens conducted most of the game and fish operations. These men were C. A. Hale and H. C. Stenshoel and they appointed deputy wardens to aid them.
1905-06	Two State Wardens, C. A. Hale and F. W. Schlechter, conducted game and fish operations. Schlechter resigned and was replaced by William McKean in 1906. Deputies were appointed by the two state wardens.
1907-08	The two state wardens who conducted game and fish work were W. N. Smith and Olaf Bjorke and their appointed deputies.
1909-10	A state game and fish board of control was appointed for the first time. Five men and two chief wardens served under Board President Herman Winterer.
1911-12	State game and fish board of control. The three man board and two chief wardens acted under President W. E. Byerly.
1913-16	State game and fish board of control. The four man board and two chief wardens worked under President J. P. Reeve.
1917-18	Same as 1913-16 except the board president was Charles F. MacLachlan.
1919-20	Same as 1917-18 except the board was increased to five men and two chief wardens with MacLachlan acting as president.
1921-22	Same as 1919-20 except C. E. Manning was the board president.
1923-26	Same as 1921-22 except W. C. Taylor was board president.
1927-28	Same as 1923-26 except C. H. Noltimier was board president.
1929-32	First one man game and fish commissioner appointed by the Governor. This man was B. W. Maurek.
1933-34	Commissioner Thoralf Swenson.
1935-36	Commissioner Arthur I. Peterson.
1937-38	Commissioner D. W. Hulterstrum.
1939-47	Commissioner William J. Lowe.
1948-56	Commissioner H. R. Morgan.
1957-60	Commissioner Dr. I. G. Bue.
1961-	Commissioner Russell W. Stuart.

10

Shotguns for Upland Game

Early History

Mention has been made that the rifle was more widely used than the shotgun in North Dakota during the 1800's. In fact, the rifle was more popular than the shotgun until after 1900, or when hunting changed from necessity to sport. The much sought big game that was so common in the fur trader period was largely taken by bow and arrow or rifle. Waterfowl, grouse, and other birds were trapped or taken with the rifle; a good example was the step-by-step "perch shooting" described by Boller, De Trobriand, Roosevelt, and others.

Although muzzle-loading and percussion rifles were used and coveted by fur traders of the mid-1800's, many of the Indians used just about any firearms they could get their hands on. White men were reluctant to put quality weapons into the hands of Indians for fear they would be used against the white man. This was particularly true after the metallic cartridge rifles were developed and carried to western United States after the Civil War.

Denig left some good accounts of the weapons and methods used by various tribes in the Ft. Union area in the mid-1800's. He stated that the Cree "shoot their northwest [shot] guns with nearly the certainty of rifles."[228] While describing the Assiniboine Indians, the same author wrote, "They never use the gun on horseback or the bow on foot after game. The former they cannot load while running and the latter is not calculated to shoot with certainty any distance over 10 paces."[229]

In summing up the hunting of five major Indian tribes of the Upper Missouri, Denig stated that they used the bow and arrow when hunting from horseback and, "the northwest shotgun is the only arm employed in killing any and all game on foot."[230]

---

[228]Denig, E. T., *Five Indian Tribes of the Upper Missouri*, 1961, p. 130.
[229]Denig, E. T., *Indian Tribes of the Upper Missouri*, 1930, p. 542.
[230]Ibid., p. 542.

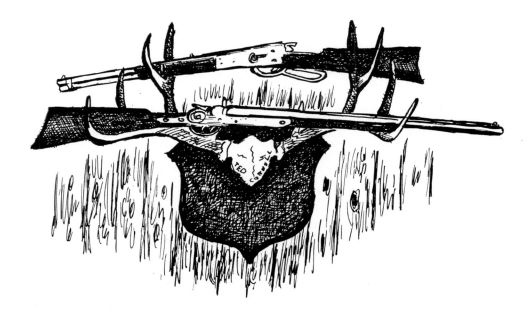

The most significant development in the shotgun was the designation of the weapon for breech-loading and metal or paper cartridges. Huntington stressed this fact:

> Forester [Frank] doubted if the breech loader would ever come into general use on account of the inconvenience of the little case in which the loads were carried. I spent a whole day in New York recently in a fruitless effort to find one of the old single muzzle loaders to be used making an illustration. The muzzle loading double gun is rapidly becoming a curiosity.[231]

From the 1880's until 1900 most of the shotguns used in waterfowl and upland game bird hunting were single and double-barreled. Practical from the standpoint of killing game they were, nevertheless, too expensive for the average hunter. Several North Dakota old-timers mentioned that they could not afford a shotgun until about 1900.

Only the old-timers will remember the controversy that burst forth when the first repeating and automatic shotguns were introduced around 1900. There has been little mention made of game destruction or over-kill by these guns the past twenty years, but in the period 1900-35 many persons criticized these multiple-shot weapons and legislated against their use. Newspapers and magazines printed hundreds of articles on the subject and state legislators were involved in the issue. Since the repeaters and automatics were something entirely new and efficient, and because they could fire five or six shots in a few seconds, considerable criticism could be expected. Their critics soon tagged these weapons with such ignoble names as "slaughtering machines," "pot-hunter's tools," and "just the thing for the market hunters and game hogs." The famous naturalist, Ernest T. Seton advocated the restriction of these guns in *Recreation Magazine:*

---

[231]Huntington, op. cit., intro.

I have just returned from Manitoba and while there I saw many of the sportsmen and others interested in the preservation of game. I was glad to meet Dr. George Bell, who was the leader in the fight against the automatic gun, which, as you know has been declared illegal in the province of Manitoba. . . . We went around in Winnipeg and got practically every sportsman to sign a protest against the automatic gun. Armed with this we went before the Legislature. . . . The thing was easily carried in the House.[232]

Another critic in the same magazine wrote:

. . . I am sorry the Winchester Company intends to put an automatic gun on the market. Such a slaughtering machine should not be put within the reach of the bristlebacks.* No true sportsman would be caught dead with an automatic gun. If such a weapon is put on the market, I shall never own one, and shall do all I can to prevent my friends buying one.[233]

The defenders of the new weapons expressed themselves as eloquently. One hunter philosophically said, "Do not call the gun the game hog, but the man behind it,"[234] Another enthusiast defended the repeating shotgun:

Because a man prefers a pump gun it is no sign he has bristles and desires to exterminate the game. A sportsman is not made or unmade by the gun he carries. I see no excuse for this tirade against the repeater. Limit the number of birds to the gun, or fish to the rod, if you will, but never undertake to dictate to the sportsmen of this great country that they must use a certain kind of gun to be called true sportsmen, or refrain from using another kind for fear of being called game hogs. . . .[235]

So a legislative tug-of-war, similar to the one that revolved around the use of bird dogs, was created between the advocates of repeater and automatic shotguns and those who believed in using only one and two shot weapons. Dogs and guns were favorite targets for the "do-gooders" to blame for the decreases in pioneer game in many parts of the nation.

A few years after the repeating and automatic shotguns were placed on the market there was talk of a magnum shotgun that would prove an aid to the hunter. As early as 1923 the following appeared in *Hunter, Trader and Trapper Magazine:*

Why not produce a longer shooting weapon for the shotgun crank? . . . The conditions which have brought about the need for a hi-powered rifle in the hunting fields are bringing, in fact, have brought about the need for a shotgun of greater range than those which can be purchased off of the manufacturers in the country . . . Why? For the reason that the remaining game is educated to the human wiles and their boomsticks, calling into use the longer range weapons. . . . One English firm has brought out a gun along these lines which they call "Magnum." These guns are made in ten and twelve gauge and weigh from eight to ten pounds which shoot a special case known as the "Perfect."

You ask 'where could such a type gun be in demand?' Were you ever out after grouse to have them flush thirty to thirty-five yards in the lead of you? That would be the time to swing up an American made gun with a range of eighty or more yards, would it not?[236]

*Favorite reference to the "game hog" in the early 1900's.
[232]*Recreation Magazine, Jan., 1905,* p. 47.
[233]Ibid., p. 49.
[234]*Recreation Magazine, April, 1900,* p. 299.
[235]Ibid., p. 297.
[236]*Hunter, Trader and Trapper Magazine, Jan., 1923,* p. 58.

As time went by the repeater, automatic, and magnum guns were accepted by the sportsmen with only one reservation — the Federal Act of 1935 which restricted the hunting of migratory birds to a shotgun which held more than three shells. This regulation was approved by President F. D. Roosevelt on February 2, 1935, and was written up in the March, 1935, issue of *North Dakota Outdoors*. The article quoted the Federal Bureau of Biological Survey as believing that the magazine shotgun, holding five or six shells, "contributed both to careless marksmanship and to excessive destruction of birds . . . Canada in six provinces and the Northwest Territories has legislated a prohibition against them, [guns holding more than three shells] similar action has been taken by two states . . ."[237]

This three shot limitation has been in effect until 1964 and many states, including North Dakota since 1935, have extended the regulation to the hunting of upland game birds.

First gun regulations in North Dakota went into effect after 1887 when the Territorial Legislature passed a law specifying that it would be unlawful to kill any wild duck, goose, or brant, "with a swivel gun, or any kind of gun, except such is commonly shot from the shoulder . . ."[238]

After 1909 North Dakota law prohibited the carrying of a shotgun in the field between June and the opening of the hunting season. Wardens often pointed out that it was difficult to prosecute violators under this law because of the conflicting federal law which permits citizens of the United States the right to bear arms at all times.

The practice of shooting waterfowl with a rifle was outlawed for the first time during the legislation of 1911-12.[239] This was extended to cover upland game birds in 1931.[240] The State Legislature of 1927 passed a law stating that "no gun larger than 10 gauge shotgun" shall be used for the hunting of game birds.[241]

Present Day

In the period around 1900 there were many small companies engaged in the manufacture of shotguns in the United States and overseas. But, like the hundreds of automobile makers, so common during the early years of the automobile's development, gunmakers flourished for a few years, and then dropped out of existence, or were incorporated into the few remaining large companies that we have today. With the passing of these small companies went many nostalgic names and unique guns — guns found today in museums or in the hands of private collectors.

We will never know what guns were most popular in North Dakota in the years gone by. Probably the list would have been more diversified, with more makers' names, than it is today. There would certainly have been names like Greener, Syracuse, Parker, LeFever, Davenport, and Baker. They were popular makers of fine double-barrels. The well-known names of today like Winchester, Remington, and Savage were also the choice of many hunters.

[237]North Dakota Outdoors, March, 1935, p. 7.
[238]*North Dakota State Game and Fish Dept., First Biennial Report*, 1893-94, p. 385.
[239]*North Dakota State Game and Fish Dept., Second Biennial Report*, 1911-12, p. 64.
[240]*North Dakota State Laws, 22nd Session, 1931*, p. 238.
[241]*North Dakota State Laws, 20th Session, 1927*, p. 201.

By 1900 the first repeaters and automatics were being used by hunters and, contrary to the wishes of their many critics, they were not ridiculed out of existence. The companies that made them, such as Winchester, Browning, and Savage, were not "blackballed" but are leading gunmakers of the 1960's.

In 1961 questions relative to the hunting of upland game were included on the annual fall hunter questionnaire. Approximately two thousand North Dakota hunters responded with information that gives us some idea of the types and makes of shotguns used for upland game hunting in this state. With the help of Jim Stewart of Bismarck, a veteran of over fifty years in the gun repair business, the returns from the two thousand hunters were tabulated. The results follow:

Shotgun gauge

The 12 gauge shotgun has probably been the most popular size for upland game shooting in the past and in the present. The following returns show three out of four shooters today prefer it to all other gauges.

1.	12	gauge —	1540 (76.9%)
2.	16	gauge —	225 (11.2%)
3.	20	gauge —	192 (9.6%)
4.	410	gauge —	40 (2.0%)
5.	28	gauge —	3 (trace)
6.	10	gauge —	2 (trace)

2002 hunters reporting

Shotgun action

Apparently two-thirds of the North Dakota hunters use one of the various repeating shotguns in the field. Generally, they are of lever, bolt, or pump action. Automatics may be regular or gas-operated action. Double-barrels include side-by-side and over-and under. Single-shots are either top lever or bolt action.

All repeaters	958 (62.3%)
All automatics	354 (23.0%)
All double-barrels	149 (9.7%)
All single-shots	76 (5.0%)

1537 hunters reporting

Shotgun makes

This section was not intended for commercial purposes but the results indicated the following manufacturer popularity:

1.	Winchester	724 (37.5%)
2.	Remington	471 (24.4%)
3.	Browning	164 (8.5%)
4.	Stevens	148 (7.7%)
5.	Ithaca	107 (5.5%)
6.	J. C. Higgins	94 (4.9%)
7.	Western Field	40 (2.1%)
8.	Savage	25 (1.3%)
9.	Mossberg	20 (1.0%)
10.	Marlin, H&R, I. Johnson, and L. C. Smith	52 (2+%)
11.	Odd United States and foreign makes	86 (4.5%)

1931 hunters reporting

The preceding group listed as "odd United States and foreign makes" includes a motley array of companies, models and gauges. It is an interesting group because here were placed many of the obsolete companies and guns. Such admirable and finely tooled weapons as Parker, Ithaca, L. C. Smith, Fox, and LeFever double-barrels fell into this category. The same might be said of uncommon and nearly forgotten names like Hercules, Fulton, Riverside, Ranger, Valiant, Meriden, Triumph, Columbia, Crescent-Davis, Hopkins-Allen, Invincible, Harper and many others. There were a few foreign made guns such as Beretta, Franchi and Aya Matador.

Shotgun models

The Winchester Model 12 has long been recognized as the most widely used shotgun in North Dakota. Table 27 below points out the fact that one of every five upland game hunters used this particular gun in 1961. Note, too, the popularity of the old Model 97 after a period of over sixty years on the market.

TABLE 27   POPULAR SHOTGUN MAKES AND MODELS IN
NORTH DAKOTA

	Make	Model	Action	No. of Hunters	Percent
1.	Winchester	No. 12	(pump)	372	19.3
2.	Remington	No. 870	(pump)	148	7.7
3.	Winchester	No. 97	(pump)	113	5.9
4.	Browning Lgt. 12, Std. 5 and Sweet 16		(auto.)	89	4.6
6.	Remington	No. 11 and No. 11-48	(auto.)	76	3.9
6.	Ithaca	No. 37	(pump)	64	3.3
7.	Winchester	No. 50	(auto.)	60	3.1
8.	Stevens	No. 311	(d. b.)	41	2.1
9.	J. C. Higgins	No. 20	(pump)	33	1.7
				996	51.6
10.	All other shotguns			935	48.4
	Total			1931	100.0

Double-barrels

There were only 149 double-barrels reported so the reliability of the following information is questionable. It is apparent, however, that the Stevens Model 311 is widely used.

1. Stevens 43
2. L. C. Smith 17
3. Browning 16
4. Winchester 15
5. Ithaca 7

98
6. All others 51

149 hunters reporting

Three hunters in the double-barrel class reported the use of the Winchester Model 21 for upland game. This gun, priced from $1,000 to $3,500, probably represents the "cream of the crop" as far as price is concerned at the present time.

11

Dogs and Upland Game Birds

Ever since the first half-wild, half-starved, wolf dogs of the Mandan Indians snapped angrily at the heels of the Lewis and Clark party, dogs have been a controversial subject among the outdoorsmen of North Dakota. Hunting dogs have been alternately blamed for game bird losses out of season or acclaimed for their usefulness in finding and retrieving crippled birds in season.

In the period around 1900 local hunters, market-hunters, and well-heeled nonresident sportsmen hunted at all seasons to take more than the accepted limits of birds. Dogs were universally employed by these men. As recently as the 1920's wealthy eastern and southern nonresident professional dog trainers traveled great distances to work their purebred dogs on prairie chickens and waterfowl. The general public was critical, perhaps jealous, of these groups of men and hastened to pass laws curtailing their activities. Only in the past twenty years, during which time many laws were passed to restrict hunting in other ways, has the general public accepted the legal employment of dogs for hunting upland game birds and waterfowl.

TED CORNELL

W. E. Webb, who hunted prairie chickens with dogs in Kansas, undoubtedly spoke objectively for many sportsmen of the 1870's:

> If any of my readers are fond of field sports, and have not yet shot prairie chickens over a dog, let them take their guns and hie to the West, and taste for themselves of this rare sport. . . . But with denser settlement come more guns, and, what is a far more destructive agent, trained dogs also. . . . With double-barrelled gun and keen-scented pointer, the sportsman and pot-hunter think nothing of fifty or sixty birds for a day's work. It seems almost impossible, under such combination, for a covey to escape total annihilation . . . without this useful animal [dog] the chickens would multiply, despite any number of hunters.[242]

This universal feeling that dogs were responsible for the over-kill of prairie chickens in North Dakota was voiced by H. V. Williams:

> During the years when the hunting dog was used the chicken decreased in numbers quite noticeably until they became very scarce. Added to the dog was the increase in the acreage of land put under cultivation, causing the destruction of most of their nesting grounds; but since the dog was prohibited and with the increase in the growing of alfalfa and like crops, this grand bird has made great strides towards increasing and is now rapidly coming back to former numbers. . . . In 1918, I think, the State Legislature passed the law prohibiting the use of so-called bird dogs and limiting the bag to five birds a day, and this fact alone meant the salvation of the Pinnated Grouse, which had no show whatsoever against the combination of dog and magazine shotgun.[243]

Shortly after restrictions were placed on hunting with bird dogs in 1919 (see Table 28) the North Dakota Game and Fish Board commented in its 1919-20 Biennial Report:

> It is conceded by everybody that grouse and prairie chickens were never more plentiful than they were the past two seasons and all true sportsmen together with a good many of those who at first opposed the law now are agreed that the bill cutting out the use of dogs was one of the most far-sighted pieces of legislation ever passed by a North Dakota Legislative Assembly for the conservation of game and should never be repealed if we want the growing generations to enjoy this great game bird.[244]

Although there were certain members of the Board of Control who were against hunting with dogs there were many who believed fewer birds were crippled, killed, or lost in this practice. This hassle continued until 1933 when the law was modified to permit the use of dogs for "retrieving" upland game birds. And finally, ten years later (1943), restrictions were further clarified when the laws stated any dog could be used for hunting upland game birds in season. By this time game bird populations were rapidly increasing and it was not difficult to ease up on practically all restrictions.

The percent of sportsmen who use a dog has not varied much since the early 1940's. In 1941 a sample of one hundred hunters reporting under the "retriever only" law showed that 11 percent were using dogs. And the following year (1942), the last for the "retriever only" law, 17 percent of a 1,500 hunter

[242]Webb, op. cit., p. 63.

[243]Williams, H. V., *Birds of the Red River Valley of Northeastern North Dakota*, p. 13.

[244]*North Dakota State Game and Fish Dept., Sixth Biennial Report*, 1919-20, p. 11.

sample reported they were using dogs for upland game hunting. A check of 721 parties at pheasant checking stations in western North Dakota in 1954 showed that one dog was being used for every eighteen hunters. During the 1963 hunting season the annual questionnaire, answered by approximately two thousand hunters, showed that a dog was used by one in six. This was a somewhat biased report, however, since all upland game and waterfowl were included in the questionnaire; only hunters who actually hunted in 1963 were tabulated in the total and not those who purchased a license but did not hunt.

No doubt the popularity of certain breeds of hunting dogs has changed considerably since 1900. Some of the now little known, seldom seen, breeds like the Irish Water Spaniel, widely used by the market hunters on waterfowl, and the pointers and setters, used so much for market hunting of prairie chickens, have declined in popularity. Meanwhile, breeds such as the Weimeraner and Brittany Spaniel, recently introduced to the United States from Europe, have gained in popularity. The current emphasis has been placed on the all-around dog for hunting. In 1954 the North Dakota Game Department interrogated owners of 125 dogs at pheasant checking stations and learned that the Labrador was the most popular breed (25 percent of the sample). Next in order in 1954 were the Cocker Spaniel, the Pointers, Weimeraner, Chesapeake Bay Retriever, the Setters, Golden Retriever, and the mixed group. The results of a larger sample in 1963 are shown in the accompanying table (Table 29) in which the Labrador is rated the most popular in this state.

TABLE 28

MAJOR DOG HUNTING REGULATION CHANGES IN NORTH DAKOTA
THROUGH THE YEARS

1891	First regulation on dogs. The state legislature restricted the use of dogs in the hunting of big game (deer, antelope, etc.). Hunting upland game birds *legal* in season.
1896-1908	A .75¢ license was required to hunt with a dog on one's own land or on another's. One could hunt his own land without a permit if he did not use a dog. Hunting upland game birds with dogs in season *legal*.
1909-14	Bird dogs were not allowed in the field with, or without, the owner between April 1 - August 15. Professional dog trainers not permitted in field with dogs between May 1 and August 15. Hunting upland game birds with dogs in season *legal*.
1915-18	Bird dogs not permitted to run loose with, or without, their owners between April 1 and August 1. Professional dog trainer's license required for the first time at the cost of $1.00 (res.) and $25.00 (nonres.). Hunting upland game birds with dogs in season *legal*.
1919-32	Bird dogs outlawed except for retrieving waterfowl. No bird dogs allowed to run loose, or with owners, in the field between April 1 and November 1. Hunting upland game birds with any type dog *illegal*.
1933-42	The hunting proclamation stated: "It is illegal to use dogs for hunting upland game birds EXCEPT that a SPANIEL or RETRIEVER may be used to RETRIEVE dead or wounded upland game birds. Use of Pointers, Setters, and Droppers is unlawful." Hunting upland game birds was *legal* but discriminatory as to breeds and methods of hunting.
1943-51	The State Legislature repealed the law prohibiting the use of certain bird dogs. House Bill No. 44 stated all types of dogs were *legal* to hunt upland game in season. Bird dogs were not allowed to run loose, or with owners, between April 1 and August 1.
1952-63	Nonresident hunters required to vaccinate dogs for rabies thirty days before their arrival in North Dakota. They must have the legal papers to show proof of vaccination. Hunting upland game birds with any type dog *legal* in season. Bird dogs not permitted to run loose, or with owners, between April 1 and August 1.

TABLE 29

BREEDS OF DOGS USED FOR HUNTING UPLAND GAME IN
NORTH DAKOTA DURING THE 1963 HUNTING SEASON
(Sample of approximately 2,050 hunters)

Purebred Labradors		99
Black Labrador	40	
Golden Labrador	12	
Unspecified Purebred Labradors	47	
Golden Retriever		25
German Short-haired Pointer		20
Cocker Spaniel		20
Springer Spaniel		18
Weimeraner		13
Brittany Spaniel		12
Chesapeake Bay Retriever		12
Setters (English, Irish, Llewellin)		9
Beagle		8
German Shepherd		6
Other Pureblood Breeds:		
Water Spaniel (3), Greyhound (3), Pointer (3), Coonhound (3), Poodle (2), Dalmatian (2), Norwegian Elkhound (1), Fox Terrier (1), Airedale (1), Collie (1), Border Collie (1), Dachshund (1), Sussex Spaniel (1)		23
Crossbreeds (mixed mutts, and mongrels)		36
TOTAL		301

12

Hunting Humor

Hunting is a hobby or pastime; few persons make it a business in North Dakota. And since it is a hobby there is ample time to laugh and have fun. North Dakota hunters have told their share of humorous anecdotes through the years. Some of the jokes have been repeated until they are a humdrum. What Department employee or farmer hasn't heard too many times the hunter's query, "Where have you got 'em tied up?" Or, "I wish I'd have bought a license!" just as the warden approaches a hunter in the field. The hunter has his license, of course, or he wouldn't have mentioned it.

A day's check by the warden or biologist means listening to all kinds of stories, many laced with humor. Perhaps he'll hear the one about the big city slicker who came to hunt pheasants but filled up the car trunk with meadowlarks. Or perhaps he was after deer but bagged a jackass and then drove proudly down main street with it draped across the hood of his "Caddy." Meadowlarks or donkeys, supposedly the hunter was so dumb he didn't know the difference between game and garbage and his mistake gave the locals and pros a real, live joke to pantomime at the corner bar.

Many of the celebrated humorists of our time have stated that comedy is not widely separated from tragedy. This is evident when we hear hunters' tall tales. In many cases a particular event only became humorous after a certain crisis was reached. When a man breaks through ice at 15° above zero while duck hunting the humor doesn't show up until later, at least not until he has scrambled out of the water and warmed up someplace. The shotgun that went off in the car and tore a hole in the floorboard wasn't a funny episode when it happened. Four hunters may have breathed a sigh of relief and then laughed heartily a few days later. Running onto a skunk in a buckbrush patch isn't exactly a joke at the time, especially if old Duke, the setter, forgot about pheasants and started nipping at the skunk. And is that the same Duke that found and gobbled down the lunch before you reached your favorite hunting spot last fall?

Some of the following incidents may not be as humorous as others but most of them could have happened to anyone.

Probably one of the earliest comic accounts to be written into North Dakota history concerned an incident which took place at Ft. Union August 7, 1843. Audubon, generally businesslike and serious in his diaries, wrote the following about his eastern taxidermist colleague Dr. John Bell as he was preparing to go on a collecting trip with two veteran frontiersmen:

> When Bell was fixing his traps on his horse this morning I was aroused to see Provost and LaFleur laughing outright at him, as he put on a Buffalo robe under his saddle, a blanket over it, and over that his mosquito bar and his rain protector. These old hunters could not understand why he needed these things to be comfortable; then besides he took a sack of ship-biscuit. Provost took only an old blanket, a few pounds of dried meat, and his tin cup, and rode off in his shirt and dirty breeches. LaFleur was worse off still, for he took no blanket, and said he could borrow Provost's tin cup; but he being a most temperate man, carried a bottle of whiskey to mix with the brackish water found in the Mauvaises Terres [Badlands] among which they have to travel till their return.[245]

---

[245]Audubon, op. cit., p. 137.

A modern parallel to this episode could well be a pair of unshaven, dungaree-clad, near-poachers armed with "Long Tom" shotguns, accompanied by their once-a-year city, hunting friend attired in a shell-laden nylon vest and dark shooter's glasses, and carrying the bluest of magnum shotguns.

Guns and the art of shooting have motivated many humorous anecdotes through the years. Henry Boller, an early fur trading agent stationed at Ft. Berthold in the 1850's and 1860's, left us one of the first good gun tales:

> I was greatly amused at watching one of the Indians load his fusee. After a double handful of powder, he put in nine half-ounce balls, one upon another, with a large wad of red flannel between each. The gun was literally loaded halfway up to the muzzle, and it seemed to me as if the safest place when fired off would have been directly in front.[246]

Easterner William Webb did not hunt prairie chickens in North Dakota but the events he described while hunting them in Kansas in the 1870's could have happened in this state. One hunter in Webb's party nicknamed "the Professor" offered this sage advice about bird shooting:

> In my father's day the rule was, when a bird rose, for a hunter to take out his snuff box, take snuff, replace the box, aim, and fire. You may find the advice yet in some works. The shot then has distance in which to spread.

An Irishman in the Webb party named Dobeen:

> . . . begged leave to inform our 'honors' that in Ireland, after a bird rose, the rule was, instead of taking snuff, to take off the boots before firing. The Professor thought that such a habit related to out-running the game keeper, and was intended to procure distance for the poacher rather than the bird.

Still another hunter in the Webb Expedition referred to an old-timer who hunted with a Revolutionary War musket:

> The recoil was tremendous, and the old man often went down before the bird; but such positions, he asserted, were taken voluntarily, as ones of rest. Some said that the gun had been known to kick him again after he was down.[247]

The famous frontier artist Frederic Remington visited North Dakota to hunt in the 1890's and while after prairie chickens in the Valley City area, could not resist making light of his own shooting mistakes:

> The Doctor shoots well and indeed prairie chickens are not difficult, but I am discouraged. As the great sportsman Soapy Sponge used to say, 'I'm a good shooter, but a bad hitter.' It was in this distressful time that I remembered the words of the old hunter who had charge of my early education in .45 calibres, which ran, 'Take yer time, sonny, and always see your hind sight.' and by dint of doing this I soon improved to a satisfactory extent.[248]

Another visitor who recognized the comic in North Dakota hunting was J. H. Tuttle, writer of *Wam-Dus-Ky*, an account of a well-heeled Minneapolis-St. Paul

---

[246]Boller, op. cit., p. 36.
[247]Webb, op. cit., p. 70.
[248]Remington, op. cit., p. 104.

party that visited Stump Lake in the fall of 1892.   Concerning the dismal success of some of his hunting companions (or himself) he wrote:

> Dr. and Mrs. Lutett made a good many holes in the sky, but none in the birds; at least not one of them came down to testify to any harm it received.   The Dr. did, however, during the day, as a mere experiment, aim and fire at a snipe sitting on the opposite shore of the stream, and strangely enough, with fatal results.   The mistake haunted him.   He thought it singular that he should miss what he tried to shoot and shoot what he wanted to miss.[249]

At another point in this book Tuttle commented on one of the lady hunters who employed a light gauge gun with woeful success:

> The results on this and other occasions indicated, to be sure, more boldness than skill, but it should be remembered that she had had no practice of this kind, that these were her first lessons in the art of shooting.   And, besides, she insisted, with some reason, that her capacity for duck hunting had been slightly insulted by the very small, light gun which had been given her.   'Who,' she asked, 'can shoot ducks, geese, especially with such a pop-gun as this?'   It was doubtless an efficient gun for that size and weight, but its leaden pellets were too short-winded for a long race. If the holes they made in the sky could have been left and seen, as in a target, they would have shown that Nellie had, after all, a great deal of faith in the power of these pellets, and that she did not sit and sulk because she was not considered mature enough to use a larger gun.[250]

Old-timer Ben Baenen of Jamestown was loyal to his old muzzle-loading shotgun for some time after most other hunters were changing over to more modern guns.   His final trip with the weapon ended abruptly:

> When I had the old muzzle-loading 12 gauge shotgun I bought my shot and powder and used three drams of black powder per load.   The best wadding I ever found was hornets' nests; they wadded down real good.   I gathered them whenever I found one and took them home.   Anyway, I kept this old muzzle-loader until the late 1890's when I went hunting geese with my brother Tony south of Jamestown. When Tony shot seven geese with his new breech-loading gun while I was still loading up that did it!   I got mad and slammed down the muzzle-loader and broke the stock. That was the last time I ever used that gun.

When John Bert Johnstone was a young fellow at the family farm near Emerado in 1898 his mother called him out of bed one night to do something about a commotion in the family chicken house.   For several nights an unknown marauder had been giving the chickens fits.   As young John Bert charged out the back door he grabbed a trusty double-barreled shotgun.   He had no sooner stepped into the dim light when he saw a movement and, raising his gun, fired both barrels.   Then he went on to the chicken house where he saw a skunk chasing the chickens.   He reloaded the gun and killed the skunk.

The next morning as the family came to the breakfast table John Bert's father looked out the kitchen window and saw his favorite yellow corduroy pants waving in the morning breeze with the seat shot out.   John Bert's mother could see what was coming and hastened to temper her husband by saying,

---

[249]Tuttle, op. cit., p. 51.

[250]Ibid., p. 84.

"Now don't get mad, dad, Bert shot the skunk!" The elder Johnstone growled back, "Well, did he think it had wings?" It was one time the father didn't appreciate John Bert's shooting!

Pioneer lawyer H. B. Spiller of Cavalier tells of the hunting trip he made with a friend in the early 1900's:

> Our hunt was to be a goose hunt at Glasston Slough in Pembina County. We stopped at the Olson Shanty, a cabin used by hunters for sleeping or getting out of the weather. We had a bottle of whiskey with us and didn't dare leave it in the shack where other hunters would find it. I hid the bottle in the grass outside the building and Gill took off north while I went south to do my hunting. A few hours later I returned to find Gill standing outside the shack yelling excitedly, 'Is kerosene poison? Is kerosene poison?' He explained that he'd found a whiskey bottle on the cabin table and it had the same label as ours. He took a drink before he realized the contents. Although upset for an hour or two he soon recovered from the ordeal.

Veteran trapper John Aarestad of McHenry recalled an eventful winter day in 1906 when he trapped five skunks on the James River near Bordulac and decided to take them with him by train from Bordulac to Rodgers and on to Hannaford:

> I did not have time to skin the skunks, so they were dumped into a gunny sack and tied with binder twine. I had a sack of furs, a sack of traps, the sack of un-skinned skunks, a bicycle, two guns, and a dog to take home. Towards evening it started snowing from the southeast and the train from the west was several hours late. I told the depot agent I had some packages, a bicycle, and a dog I wanted to check on my ticket. I also put a tag on the skunk package.
>
> When the train came I barely got on with all my luggage. Since we were traveling against the wind the train was soon filled with the skunk smell. Some highfalutin' ladies seated near me started twisting their noses and some gentlemen began laughing at the ladies. Nearly everyone thought the train had run over a skunk. Two who knew differently were the baggage man and me. I don't know how he stood it in that car!
>
> We got to Rogers at 2:00 a.m. and unloaded. It was time to change trains now. When I tried to check the packages on the train for Hannaford the agent wouldn't do it. I had come as far as I could with my package of skunks.

The same year (1906), and at about the same time trapper Aarestad was having his troubles transporting skunks by rail, Glen Wood of Emmonsburg was off on his annual deer hunt in the Glencoe Bottoms of the Missouri River with

Charlie Coventry and Wallace Kyes.   This period was the worst in history for the deer population but Glen says there was still some humor left in the situation:

> We'd hunted for about six days in the willows and hadn't seen a deer. Bill Jones and Pete Shier were hunting there, too, and Bill said, 'Let's have some fun!' and fired his gun into the air three times.   As the shots reverberated in the bottoms he hallooed 'there he goes — going north!'   Believe it or not we counted thirty-four hunters who'd climbed the small cottonwoods trying to spot the deer that wasn't there.

One of the most famous coyote and wolf hunters in the United States around the turn of the century was Adam Lesmeister of Harvey, a powerfully built German emigrant carrying 250 pounds on a five foot eight inch frame.   He hunted strictly with dogs and never killed a coyote or wolf with a gun although he accounted for over 18,000 of these predators in the years 1889-1931.   After 1915 he was accompanied on hunts by his sons Frank and Wendelin, and Frank passed along this amusing episode in July, 1960.

> It was in the period around 1920 and the three of us were hunting with a two horse, four-wheeled, spring buggy when suddenly we spotted a coyote and let the hounds out of their cage.   They took off with us right after them at top speed.   Our little team of half-Belgian, half-Arabian horses were about as smart as the dogs on the chase.   My father often stood upright and let the reins lay in the seat.   Suddenly on this particular chase the buggy pitched after hitting a rock or a hole and my father was thrown out backwards landing on the back of his neck and shoulders.   By the time my brother and I got the horses stopped and turned around Adam was just rolling back to a sitting position.   As we came up to him expecting the worst he gazed off in the general direction of the chase and uttered in a husky, almost unintelligible voice, 'Where's the dogs?'   He was still very much in the hunt even though the fall laid him up for three or four days with bumps and bruises.

The North Dakota Badlands have always been a celebrated area when it comes to hunting.   Since the ranchers who live there are particularly adept at relating humorous stories, it is only natural that the hunting tales from this region are some of the best.   Old-timer Arthur Parker of Dickinson knew many of the buffalo hunters and trail drivers that lived in the Badlands in the 1870's and 80's.   One of his best anecdotes concerns Johnny Davis, a man still remembered by many people in the ranch country:

> Johnny Davis was one of the early buffalo hunters who came here from Pennsylvania in 1882.   The hunt was just about over by this time but he got in on the tail end of it.   One evening about dusk he was sitting alone at his camp near Black Butte when he saw a rider in the distance zig-zagging toward him.   As the heavily-bearded stranger drew near, Johnny noted he was a rough looking fellow and the thought of how to get rid of him as quickly as possible ran through Johnny's mind.   The stranger spoke first 'Well, you've got company,' in a bold tone.   Johnny's curt reply was, 'I'll feed you but you can't stay!'   The stranger asked, 'Why?' in a gruff voice.   Quick-thinking Johnny, momentarily elated by his own resourcefulness, answered clearly and deliberately, 'Because I've got lice!'   There was a pause as the unruffled visitor took his gaze off his host for the first time, threw a leg over the saddle, and with his back to Johnny began taking down his bed roll.   Suddenly, as though inspired by thought, he turned, and with a twinkle in his eye calmly said 'That's all right kid, I've got 'em, too!'   The two men spent the night together without further incident.

North Dakota Counties and Towns Mentioned in This Book.

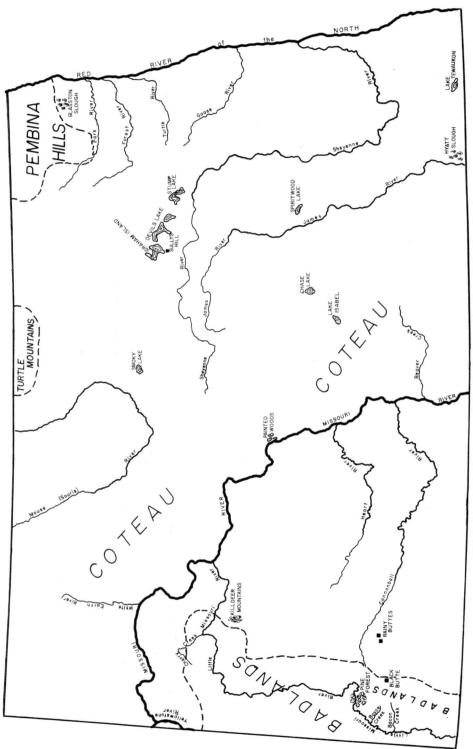

Chief Physical Features of North Dakota Mentioned in the Text.

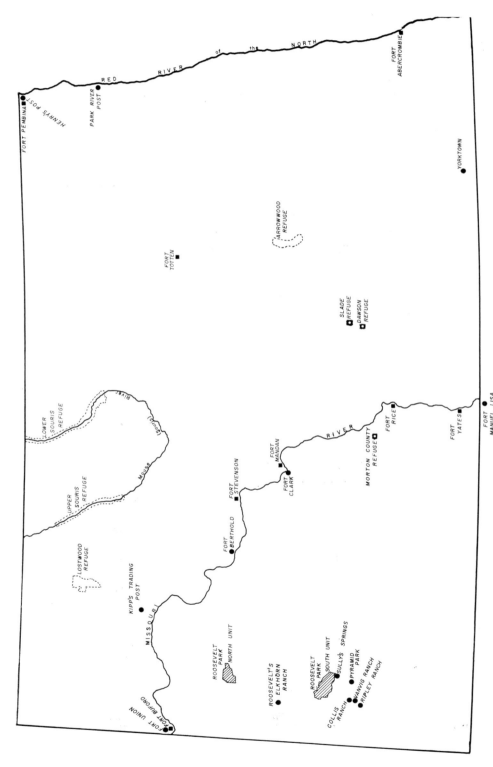

Early Settlements, Refuges, and Parks Mentioned in This Book.

Books and Periodicals

Adams, Arthur W. 1961. *Furbearers of North Dakota.* N. Dak. State Game and Fish Dept., 102 pp.

Aldous, Shaler. 1943. "Sharp-tailed Grouse in the Sand Dune Country of North-central North Dakota." Reprinted from the *Jour. of Wildl. Mgmt.,* Vol. 7, No. 1, Jan., pp. 23-31.

Allen, Durward. 1956. *Pheasants in North America.* Harrisburg, Penn.: Stackpole Co., 490 pp.

Allen, William A. 1903. *Adventures with Indians and Game, or Twenty Years in the Rocky Mountains.* Chicago: A. W. Bowen Co., 302 pp.

Ammann, G. A. 1957. *The Prairie Grouse of Michigan.* Lansing: Mich. Dept. of Cons., Game Div., 200 pp.

Anonymous. 1942. *The Wild Turkey in Virginia, its Habits and Management.* Richmond: Va. Comm. of Game and Inland Fisheries, 45 pp.

Anonymous. 1943. *North Dakota Offers Variety in Hunting.* Bismarck: N. Dak. State Game and Fish Dept., 31 pp.

Anonymous. 1955. *North Dakota Wild Turkey Story.* Bismarck-Mandan: Mo. Slope Chapt. Izaak Walton League of Amer., 4 pp.

Audubon, Maria. 1960. *Audubon and His Journals.* New York: Dover Publ., Inc. 2 vols., 1086 pp.

Bach, Roy N. 1949. *The Red Fox in North Dakota.* Bismarck: N. Dak. State Game and Fish Dept., 31 pp.

——————————. 1944. *Comparative Data, North Dakota Upland Game, 1942-44.* Bismarck, N. Dak. State Game and Fish Dept., 24 pp.

Baker, Maurice F. 1953. *Prairie Chickens of Kansas.* Lawrence: Univ. of Kans., Misc. Publ. No. 5, 68 pp.

Barton, O. A. 1939. *Turkeys, Origin, and History and Distribution.* Fargo: N. Dak. State Coll. Ext. Serv., Circ. No. 167, 11 pp.

Bendire, Capt. Charles. 1892. *Life Histories of North American Birds.* Washington, D. C.: Govt. Printing Office, U. S. Natl. Mus., Spec. Bull. No. 1, 446 pp.

Bent, Arthur C. 1963. *Life Histories of North American Gallinaceous Birds.* New York: Dover Publ., Inc., 490 pp.

Bismarck Tribune Newspaper. 1960-63. Bismarck, N. Dak. Excerpts from "Way Back When" column.

Black, R. M. 1929. *History of Dickey County, North Dakota.* Ellendale: N. Dak. State Normal Coll., 333 pp.

Bogardus, Adam H. 1874. *Field, Cover and Trap Shooting.* New York: J. B. Ford Co., 343 pp.

Boller, Henry A. 1868. *Among the Indians, Eight Years in the Far West — 1858-1866.* Philadelphia: T. Ellwood Zell, 428 pp.

Boom. Feb., 1964. Milwaukee, Wisc. Vol. 3, No. 1, (Quarterly Report of Soc. of Tympanuchus cupido pinnatus Ltd.).

Brackenridge, H. M. 1904. *Journal of a Voyage up the Missouri.* 1811. Edited by R. G. Thwaites. Cleveland, Ohio: Arthur Clark Co., 163 pp.

Brower, J. V. 1904. *Mandan Contributions by E. R. Steinbreuck. Mem. of Explor. in the Basin of the Miss.,* Vol. VIII. St. Paul, Minn: McGill-Warner Co., 158 pp.

Bryant, William C. n.d., *Poems.* New York: Hurst and Co., 337 pp.

Burroughs, Raymond D. 1961. *The Natural History of the Lewis and Clark Expedition.* Lansing: Mich. State Univ. Press, 340 pp.

Coffin, Charles C. 1870. *The Seat of Empire.* Boston: Fields, Osgood and Co., 232 pp.

Cooke, W. W. 1888. *Report on Bird Migration in the Mississippi Valley in the Years 1884 and 1885.* Edited by C. H. Merriam. Washington, D. C.: U. S. Govt. Printing Office, Dept. of Agric. Ornith. Bull., No. 2, 313 pp.

Coues, Elliott. 1874. *Birds of the Northwest.* Washington, D. C.: U. S. Govt. Printing Office, Dept. of Inter. Misc. Publ., No. 3, 791 pp.

Cowdrey, Mary B. 1937. *The Checkered Years.* Caldwell, Idaho: Caxton Printers Ltd., 265 pp.

Crawford, Lewis F. 1931. *History of North Dakota.* Chicago and New York: Amer. Hist. Soc., Inc., 3 vols., 1911 pp.

Dakota Legislative Assembly Laws, 1869-89. (In N. Dak. State Hist. Soc. Lib.)

Dale, Fred H. 1943. "History and Status of the Hungarian Partridge in Michigan." Reprinted from the *Jour. of Wildl. Mgmt.,* Vol. 7, No. 4, Oct., pp. 368-377.

Denig, E. T. 1930. *Indian Tribes of the Upper Missouri.* Washington, D. C.: U. S. Govt. Printing Office, Bur. of Amer. Ethnol., 46th Annual Report, 1928-29, pp. 375-628.

------------------------------------. 1961. *Five Indian Tribes of the Upper Missouri.* Edited by John Ewers. Norman: Univ. of Okla. Press, 217 pp.

Dickinson Press Newspaper. July 2, 1957. Dickinson, N. Dak.

Dictionary of Americanisms. 1951. Edited by M. M. Matthews. Univ. of Chicago Press, 2 vols., 1946 pp.

Eastman, Frank C. 1936. *Enjoyment of Laughter.* New York: Simon and Schuster Co., 368 pp.

Edminster, Frank C. 1954. *American Game Birds of Field and Forest.* New York: Scribner's and Sons, 490 pp.

Elton, Charles S. 1958. *The Ecology of Invasions by Animals and Plants.* London, Eng.: Methuen and Co. Ltd., 181 pp.

Errington, Paul L. and F. N. Hamerstrom, Jr. 1938. "Observations on the Effect of a Spring Drought on Reproduction in the Hungarian Partridge." Reprinted from *The Condor,* Vol. XL, Mar-Apr., pp. 71-73.

Fernald, M. L. 1950. *Gray's Manual of Botany.* (8th ed.) New York: American Book Co., 1632 pp.

Flandrau, Grace. 1925. "The Verendrye Overland Quest of the Pacific." Reprinted from the *Oreg. Hist. Soc.,* Vol. XXVI, No. 2, Great Northern Railway, 64 pp.

Forester, Frank. 1848. *Field Sports in the United States and the British Provinces of America.* London, Eng.: R. Bentley, Vol. 1, 344 pp.

Gier, H. T. 1957. *Coyotes in Kansas.* Manhattan: Kans. Exp. Stat. Bull. No. 393. 95 pp.

Gillmore, Parker. 1874. *Prairie and Forest, A Description of the Game of North America.* New York: Harper and Bros., 378 pp.

Grange, Wallace B. 1948. *Wisconsin Grouse Problems.* Madison: Wisc. Cons. Dept. Publ. No. 328, 318 pp.

Hamerstrom, F. N., Jr. 1939 "A Study of Wisconsin Prairie Chicken and Sharp-tailed Grouse." Reprinted from *The Wilson Bull.,* Vol. 51, No. 2, June, pp. 105-120.

------------------------------------ and Frances Hamerstrom. 1949. "Daily and Seasonal Movements of Wisconsin Prairie Chickens." Reprinted from *The Auk,* Vol. 66, Oct., 313-337 pp.

-----------------------------, Oswald E. Mattson and Frances Hamerstrom. 1957. *A Guide to Prairie Chicken Management.* Madison: Wisc. Cons. Dept., Tech. Wildl. Bull. No. 15, 128 pp.

Hammond, Merrill C. 1941. "Fall and Winter Mortality Among Hungarian Partridges in Bottineau and McHenry Counties, North Dakota." Reprinted from the *Jour. of Wildl. Mgmt.*, Vol. 5, No. 4, Oct., 375-382 pp.

Harper's Weekly, A Journal of Civilization. 1871-78. Vols. XV, XVII, XVIII, XIX, XX, XXII. New York: Harpers Bros.

Hatch, P. L. 1892. *First Report of the State Zoologist accompanied with notes on the Birds of Minnesota.* Minneapolis: Harrison and Smith, 487 pp.

Henry, Alexander. 1897. *The Manuscript Journals of Alexander Henry, Fur Trader of the Northwest Company and David Thompson, years 1799-1814.* Edited by Elliott Coues. New York: F. P. Harper, 3 vols., 1027 pp.

Henshaw, Henry W. 1918. *The Book of Birds, Common Birds of Town and Country and American Game Birds.* Washington, D. C.: Publ. of Natl. Geog. Soc., 195 pp.

Hornaday, William T. 1931. *Thirty Years War for Wild Life.* Stamford, Conn.: Gillespie Bros., Inc., 292 pp.

Hunter, Trader and Trapper Magazine, Jan., 1923, Vol. XLVIII, No. 4.

Huntington, Dwight W. 1907. *Our Feathered Game, A Handbook of North American Game Birds.* New York: Scribner's and Sons, 396 pp.

Irving, Washington. 1956. *A Tour of the Prairies.* Edited by John F. McDermott. Norman: Univ. of Okla. Press, 214 pp.

Jamestown's Diamond Jubilee, 1883-1958. 1958. n.p., 93 pps.

Judd, Elmer T. 1917. *List of North Dakota Birds found in the Big Coulee, Turtle Mountains and Devils Lake Region.* Cando, N. Dak.: Publ. by the author, 29 pp.

Judd, S. D. 1905. *The Bobwhite and Other Quails of the United States and Their Economic Relations.* Washington, D. C.: U. S. Govt. Printing Office, U. S. Dept. of Agric. Bull. No. 21, 66 pp.

-----------------------------. 1905. *The Grouse and Wild Turkeys of the United States and Their Economic Value.* Washington, D. C.: U. S. Govt. Printing Office, U. S. Dept. of Agric. Bull. No. 24, 55 pp.

Klett, A. T. 1957. *Banding and Marking Methods in Studying Seasonal Movements of the Sharp-tailed Grouse in Morton County, North Dakota.* Logan: Utah State Coll. Unpubl. Master's thesis, 53 pp.

Kokes, Otakar and Eduard Knobloch. 1947. *KOROPTEV. The Partridge, Its Life History, Propagation and Hunting.* Prague, Czechoslovakia: Scientific Text Publ., Eng. Trans. by Canad. Wildl. Serv., 278 pp.

Kurz, Rudolph F. 1937. *Journal of Rudolph Friederich Kurz, 1846-1852.* Edited by J. N. B. Hewitt. Washington, D. C.: U. S. Govt. Printing Office, Bur. of Amer. Ethnol. Bull. No. 115, 382 pp.

Larson, Adrian. 1928. "Birds of Eastern McKenzie County, North Dakota." Reprinted from *The Wilson Bull.*, Vol. XV, Mar. pp. 39-48, June, pp. 100-110.

Lee, Charles. 1899. *The Long Ago.* Walhalla, N. Dak.: The Mountaineer Press, 7 pp.

Leopold, Aldo. 1931. *Report on a Game Survey of the North Central States,* Madison, Wisc.: Sporting Arms and Ammo. Manuf. Inst., 299 pp.

-----------------------------. 1933. *Game Management.* New York: Scribner's and Sons, 481 pp.

-----------------------------. 1936. "Farm Game Management in Silesia." Reprinted from *Amer. Wildl.*, Sept.-Oct., 10 pp.

Lewis and Clark Expedition, 1804-1806. 1952. Omaha, Nebr.: Publ. of the Corps of Engineers, U. S. Army Office of Dist. Engin., Aug., 201 pp.

Lewis, Elisha J. 1857. *The American Sportsman.* Philadelphia: J. B. Lippencott and Co., 510 pp.

Luttig, John C. 1920. *Luttig's Journal of a Fur Trading Expedition on the Upper Missouri, 1812-1813.* Edited by Stella M. Drumm. St. Louis: Mo. Hist. Soc., 192 pp.

Maximilian, Prince of Wied. 1905. *Travels in the Interior of North America, Maximilian of Wied.* Edited by R. G. Thwaites. Cleveland, Ohio: Arthur H. Clark Co., 3 vols., 1134 pp.

Mershon, William B. 1923. *Recollections of my Fifty Years Hunting and Fishing.* Boston: The Stratford Co., 259 pp.

Migration of Birds. May, 1962. Washington, D. C.: U. S. Dept. of Inter., Fish and Wildl. Serv., Cons. Note No. 8, 8 pp.

Monson, Gale W. 1934. "Birds of Berlin and Harwood Townships, Cass County, North Dakota." Reprinted from *The Wilson Bull.,* Vol. XLV, Mar., pp. 37-58.

Museum Review. Oct., 1946. Bismarck State Hist. Soc. of N. Dak., Vol. 1, No. 10, 8 pp.

North Dakota History. 1928-49. Vols. 1, 2, 15 and 16. State Hist. Soc. of N. Dak.

North Dakota Legislative Assembly Laws. 1889-1963.

North Dakota Outdoors. 1931-63. Bismarck, N. Dak.: Monthly publ. of the State Game and Fish Dept.

North Dakota State Game and Fish Department Annual and Biennial Reports. 1891-1963.

North Dakota State Game and Fish Department. 1940-64. *Pittman-Robertson Project Reports.*

Ord, George. 1894. *A reprint of North American Zoology . . .* Edited by Samuel Rhoads. Haddonfield, N. J.: Publ. by the editor, 2 vols., 290-360 pp.

Ordal, Norman J. 1952. "The Hungarian Partridge." Reprinted from the *Cons. Volunteer* (Minn.), Vol. 15, Jan.-Feb., pp. 26-32.

Outdoor Life. Jan., 1905. Denver, Colo.: Vol. XV, No. 1.

Over, W. H. and C. S. Thomas. 1946. *Birds of South Dakota.* Vermillion, S. Dak.: Univ. of S. Dak. Mus. Natural Hist. Studies No. 1, 200+ pp.

Palliser, John. 1856. *The Solitary Hunter, or Sporting Adventures in the Prairies.* London, Eng.: George Routledge and Co., 234 pp.

Patterson, Robert L. 1952. *The Sage Grouse in Wyoming.* Denver, Colo.: Sage Books Inc., Wyo. Game and Fish Comm., Fed. Aid Proj. 28-R, 341 pp.

Pennsylvania Game News. April, 1963. Harrisburg: Monthly magazine of the Penn. Game Comm.

Petrides, George A. 1951. "Notes on Age Determination in Juvenal European Quail," *Jour. of Wildl. Mgmt.,* Vol. 15, No. 1, Jan., pp. 116-117.

Phillips, John C. 1928. *Wild Birds Introduced or Transplanted in North America.* Washington, D. C.: U. S. Govt. Printing Office, U. S. Dept. of Agric., Tech. Bull. No. 61, 64 pp.

Porter, Richard. 1955. "The Hungarian Partridge in Utah." Salt Lake City: Reprinted from the *Jour. of Wildl. Mgmt.,* Vol. 19, No. 1, pp. 93-109.

Recreation Magazine. 1897-1905. New York: G. O. Shields, Vol. VII, XII, XIII and XXII.

Remington, Frederic. 1961. *Pony Tracks.* Norman: Univ. of Okla. Press, 176 pp.

Roberts, T. S. 1932. *The Birds of Minnesota.* Minneapolis: Univ. of Minn. Press, 2 vols., 1512 pp.

Roe, Frank G. 1951. *The North American Buffalo, a critical study of the species in its wild state.* Toronto, Canad.: Univ. of Toronto Press, 957 pp.

Roosevelt, Theodore. 1885. *Hunting Trips of a Ranchman.* New York: G. P. Putnam's Sons, 328+ pp.

Rowan, William. 1961. *The Ten Year Cycle.* Calgary, Alberta: P. F. Collier and Son, 384 pp.

Ruffed Grouse Society of America (Newsletter). April, 1963. Monterey, Va.: Vol. 1, No. 1, 8 pp.

Scott, T. C. and G. O. Hendrickson. 1936. *Upland Game Birds of Iowa.* Ames: Iowa State Coll. Ext. Serv., Circ. No. 228, 32 pp.

Sears, Robert. 1847. *Information for the People, or Treasury of Useful Knowledge,* New York: J. S. Redfield, Clinton Hall, 530 pp.

Sharp, Ward M. 1957. "Social and Range Dominance in Gallinaceous Birds, Pheasants and Prairie Grouse," *Jour. of Wildl. Mgmt.,* Vol. 21, No. 2, April, pp. 242-244.

Shields, G. O. 1883. *Hunting in the Great West.* Chicago and New York: Belford, Clarke, and Co., 306 pp.

Shoenberger, J. H. 1934. *From the Great Lakes to the Pacific.* San Antonio, Texas: Naylor Co., 211 pp.

Shrader, Thomas A. and Arnold B. Erickson. 1944. *Upland Game Birds of Minnesota.* St. Paul: Minn. Dept. of Cons., Bull. No. 8, 39 pp.

Silvonen, Lauri. 1956. *The Correlation between the Fluctuations of Partridges and European Hare Populations and the Climatic Conditions of Winters in Southwest Finland during the Last Thirty Years.* Helsinki, Finland: Finnish Game Foundation, Bull. No. 17, 30 pp.

South Dakota Game and Fish Dept. 1941. *Fifty Million Pheasants in South Dakota.* WPA project. Pierre, publ. by S. Dak. Game Dept., 90 pp.

South Dakota Department of Game Fish and Parks. 1959. *Looking Back Past 50 Years.* Edited by Don Hipschman. Pierre: S. Dak. Dept. of Game, Fish and Parks Annual Report, 1954 pp.

Stevens, O. A. 1963. *Handbook of North Dakota Plants.* Fargo: N. Dak. State Univ. Inst. of Regional Studies, 324 pp.

Stewart, Omer C. 1953. "Why the Great Plains are Treeless." Reprinted from *Colorado Quarterly,* summer, Vol. 2, No. 1, pp. 40-50.

Stone, Howard L. 1945. *A Letter to the Lover of the Outdoors, a History of the North Dakota Wildlife Federation,* 8 pp.

Tabeau, Pierre-Antoine. 1939. *Tabeau's Narrative of Loisel's Expedition to the Upper Missouri.* Edited by Annie H. Abel. Norman: Univ. of Okla. Press, 272 pp.

Taverner, P. A. 1940. *Birds of Canada.* Ottawa: Nat. Mus. of Canad., 446 pp.

Taylor, Joseph H. 1906. *Beavers and Their Ways.* Washburn, N. Dak.: Publ. by the author, 218 pp.

Trippensee, Reuben E. 1948. *Wildlife Management, Upland Game and General Principles.* New York: McGraw-Hill Book Co., Inc., 479 pp.

Trobriand, Phillippe Regis de. 1951. *Military Life in Dakota, the Journal of Phillippe Regis de Trobriand.* Edited by Lucile M. Kane. St. Paul, Minn.: Alvord Memorial Comm., 395+ pp.

Tuttle, J. H. 1893. *Wam-dus-ky.* Descriptive record of a hunting trip to N. Dak. in 1892. Minneapolis; Hall, Black and Co., 178 pp.

Van Tramp, John C. 1860. *Prairie and Rocky Mountain Adventures, or Life in the West.* St. Louis, Mo.: H. Miller, 640 pp.

Webb, William E. 1872. *Buffalo Land.* Philadelphia: Hubbard Bros., 503 pp.

Westerskov, Kaj.   1948.   *Management Practices for the European Partridge in Ohio and Denmark and Remarks on General Decline Factors.*   Ann Arbor, Mich.: (Mimeo. presentation at 10th Midwest Wildl. Conf.) 4 pp.

————————————————.   1958.   "The Partridge as a Game Bird."   Wellington, New Zealand: Reprinted from *New Zealand Outdoors*, Vol. 22, No. 12, Feb., 10 pp.

Williams, H. V.   1926.   "Birds of the Red River Valley of Northeastern North Dakota."   Reprinted from *The Wilson Bull.*, Mar.-June, 37 pp.

Wood, Norman A.   1923.   *A Preliminary Survey of the Bird Life of North Dakota.*   Ann Arbor: Univ. of Mich., Misc. Publ. No. 10, 97 pp.

Woolworth, Alan R. and W. Raymond Wood.   1960.   *The Archeology of a Small Trading Post (Kipp's) in the Garrison Reservoir, North Dakota.*   Washington, D. C.: U. S. Govt. Printing Office, Bur. of Amer. Ethnol., Bull. No. 176, pp. 239-305.

Yaggy, L. W.   1903.   *How to Do.*   Chicago and Valparaiso, Ind.: Powers, Higley and Co., 1012 pp.

Yeatter, Ralph E.   1948.   *Bird Dogs in Sport and Conservation.*   Urbana: Ill. Natural Hist. Survey, Circ. 42, 64 pp.

Yocum, Charles F.   1943.   "The Hungarian Partridge in the Palouse Region, Washington."   Pullman, Wash.: Reprinted from *Ecological Monographs* No. 13, April, pp. 167-202.

Letters, Manuscripts

Berg, Howard O., Devils Lake, N. Dak., *Letter,* July 24, 1963.

Bossenmaier, Eugene F., Dept. of Mines and Natural Resources, Game Branch, Winnipeg, Manitoba, Canad., *Letter,* March 14, 1961.

Coleman, David C., State of Kansas Forestry, Fish and Game Commission, Pratt, Kans., *Letter,* Dec. 3, 1963.

Craig, Vernon, I and E Div. of Montana Dept. of Fish and Game, Helena, Mont., *Letter,* March 22, 1961.

North Dakota Game and Fish Dept. Records, 1896-98 (In State Hist. Soc. Library, Bismarck).

Duebbert, Harold, U. S. Fish and Wildl. Serv., Devils Lake, N. Dak., *Letter,* March 27, 1964.

Eng, Robert L., State of Montana Dept. of Fish and Game, Helena, Mont., *Letters,* May 6 and July 26, 1963.

Erickson, Arnold B., Minnesota Dept. of Conservation, St. Paul, Minn., *Letter,* Sept. 11, 1961.

Green, Duane L., Deputy State Forester, Bottineau, N. Dak., *Letters,* May 28 and June 24, 1963. N. Dak., *Letter,* May 9, 1963.

Hamerstrom, F. N., Jr., Trans. of Midwest Prairie Chicken Conf., *Unpubl. Paper* at Emporia, Kans., March 16-18, 1959.

Hoffman, Donald M., State of Colorado, Dept. of Game and Fish, Denver, Colo., *Letter,* April 4, 1963.

Howard, Dr. James, University of North Dakota, Dept. of Sociol. and Anthrop., Grand Forks, N. Dak., *Letter,* May 9, 1963.

Hyatt, Everett G., Ludden, N. Dak., *Letter,* April 6, 1961.

Johnson, Leslie W., Cooperstown, N. Dak., *Letter,* May 18, 1946.

Jones, Pierre E., Robbinsdale, Minn., *Letter,* Sept. 7, 1961.

Klett, Albert T., U. S. Fish and Wildl. Serv., Devils Lake, N. Dak., *Letter,* Sept. 3, 1963.

Martin, Frank, Refuge Mgr., Upper Souris Natl. Wildl. Refuge, U. S. Fish and Wildl. Serv., Foxholm, N. Dak., *Letter,* Oct. 29, 1956.

McClintock, John C., Rugby, N. Dak., *Letter,* April 23, 1964.

Moberg, Verne, Editorial Section, *Harpers Magazine,* New York City, *Letter,* July 31, 1963.

Moore, Charles, Exec. Assist., Great Northern Railway, St. Paul, Minn., *Letter,* Dec. 8, 1960.

Nelson, Bernard A., Dept. of Natural Resources, Wildl. Research Div., Regina, Sask., Canad., *Letter,* March 20, 1961.

North Dakota Game and Fish Records, 1891-1935, 2 vols., (In State Game and Fish Files, Bismarck).

Olson, Mrs. Louise, Rolla, N. Dak., *Letter,* May 26, 1963.

Randall, Robert, U. S. Fish and Wildl. Serv., River Basin Branch, Bismarck, N. Dak., *Notes,* Sept. 17, 1963.

Stevens, Dr. O. A., North Dakota State University, Fargo, N. Dak., *Letter,* March 29, 1963.

Webb, R., Dept. of Lands and Forests, Fish and Wildl. Div., Edmonton, Alberta, Canad., *Letter,* Nov. 14, 1961.

Wood, Dr. Ray, Univ. of Arkansas, Dept. of Sociol. and Anthrop., Fayetteville, Ark., *Letter,* April 2, 1963.

WPA Historic Data Project Biography File, 1938. *Reuben Humes,* (In State Hist. Soc. Library of N. Dak., Bismarck) 3 pp.

Interviews

The following old-timers furnished statements on the wildlife of North Dakota. Their statements were made on a personal contact basis during the period 1960-63 and several have passed on since the project has begun. I wish to thank them for their cooperative assistance.

Aarestad, John, McHenry, N. Dak. (Nov. 25, 1899 ....). Born: Cooperstown, N. Dak. Has lived in North Dakota all his life. Mercantile business.

Almquist, Martin, Fullerton, N. Dak. (April 3, 1899 ....). Born: Stromberg, Nebr. Lived in North Dakota since 1905. Mercantile and Postal service.

Anderson, Arthur H., Belfield, N. Dak. (Oct. 14, 1881 ....). Born: Chicago, Ill. Lived In Belfield, N. Dak. since 1883. Mercantile business and rancher.

Atkins, S. J., Cando, N. Dak. (Oct. 21, 1874 ....). Born: Louisiana, Mo. Lived in North Dakota since 1885. Farmer and Mercantile business.

Baenen, Bernard J., Jamestown, N. Dak. (July 19, 1869 ....). Born: Green Bay, Wisc. Lived in North Dakota since 1882. Farmer.

Bird, Ben, Medora, N. Dak. (Dec. 7, 1864 - April 1, 1962). Born: Dennison, Tex. Lived in North Dakota since 1884. Old-time cowboy and trail driver.

Bjornseth, J. J., Dunseith, N. Dak. (April 13, 1888 ....). Born: Evansville, Minn. Lived in Dunseith, N. Dak. since 1889. Farmer and professional hunter.

Carroll, Virgil, Dhame, N. Dak. (Dec. 4, 1888 ....). Born: Hampton, Iowa. Lived in North Dakota since 1914. Farmer.

Cornell, Charles, Medora, N. Dak. (May 27, 1884 ....). Born: Gladstone, N. Dak. and has lived in the state all his life. Rancher.

Foreman, A. T., Marmarth, N. Dak. (Sept. 5, 1878 ....). Born: Gallagherville, Penn. Lived in North Dakota since 1889. Rancher and mercantile business.

Gross, E. H., Kenmare, N. Dak. (Nov. 8, 1879 ....). Born: Shakopee, Minn. Lived in North Dakota since 1902. Jeweler and photographer.

Hansen, Thomas, Valley City, N. Dak. (April 27, 1895 ....). Born Valley City, N. Dak. and has lived in the state all his life. Farmer.

Harvey, George, Williston, N. Dak. (Sept. 29, 1886 ....). Born: Cedar Rapids, Iowa. Lived in North Dakota since 1892. Railroading.

Haugland, Henry, Ioma, N. Dak. (1872-1957). Lived in North Dakota since 1895. Grain buyer. Statements from letters April 36 and October 31, 1957.

Hyatt, Everett, Ludden, N. Dak. (Aug. 9, 1893 ....). Born: Kokomo, Ind. Lived in North Dakota since 1898. Farmer.

Jensen, Edward, Esmund, N. Dak. (April 16, 1894 ....). Born: Oberon, N. Dak. and has lived in the state all his life. Painter.

Johnstone, J. Bert, Hansboro, N. Dak. (Mar. 27, 1877 ....). Born: Glencoe, Minn. Lived in North Dakota since 1882. Farmer.

Kretschmar, Otto, Venturia, N. Dak. (July 19, 1897 ....). Born: Venturia, N. Dak. and has lived in the state all his life. Manager, Lumber yard.

Lee, Bert J., Williston, N. Dak. (Jan. 4, 1879 ....). Born: Springfield, Ohio. Lived in North Dakota since 1903. Painter.

Lesmeister, Frank, Harvey. N. Dak. (May 24, 1905). Born: Harvey and has lived in the state all his life. Farmer.

Lesmeister, Ludwig F., Harvey, N. Dak. (Nov. 20, 1885 ....). Born: Kandel, Odessa, Russia. Lived in North Dakota since 1895. Farmer.

Lyon, J. B., Williston, N. Dak. (June 28, 1879 _____). Born: Evansville, Ind. Lived in North Dakota since 1899. Mercantile business.

McBrideg Vern, Kenmare, N. Dak. (Mar. 29, 1907 _____). Born: Kenmare, N. Dak. and has lived in this state all his life. Butcher.

McConnell, Harvey, Kenmare, N. Dak. (Jan. 3, 1880 _____). Born: Paisley, Ontario. Lived in North Dakota since 1900. Butcher.

McMahon, Patrick E., Rugby, N. Dak. (April 19, 1893 _____). Born: Grand Forks, N. Dak. and has lived in North Dakota all his life. Railroading.

Maddock, Charles B., Guelph, N. Dak. (Sept. 27, 1877 _____). Born: Champaign Co., Ill. Lived in North Dakota since 1906. Farmer.

Malone, Patrick T., Linton, N. Dak. (April 11, 1874 _____). Born: England. Lived in North Dakota since 1901. Farmer.

Ness, C. J., Cando, N. Dak. (Feb. 21, 1888 _____). Born: Spokane, Wash. Lived in North Dakota since 1912. County Judge.

Nostdal, Louis R., Rugby, N. Dak. (1873 - 1962). Born: Minnesota. Lived in North Dakota since 1898. Attorney.

Odegard, Albert O., Heimdal, N. Dak. (Dec. 9, 1881 - Mar. 30, 1964). Born, Buxton, N. Dak. Lived in North Dakota all his life. Farmer and hardware store business.

Parker, Arthur, Dickinson, N. Dak. (Jply 9, 1889 _____). Born: Wibaux, Mont. Lived in North Dakota since 1893. Grocer.

Peterson, Edwin, Rugby, N. Dak. (May, 1882 _____). Born: Ottertail Co., Minn. Lived in North Dakota since 1906. Grocer.

Petrie, Fred, Linton, N. Dak. (Dec. 15, 1891 _____). Born: Alma, Mich. and moved to North Dakota when he was but a few months of age. Mercantile.

Quamme, Joseph, Westhope, N. Dak. (Jan. 3, 1878 _____). Born: Hayfield, Minn. Lived in North Dakota since 1881. Printer.

Rasmussen, Chris, Medora, N. Dak. (Nov. 26, 1873 _____). Lived in North Dakota since 1893. Rancher.

Roberts, Mrs. Elizabeth, Dickinson, N. Dak. (Mar. 7, 1872 _____). Born: Waterloo, Iowa. Lived in North Dakota since 1877. Rancher and lady game warden.

Robinson, Harv, Dickinson, N. Dak. (Jan. 31, 1867 _____). Born: Renselaar, Ind. Lived in North Dakota since 1891. Old-time cowboy and trail driver.

Schiefer, George, Kenmare, N. Dak. (Nov. 24, 1869 _____). Born: Sauk Centre, Minn. Lived in North Dakota since 1893. Farmer.

Sheltrau, James, Walhalla, N. Dak. (Mar. 20, 1965 _____). Born: Milk River, Mont. Lived in North Dakota since 1872. Farmer, professional trapper and hunter.

Sihler, W. F., Devils Lake, N. Dak. (June 13, 1876 _____). Born: Simcoe, Ontario. Lived in North Dakota since 1899. Doctor.

Snyder, Bill, Bowman, N. Dak. (April 3, 1883 _____). Born: Inkster, N. Dak. Lived in North Dakota all his life. Farmer and rancher.

Spiller, H. B., Cavalier, N. Dak. (Sept. 13, 1875 _____). Born: New York. Lived in North Dakota since 1885. Attorney.

Spire, A. J., Marmarth, N. Dak. (Oct. 1, 1881 _____). Born: Denison, Iowa. Lived in North Dakota since 1907. City and county official.

Stewart, Charles, Carson, N. Dak. (Dec. 28, 1894 _____). Born: Dale (Emmons Co.), N. Dak. Lived in North Dakota all his life. Rancher.

Swett, Herb, Dickinson, N. Dak. (Sept. 17, 1888 _____). Born: Bismarck, N. Dak. Lived in North Dakota all his life. Dakota Maid Elevator manager.

Wenz, Charles C., New Rockford, N. Dak.   (Mar. 1888 ....).   Lived in New Rockford all his life.   City employee.

Westlake, Cecil, Kenmare, N. Dak.   (Mar. 1899 ....).   Born: Inkster, N. Dak.   Lived in North Dakota all his life.   Farmer, grain buyer and hardware business.

Williams, Henry V., Grafton, N. Dak.   (July 31, 1891 ....).   Born: Glasston, N. Dak. and has lived in North Dakota all his life.   Taxidermist.

Wingstrand, G. L., Rhame, N. Dak.   (Oct. 6, 1885 ....).   Born: St. Peter, Minn.   Lived in North Dakota since 1907.   Mercantile business.

Wood, Glen, Emmonsburg, N. Dak.   (Sept. 5, 1885 ....).   Born: Michigan.   Lived in North Dakota since 1905.   Farmer.

Wright, Dana, St. Johns, N. Dak.   (Aug. 30, 1878 - Feb. 16, 1964).   Retired U. S. Army Officer and historian.

TABLES IN THIS BOOK

PHOTO CREDITS

Berg, Howard O., Devils Lake, pages 4, 65, 99, 101.

Bry, Ed, Game and Fish Department, pages 1, 8, 22, 59, 73, 76, 190, 203.

Cave, Frank, Bismarck, page 121.

Fox, Al, Game and Fish Department, page 153.

Grondahl, C. R., Game and Fish Department, page 101.

Gross, E. H., Kenmare, pages 18, 111 .

Harpers Magazine, New York (contributed by Robert Johnson, Fullerton), pages 94, 154.

Johnson, Frank, Fullerton, page 96.

Klett, A. T., Game and Fish Department, page 219.

Koyama, Shin, Game and Fish Department, pages 41, 72, 144, 149, 179, 182, 185, 195, 196, 197.

McConn, A. W., Pelican, Minnesota (contributed by Doug Burtell, Fargo), page 120.

Mattson, Conrad, Pleasant Lake, page 159.

Miller, Bill, Bismarck, pages 43, 45, 57, 81, 109, 140.

Odegard, Albert, Heimdal, page 207.

O'Hearn, Mrs. Nora, Dickinson, page 17.

Osborn Studio, Dickinson, page 15.

Pfiefer, Carl, Oakes, page 113.

State Game and Fish Department Photo, pages 116, 142, 193.

State Historical Society Library, Bismarck, pages 89, 102.

Westlake, Cecil, Kenmare, page 84.